WORDSWORTH AND THE
HUMAN HEART

WORDSWORTH AND THE HUMAN HEART

JOHN BEER

Columbia University Press
New York 1978

Printed in Great Britain

Library of Congress Cataloging in Publication Data

Beer, John B
    Wordsworth and the human heart.

    Includes bibliographical references and index.
    1. Wordsworth, William, 1770–1850 – Criticism and interpretation.
    2. Emotions in literature.
    I. Title.
    PR5892.E5B43   821'.7   78–17567

ISBN 0–231–04646–4

In memory of my parents

Contents

Abbreviations

BW   Blake, *Complete Writings*. Edited by Geoffrey
                Keynes (Oxford, 1966). Oxford Standard
                Authors edition, reprinted with correc-
                tions and additions from the 1957
                Nonesuch Variorum edition.

CBL   Coleridge, *Biographia Literaria*. Edited by J.
                Shawcross, 2 vols (Oxford, 1907).

Chronology   M. L. Reed, *Wordsworth: The Chronology of
                the Early Years, 1770–1799* (Cambridge,
                Mass., 1967).

CL   *Collected Letters of Samuel Taylor Coleridge*.
                Edited by E. L. Griggs, 6 vols (Oxford,
                1956–71).

CN   *The Notebooks of Samuel Taylor Coleridge*.
                Edited by Kathleen Coburn, vol I–
                (1957–).

CPW   *The Complete Poetical Works of Samuel Taylor
                Coleridge*. Edited by E. H. Coleridge. 2
                vols (Oxford, 1912).

DQW   De Quincey, *Works*, 15 vols (Edinburgh,
                1862–3).

DWJ   *Journals of Dorothy Wordsworth* (1798–1803).
                Second Edition. Edited by Mary Moor-
                man (Oxford, 1971).

DWJ (De Sel)   *Journals of Dorothy Wordsworth*. Edited by E.
                de Selincourt. 2 vols (1959).

Exc.   *The Excursion* (1814). (Text from PW, vol V).

HCR   *Henry Crabb Robinson on Books and their*

	Writers. Edited by Edith J. Morley. 3 vols (1938).
HCR *Corr*	*The Correspondence of Henry Crabb Robinson with the Wordsworth Circle.* Edited by Edith J. Morley. 2 vols (Oxford, 1927).
HW	*The Complete Works of William Hazlitt.* Edited by P. P. Howe. 21 vols (1930–4).
LB (1798)	Wordsworth (and Coleridge), *Lyrical Ballads, with a few other poems* (1798).
LB	Wordsworth (and Coleridge), *Lyrical Ballads* with other poems in two volumes (1800).
Moorman	Mary Moorman, *William Wordsworth: a Biography.* 2 vols (Oxford, 1965).
PL	Milton, *Paradise Lost.*
Prel.	Wordsworth, *The Prelude.* Edited by E. de Selincourt, revised by Helen Darbishire, 2nd ed. (Oxford, 1959). (See also 1799, 1805, 1850.)
PrW	*The Prose Works of William Wordsworth.* Edited by W. J. B. Owen and Jane Worthington Smyser. 3 vols (Oxford, 1974).
PrW (Gr)	*The Prose Works of William Wordsworth.* Edited by A. B. Grosart. 3 vols (1876).
PW	*The Poetical Works of William Wordsworth.* Edited by E. de Selincourt and Helen Darbishire. 5 vols (Oxford, 1940–9).
Salisbury Plain Poems	*The Salisbury Plain Poems of William Wordsworth.* Edited by Stephen Gill (The Cornell Wordsworth I) (Ithaca, N.Y., and Hassocks, Sussex, 1975). See Note on Texts.
Transactions W. Soc.	*Transactions of the Wordsworth Society* (Edinburgh, 1882–1887).
WL (1787–1805) WL (1806–11)	*The Letters of William and Dorothy Wordsworth 1787–.* Edited by E. de Selincourt, revised by C. L. Shaver and others. Vols I and II (Oxford, 1967–).
WL (L.Y)	*The Letters of William and Dorothy Wordsworth: The Later Years.* Edited by E. de Selincourt (Oxford, 1939).

1799   Wordsworth, *The Prelude, 1798–99.* Edited by Stephen Parrish (The Cornell Wordsworth II) (Ithaca, N.Y., and Hassocks, Sussex, 1977). See Note on Texts.

1805   Wordsworth, *The Prelude* (text of 1805). Edited by E. de Selincourt, corrected by Stephen Gill. 2nd ed. (1970).

1807   Wordsworth, *Poems in two volumes* (1807).

1850   Wordsworth, *The Prelude,* text of 1850 (quoted from *Prel.* above).

Preface and Acknowledgements

The exact quality of Wordsworth's humanitarianism has been a subject of contention in recent years. In studies such as those by Helen Darbishire, Mary Moorman and John Danby he is presented as one of the most human poets in the English language; other critics, notably F. W. Bateson, have taken a more quizzical view; others again, including John Jones, Jonathan Wordsworth and F. M. Todd, have contributed importantly to the debate without finally taking sides.

The main puzzle is furnished by his tendencies to isolation and self-elevation, which often seem to clash with the strong note of humanity in his writing. His decline from radicalism, similarly, a commonplace of literary history, makes it tempting to see him as a renegade from early humanitarianism – yet he himself insisted that he had actually been 'humanized' by some of his later experiences.

The following study springs from a belief that Wordsworth's sense of humanity developed in certain respects according to a pattern of its own, which owed a good deal to his relationships with Coleridge and with his sister. The fact that Dorothy's humanity could sometimes be expressed more immediately and vividly than his own stands out from the pages of her journal, but the significance of this phenomenon can, I believe, only be fully understood when set in the context of speculations about the links between human consciousness and the human heart which were at the same time reaching Wordsworth from Coleridge. 'I will not speak of other thoughts that passed through me,' he wrote to Coleridge in 1804, after hearing of his recovery from a severe illness, 'but I cannot help saying that I would gladly have given 3 fourths of my possessions for your letter on the Recluse at that time. I cannot say what a load it would be to me, should I survive you and you die without this

memorial left behind.' While this appeal has sometimes been quoted
as an illustration of Wordsworth's egotism, less attention has been
given to it as evidence of Wordsworth's sense of his own dependency
on Coleridge's ebullience of intellect, and this may reflect uncertainty as to what, exactly, Coleridge was saying during those years.
Guidance towards an understanding has been offered by Stephen
Prickett in *Wordsworth and Coleridge: the Poetry of Growth* (1970) and
by Thomas McFarland in 'The Symbiosis of Coleridge and
Wordsworth' (*Studies in Romanticism* (1972) XI 263–303), proceeding from the evidence directly available. My own further reconstruction of his thought, as set out in *Coleridge's Poetic Intelligence* and
several other places, is necessarily tentative at times;[1] yet it is hard to
resist the overall conclusion that the strong psychological element to
be traced in the drafts and poems which Wordsworth wrote when
their intimacy was at its height was in some way due to the direction
given to his thought by exposure to speculations of this kind. No
adequate alternative explanation has yet been offered.

The present study is in no way intended to present a complete
view of Wordsworth – or for that matter of his friendship with
Coleridge. Another important element in his work (and one where I
believe the influence of Coleridge can again be traced) is to be found
in his meditations upon his early visionary experiences and the light
which they might throw upon the significance of the human consciousness within the time-process. These issues are dealt with in a
complementary study, entitled *Wordsworth in Time*, to be published
at about the same time as this one. Further discussions between the
two men were evidently devoted to previous poetry and their
attitudes to language in general, issues which will be the subject of a
third study. My aim throughout, it should be repeated, is not to
argue for the superiority of Coleridge, but rather to suggest that his
speculations assisted Wordsworth to explore and bring out the full
potentialities of his own genius.

For similar reasons I have given less attention than I might
otherwise have done to critical evaluation of Wordsworth's poetry.
Although it is not difficult to 'place' some of Wordsworth's poems
at a first reading, poetry can change for the reader as he or she becomes aware of its underlying processes: the weight of individual
words, for instance, can change according to one's awareness
of their significance to the poet. It seemed better to give more
attention to those processes and significances, therefore, and leave

them for the reader to reflect upon before coming to judgement.

In the course of work over so long a period I have incurred more debts than I can easily call to mind. I should mention particularly conversations with Mr Hugh Sykes Davies, Professor Basil Willey, the late Professor John Danby, Dr Arnold Goldman, Mr John Woolford, Professor W. B. Gallie, Professor Thomas McFarland and Professor Robert Langbaum. I am especially grateful to A. S. Byatt for drawing my attention to one or two of Wordsworth's recurrent images. To Professor Frank Kermode I am indebted not only for his friendship and writings over many years, but, more specifically, for the title of my ninth chapter, a quotation from Philip Larkin under which his Mary Flexner lectures, later published as *The Sense of an Ending*, were originally delivered at Bryn Mawr. I am also grateful to Richard Wordsworth and the participants in successive sessions of the Wordsworth Summer Conference at Ambleside and Grasmere, where some of the ideas in the book (particularly those in Chapter 4) were first given an airing. Wordsworth's relationship with Dorothy, which I discuss in Chapter 6, was the subject of an interesting lecture there in 1975 by Donald Reiman, who had also taken part in a correspondence on the subject in the *Times Literary Supplement* between August and November of the previous year. My own discussion was already written by then and I did not feel any need to change what I had said, but readers who are interested in the issues involved will find it profitable to turn back to this correspondence.

I should also like to acknowledge the help of the Librarians and staff of the Cambridge University Library, the Bodleian and the British Library and of the libraries of Peterhouse and St John's College, Cambridge. I am grateful to the Trustees of the Dove Cottage Library for their kindness in allowing me to use their collection, to the curators for their kindness and help and to Mr Jonathan Wordsworth, who, as chairman of the Trust, gave me permission to quote various readings from the original manuscripts. He also facilitated my work by making available certain materials ahead of publication. I owe much to Mrs Olive Page and Mrs Hazel Dunn for their patience and accuracy in typing the various manuscripts involved. My greatest debt is, as always, to my wife.

Any study which tries to look at the whole of Wordsworth's career inevitably falls into something of an elegiac mode, commemorating as it does a poet who dwelt constantly on the theme that

>   brightest things are wont to draw
>   Sad opposites out of the inner heart.

Even more striking, however, as I try to show, is his staying power, his success in discovering and displaying the processes that sustain humanity through that recognition. My dedication is relevant on both counts.

March 1978   J.B.B.

)

A Note on Texts
and Editions

During the past few years the scholarly materials for the study of
Wordsworth have been improved by some splendid new works,
including the Owen/Smyser edition of the prose, the re-editing of
the *Letters*, M. L. Reed's *Chronology* and Mary Moorman's biog-
raphy. The volumes of the Cornell Wordsworth, which at the time
of writing have just begun to appear, are doing a similar service for
the poetry.

After some thought, I have decided wherever possible to quote the
earliest complete text of particular poems and passages. Although
this sometimes means missing a later improvement or addition, such
as the change to 'A voice so thrilling ne'er was heard. . .' in 'The
Solitary Reaper', such losses are I believe counterbalanced, in a study
explicitly devoted to Wordsworth's processes, by the advantages of
seeing Wordsworth's text nearest to the original composition. In
particular, the early versions often bring out the original *movement* of
a poem: later revisions are sometimes purchased at the expense of a
dulling of that movement.

In quoting from *The Prelude*, similarly, I have quoted from the
letters and manuscripts in which passages first appeared, from the
1799 text, and then from the text of 1805, making reference to the
1850 version only where it is a source of further illumination.

In quoting from Dorothy Wordsworth's *Journals* I have followed
recent practice in using Mary Moorman's slightly better text for the
passages covered by her Oxford Paperbacks edition and De Selincourt's for the remainder.

I wish to make grateful acknowledgements to Robert Osborn
for allowing me to use his text of *The Borderers* (forthcoming in
revised form in the Cornell Wordsworth) from his Oxford B.Litt.
thesis in the Bodleian Library. As explained above, my texts of the
'Salisbury Plain' poems and the early versions of *The Prelude* derive
from the earliest manuscripts; for the reader's convenience, however, references are given to the line-numberings of the 'reading-
text' in the Cornell Wordsworth editions.

Some important dates

xviii

1800	Second volume of *Lyrical Ballads* completed (pub. 1801); Coleridge settles with family at Keswick
1802	Burst of productivity, including part of the Immortality Ode and 'Resolution and Independence'. Visit to Annette in France; marriage to Mary Hutchinson (Oct)
1803	Scottish tour with Dorothy and Coleridge
1804	Coleridge leaves for Malta
1805	(Feb) Death of John Wordsworth; (May) completion of 1805 *Prelude*
1806	'Elegiac Stanzas' (Peele Castle) written; Return of Coleridge; beginnings of estrangement between the two poets
1807	*Poems in Two Volumes*
1807–8	'The White Doe of Rylstone' written
1808	Move to Allan Bank
1809	Tract on the Convention of Cintra
1810	'Essays upon Epitaphs' for *The Friend*; quarrel with Coleridge (Oct)
1812	Reconciliation with Coleridge; deaths of Catharine and Thomas Wordsworth
1813	Distributorship of Stamps; move to Rydal Mount.
1814	*The Excursion* published
1817	Winters in London; meets Keats and others
1819	*Peter Bell* (1798) and *The Waggoner* (1805) published
1820	Duddon Sonnets published
1828	Continental tour with Coleridge
1834	Death of Coleridge
1850	Death of William Wordsworth
1855	Death of Dorothy Wordsworth

Great spirits now on earth are sojourning;
    He of the cloud, the cataract, the lake,
    Who on Helvellyn's summit, wide awake,
Catches his freshness from Archangel's wing:
    . . .
These, these will give the world another heart,
    And other pulses.

John Keats, 1816

Those who speak of Wordsworth as the original Lost Leader (a reference which Browning, as I remember, denied) should make pause and consider that when a man takes politics and social affairs seriously the difference between revolution and reaction may be by the breadth of a hair, and that Wordsworth may possibly have been no renegade but a man who thought, so far as he thought at all, for himself.

T. S. Eliot

I

The Consenting Language

'How is it, Bill, thee doest write with such good verses? Doest thee invoke Muses?'

The wondering question, addressed to the young Wordsworth by one of his older school-mates,[1x] can be interpreted in more than one way; but it may not be fanciful to detect, among other things, a note of surprise – surprise, perhaps, that the boy whom he knew primarily either as a boisterous participant in schoolboy games or, in alternative moods, as a serious and assiduous student, should turn out to be skilled also in an art which did not quite fit either persona. What was the secret that explained this further strain and depth?

If so, the anonymous Hawkshead schoolboy was by no means the last person to sense the existence of an enigmatic play of forces in Wordsworth. Some years after their quarrel in 1810, Coleridge tried to come to terms with what he had meant to him by drawing up a kind of balance-sheet. On the credit side he set Wordsworth's feeling for nature, his possession of an eye and heart which could intuitively penetrate living things to see one life in all, his creative and modifying imagination, his strength of intellect. On the other he set qualities which he characterised briefly as Wordsworth's 'northernism', his 'attorneysonship' and his 'self-idolatry' – referring, evidently, to a canniness and tendency to self-isolation which he felt might have something to do with his Northern background and with the fact that he had been born into a legal family.[2x]

It was a rather bitter analysis, drawn out of Coleridge by a sense of betrayal which he still found hard to express openly, or even understand; but in certain respects it is more revealing than his considered and guarded formulations in *Biographia Literaria*. For of the many attempts that have been made to describe the sense of division in Wordsworth which many critics feel, this one brings us

1

closest to the recognisable facts of his early development: on the one hand the lonely, prophetic Wordsworth, the boy who roamed the Cumbrian fells and there felt himself subject to strange solitary moments of revelation; on the other the Wordsworth who was his father's son and who must be about his father's business – a humble carrying out of human processes under the law to the benefit of those with whom he came into daily contact.

As Wordsworth grew older the second side of him became proportionately stronger and it is tempting to say that as it did so he became less of a poet; Coleridge's analysis, in fact, half invites one to conclude so. Yet Coleridge knew, and we are bound to recognise, that it was not so simple a matter. The attorney's son was always a powerful presence in the poetry, from the beginning; and anyone acquainted with the contemporary inhabitants of Lakeland would understand why. Individuals who are able to live in stubborn independence are also those who know best the need for objective rules of justice to regulate their disputes and differences.

These two sides of Wordsworth's early experience foreshadow further divisions within the adult man, even deeper and subtler than one might suspect from Coleridge's account. On the one hand, he was led by his love of wild places – and the strangely self-enforcing knowledge that that opening of himself to wildness sometimes seemed to bring – to a feeling for the spontaneous and the passionate that led him to his early love affair with Annette Vallon and his involvement with the aspirations of the French Revolution. On the other, his baffling adventures in the world of passion drove him to reach back for a more comprehensible world – the steady world of law in nature that had in the eighteenth century been reinforced by the work of Locke and Newton. In a mathematically-based science there existed the promise, at least, of an order based upon certainties.

But where in all this lay the room for a poet to exist and work? Passion was too disordering and disorienting to render itself easily into a manageable verse; intellect and its devotion to law froze the forms of language into dull, featureless characters. A poet needed something more vital: a sense of life within and a nourishment from the world outside. Left to themselves, the promptings of passion and the rigour of law ground against one another too closely to allow much space for such life and growth.

There was, however, one area of the human psyche in which the conflict seemed less pressing, one space which seemed exempt from their contradictions. In many ways it corresponded to the place which Blake called Beulah:

> There is a place where Contrarieties are equally True:
> This place is called Beulah. It is a pleasant lovely Shadow
> Where no dispute can come . . .

> Beulah is evermore Created around Eternity, appearing
> To the Inhabitants of Eden around them on all sides.
> But Beulah to its Inhabitants appears within each district
> As the beloved infant in his mother's bosom round incircled
> With arms of love & pity & sweet compassion.
>
> *Milton*, 30: 1–3; 8–12

For Blake this place, the place of human affection, was at once attractive and dangerous: a necessary point of repose for those who were weary from fighting the wars of Eternity, it could be enervating and imprisoning to those who lingered there too long. It corresponded to the world of Innocence, which must atrophy in any human being who did not engage with the world of Experience, but which was a necessary source of renewing vision for those who did.

Wordsworth, less conscious of the wars of Eternity than of the more immediate conflicts just mentioned, came to find the prospect of 'Beulah' more unambiguously inviting, opening out the prospect of a place where he might actually live and work, in relative immunity from the contraries of intellect and passion. His sense of the actual could be relied upon to protect him against any false claims for the pastoral; and his knowledge of the real countryside empowered him to explore further a correspondence which was implicit in Blake's lyrical passage – a sense, that is, that the pastoral landscape, properly understood, could still be seen as the truest country of the human heart.

It is hard for a twentieth-century reader to appreciate fully the attractions involved in the latter prospect. Since Wordsworth's day, the tendency to refer to the heart vaguely and diffusely has increased to such an extent that the sensibility of the intelligent reader has become largely anaesthetised to any mention of it. For that reason such a reader may hardly respond to its presence in Wordsworth's pages either. At the time when he was growing up, on the other hand, the word was extremely fashionable. Though already compromised by sentimental usage, moreover, it continued to draw strength from older but still current connotations, as in the Bible.

How much was lost by the movement of his time which extrapolated the 'warmth' and 'softness' of the heart, as qualities to be set against the coldness and hardness associated with reason, becomes clear, in fact, when one returns to the biblical text. The use of the word there is not only complex, but noticeably lacking in specialised emotional charge. Often, indeed, the heart seems to be thought of as a place rather than a positive force – certainly it is regarded as the true locus of moral action.[3] There is also a strong suggestion of secrecy: it is there that plots may be hatched, doubts raised, evil thoughts propagated.[4] When it is thought of in more positive terms, many of the traditional associations are already there, of course: it may be softened or hardened; it may be merry or sad; it may be lifted up or broken.[5] Yet there is no implied opposition to 'the head': in the Bible the heart is referred to rather as if it marked the *centre* of being.

That note, identifying the moral force in a human being with his or her centrality of existence, had persisted in the following centuries – particularly in the puritan tradition. But side by side with it, associated with other aspects of religion and notably with the tendency to regard the devotional life as primarily an affair of the emotions, there had grown up a different attitude, which associated it not only with religious 'enthusiasm' (as in early Methodism) but, more broadly, with the tender affections as such.

In some influential Continental writers, indeed, this conception was not only accepted, but the resulting dictates were thought to be over-mastering. In his *Confessions* Rousseau described how readiness to open his heart had been a constant feature of his own conduct;[6x] he also demonstrated the power of the heart's affections at length in *La Nouvelle Héloise*. In Goethe's *The Sorrows of Young Werther*, similarly, the hero's heart was driven, and finally destroyed, by a feeling for the heroine which, he felt, transcended that evinced by her husband:

> O, he is not the man who can satisfy all the wishes of her heart. He wants that full flow of feeling – he wants – call it what you please, but his heart does not beat in unison with hers, when over a passage of a favourite author and in an hundred other cases where we happen to express our opinions, my heart and Charlotte's meet in sympathy.[7]

In England, despite the popularity of Rousseau and Goethe, the cult never rose to quite this level. One good reason was undoubtedly the different emphasis prepared by Sterne, the great English genius of the movement. In his writings, too, the heart is a touchstone, but it is also seen as paradoxically mercurial in its operation. Morality is there all the time as a standard against which the behaviour of the heart is seen as making powerful demands, but the very absurdity of some of those demands, stretching far beyond the calls of sexual affection or passion, lends to the cult a welcome touch of humour, extending the reader's sense of what is involved.[8] In the second section of *A Sentimental Journey*, nevertheless, a meditation by Sterne displays the straightforward 'sentimental' view of the heart in full physiological detail:

> When man is at peace with man, how much lighter than a feather is the heaviest of metals in his hand! he pulls out his purse, and holding it airily and uncompress'd, looks round him, as if he sought for an object to share it with – In doing this, I felt every vessel in my frame dilate – the arteries beat all chearily together, and every power which sustained life, perform'd it with so little friction, that 'twould have confounded the most *physical precieuse* in France: with all her materialism, she could scarce have called me a machine –[9]

The journey itself, also, is seen as a pilgrimage dominated by the heart's needs and affections:

> 'tis a quiet journey of the heart in pursuit of NATURE, and those affections which arise out of her, which make us love each other – and the world, better than we do.[10]

Yet the implications of the word 'quiet' turn out to be crucial. Such a journey may culminate in amorous adventure in Savoy, but it will also lead back to the domestic world of Uncle Toby and Corporal Trim. In this way, Sterne retains a close link with the primacy of 'charity' in the Christianity which he professes – even if the biblical sense of the heart has been modified in the process.

Wordsworth, who said in 1791 that *Tristram Shandy* was one of the few works of modern literature that he had recently read,[11] had reasons of another kind to be attracted by a cult of 'the heart'. His upbringing in the North of England, close to areas where many of the best older ballads were composed, had given him a delight in them which extended to the recent revival of the mode in the Scots verses of Burns. 'Familiarity with the dialect of the border counties of Cumberland and Westmoreland made it easy for me not only to understand but to feel them,' he wrote many years later.[12] There are occasional touches in his writings, such as his tribute in *The Prelude* to the 'frank-hearted Maids of rocky Cumberland' and their 'not unwelcome days of mirth',[13] which suggest a restrained version of Burns's delight in country amours, coupled with a general pleasure in village life.

This broader tradition contended vigorously for his allegiance. In Burns, as in Rousseau or Sterne, acknowledgement of the heart's claims is a touchstone of one's humanity. As in the Bible, moreover, its powers are versatile. It is warmed, or flutters; it can be broken, hardened or pierced.[14] Sentimentality is never allowed to take over, however: if Burns writes that his father had 'The pitying Heart that felt for human Woe', he immediately adds that he had also 'The dauntless heart that fear'd no human Pride'.[15] Burns has, in addition, a strong sense of the heart's actual physical working and its intimate relationship with other bodily emotions, genital or familial:

> The *life blood* streaming thro' my heart
> Or my more dear *Immortal part*,
> Is not more fondly dear!

he writes at one point; and at another,

> Wild to my heart the filial pulses glow.[16]

Over and above this, his various references to the heart and its workings are caught up by the lilt and verve of his verse as a whole. There is no room for the languishing of the drawing-room heroine. The effects of the heart's emotions may be either lively or grievous, but one thing the human being of Burns's lyrics will not do is lie back and indulge them luxuriously. The general tendency of his writing is rather to encourage a republican sense in which all men will recognise their brotherhood with one another ('A man's a man for a' that') and come to see the working of the heart as a mark of their common humanity.

An ideal of this kind hovered invitingly before Wordsworth all his life. The preface to the *Lyrical Ballads*, with its often-quoted characterisation of the poet as 'a man speaking to men', has often (and not without justice) been read as laying out the programme for a republican verse. Examination of the ballads themselves, however, shows that he was, even then, moving beyond the simple assertive warmth of Burns's lyrics.

In order to understand how and why this further movement came about, we must move from the Scottish to the English tradition. To do so is to see that, despite the remoteness of the grammar-school which Wordsworth attended, he was at a point of confluence there between two very different movements. The one, fostered by Burns and the border ballads, was characterised by a simple manliness; the other, expressed pre-eminently at that time by Cowper, was concerned to reconcile the old intellectual order with the cultivation of sensibility that was encouraged by a prosperous commercial civilisation.

Cowper, who strongly felt the appeal of sensibility, had none of Burns's raciness and larger flow. His own poetry, quiet and meditative, was more prone to encourage languorousness, therefore. In a poem to Miss Macartney, who had written a 'Prayer for Indifference', he prayed

> Oh! grant, kind Heaven, to me
> Long as I draw ethereal air,
>   Sweet Sensibility!

and elaborated the theme as follows:

> Still may my melting bosom cleave
>   To sufferings not my own;
> And still the sigh responsive heave,
>   Where'er is heard a groan.
> So Pity shall take Virtue's part,
>   Her natural ally,
> And fashioning my soften'd heart,
>   Prepare it for the sky.[17]

His metaphors of the heart, on the other hand, are more exploratory than those of Burns. He will express a wish that the Word of God will 'shoot a ray/Through all the heart's dark chambers'; or write of 'heart-shaking music'.[18] He will lament that 'The serpent Error twines round human hearts'.[19] Philosophy, he warns,

> . . . while his province is the reasoning part,
> Has still a veil of midnight on his heart.

If love were to prevail, on the other hand,

> Each heart would quit its prison in the breast,
> And flow in free communion with the rest.[20]

Inspection of the context suggests why, in spite of this, sentimentality is precluded. In almost every case Cowper is speaking of religion. As a result, references to the heart are automatically disciplined. Sometimes, indeed, he can make even the traditional pairing of the heart with the head seem abstract, desiring for instance 'An upright heart, and cultivated mind'[21] – where any attempt at literal reference would dissolve into ludicrousness. And the existence of this inbuilt discipline means that an appeal to the sensitive can be exercised with apparent impunity. Even if his constant invocations of the indulgent heart might seem to encourage a cultivation of tender feelings for their own sake, the stress is always on virtue. The centrality of the underlying concern emerges, for instance, in his attitude to landscape. The heart is there invoked specifically to a moral end:

> Acquaint thyself with God, if thou would'st taste
> His works. Admitted once to his embrace,
> Thou shalt perceive that thou wast blind before.
> Thine eye shall be instructed, and thine heart
> Made pure, shall relish with divine delight
> 'Till then unfelt what hands divine have wrought.

Cowper continues with a description of 'brutes' who

> . . . graze the mountain-top with faces prone
> And eyes intent upon the scanty herb
> It yields them; or recumbent on its brow,
> Ruminate heedless of the scene outspread
> Beneath, beyond, and stretching far away
> From inland regions to the distant main.

Finally, he speaks of a third class, who can not only admire such scenes but see in them the 'unambiguous footsteps' of God.[22]

It is instructive to turn from this to a later criticism of Burns by Wordsworth: 'He nowhere in all his poems mentions the mountains of Arran, which lay constantly before him, had he raised either his eye or his mind even so high.'[23] The terms in which Burns is being criticised, we note, are precisely those used by Cowper in the lines quoted above, and may well reflect an early influence. For whenever Cowper contended with Burns for Wordsworth's allegiance the former's greater reflectiveness and moral seriousness were likely to give him the supremacy.

Throughout Wordsworth's later comments on Burns, certainly, there runs a note of depreciation, alternating with statements of unreserved praise. It is as if he thought that Burns had never quite come to maturity; perhaps it is not accidental that his most memorable tribute to him is to

> . . . Him who walked in glory and in joy
> Following his plough, along the mountain-side

– used immediately after his discussion of Chatterton, as another example of youthful joy turning to despondency.[24] In the course of the private criticisms just mentioned, he spoke of him as a poet who 'in his own sphere, is unrivalled' but who 'never assumes the highest tone which best beseems a poet, . . . never spiritualizes, much less sanctifies his conceptions.'[25]

In comments such as these we see the germ of the demand for 'high seriousness' which could lead Matthew Arnold to hesitate about including even Chaucer in his final poetic pantheon. But if Wordsworth was led to such censures by a sense of lack at the very root of Burns's thinking – of a failure, that is, in his dealings with the heart, to link the emotional firmly to the moral in the way that Cowper did, this does not mean that he endorsed Cowper's position, either. Cowper takes his reader back, by a series of short steps, to the creator God of the Bible; Wordsworth exercises a more searching scrutiny upon the contemplation itself, which he sees primarily as an interaction between the landscape and the human being. He may take his cue from the Cowper who speaks of scenes that suggest

> By every pleasing image they present,
> Reflections such as meliorate the heart,
> Compose the passions, and exalt the mind, . . .[26]

but he then dwells upon the actual physical process that is being described, testing it and trying to judge its exact status. He is also, we feel, prepared to modify his conception of the divinity itself on the basis of what he discovers. In spite of superficial resemblances to Cowper, therefore, his position is very different. The distinction emerges still more clearly as we look at the process by which he reached it. Where Cowper was primarily concerned to bring the cultivation of sensibility into the service of a traditional religious orthodoxy, Wordsworth draws upon the resulting conciliation between mind, heart and nature, and the particular emphasis upon the role of the heart, to find an answer to threats more radical, even, than those which prompted Cowper's religious melancholia. In Burns, the heart is the badge of a common humanity; in Cowper it is the focus of a quietist religious position, combining love of liberty, love of order and cultivation of the domestic virtues. Wordsworth, who came to see how a rage for liberty might *threaten* order and the domestic virtues, was thrown more sharply upon his own individual experiences in order to find a mode of mediation between forces which he had seen raging at large, in nature and human nature alike, and which he also recognised as warring energies in his own self. While he could draw strength from a Burnsian sense of warm human community which Cowper hardly knew, his lack of religious allegiance opened him to a sense of human precariousness based not, like Cowper's, on a sense of guilt, but on an oppressive awareness of the power of the physical forces in the universe – forces by which humanity could easily be annihilated.

It was in a context of such intellectual considerations that the heart assumed for him its peculiar and crucial role. With the imposition of order upon the universe of nature through the growth of scientific laws, it had become possible to admire the mind of the maker in constructing so marvellous a system but at the same time to feel that the workings of that system might have little to do with the moral order apparently ordained by that same mind. To bridge the gap, Shaftesbury had invoked the cultivation of a state in which steady contemplation of the divine order would be combined with a response of 'enthusiasm' to it; but there was something a little contrived about this running together of the prosaic and the rhapsodic. The response of the heart, on the other hand, could be said to deal with the problem in a more satisfactory manner.

It was, among other things, a mode which honoured the new science with peculiar appropriateness. Harvey's discovery of the extraordinary processes by which the heart operated to set up a circulatory process in the human body had been one of the great glories of the previous century, often ranked with Newton's discoveries of the laws of gravity. In certain respects, moreover, it bore a direct correspondence with that, presenting a little model of dynamic order within the body to match that to be discovered in the universe at large.[27] At one point in his *Discourse on Method*, Descartes had broken off and asked his reader, before going further, to go and see an animal dissected at the heart. For the benefit of those who could not, he had given a minute account of the marvellous processes by which blood can be seen to be maintained in circulation around the body, and of the intricate system of valves which ensures that the process continues adequately for the sustenance of life.[28] In the current state of physiological knowledge, which threw very little light on the internal working of the body (knowledge of the nervous system, for instance, was rudimentary), the sense of the heart and blood and their operations was correspondingly strong. For the educated man in the eighteenth century, therefore, mention of the heart, which in some contexts would simply evoke those emotions which bound human beings together socially in sympathy and affection, could in others prompt a more detached contemplation of the wonderful mode by which processes of circulation are incessantly maintained. In the latter case the sense of the heart necessarily changed radically; it was wondered at from without rather than empathised with from within.

These and other evidences opened out the scope for a poetry which could range from accounts of simple encounters between ordinary human beings to contemplation of the universe itself and its possible significance. There was also one further and major virtue of the heart for Wordsworth. It was in its own right an *actual* physical resource: despite the elusiveness of some of the issues raised, Wordsworth had only to put his hand to his breast in order to feel its quiet work steadily and palpably continuing.

For the same reason, he valued most those emotions which were expressed directly and physiologically by it. The exaltation of the heartbeat in moments of fear or of unusual excitement was sharply felt and undeniable. If he suspected the fashionable language of sensibility of consenting too readily to some of his claims he could find these experiences, at least, directly counterchecked in the world of sense. Emotions based on fugitive and chemical changes in the body might be harder to corroborate from the experience of others; all must acknowledge such verifiable effects as these.

The same means of validation could be applied to another of Wordsworth's most deeply-held convictions: his belief that the

scope for poetry was often best provided by memory. All passionate
experience, we said earlier, was essentially unmanageable in the
moment of occurrence. When the same experience returned in a time
of remembering, however, it was more possible to hold it under
ordering control. At such moments, as he remarked in *The Prelude*,
Wordsworth could even recognise the coexistence within himself of
something like two widely varying consciousnesses:

> . . . who would not give,
> If so he might, to duty and to truth
> The eagerness of infantine desire?
> A tranquillizing spirit presses now
> On my corporeal frame, so wide appears
> The vacancy between me and those days
> Which yet have such self-presence in my heart
> That sometimes when I think of them I seem
> Two consciousnesses, conscious of myself
> And of some other being.   1799 ii 22–31

In the stress on tranquillity we glimpse something of the relationship
between heart and memory for Wordsworth. Memory is a faithful
adjunct to the organising consciousness: it may be refractory in
producing the past, but at least it knows its station. And through its
workings it can produce something akin to a spatialisation of the
past, opening out into those places which Wordsworth actually
comes to call 'spots of time'. In a typical remembered experience of
this kind, the past is restored with some experience of excitement;
the heart, remembering, beats a little faster until, with the regularisa-
tion of this onward movement (which Wordsworth, with inspired
transposition of the expected words, once described in the line 'Felt
in the blood, and felt along the heart'[29]) the spirit passes into a mood
of unusual peace. And it is at that moment that the poet may hope to
be released into composition.

Certain forces in the great intellectual centres of his time encouraged Wordsworth in this cultivation, as we shall see, taking him out
of the rural society which he knew well, where heartfelt emotion
was readily accepted, into a more sophisticated state, involving the
more refined emotions which individuals might experience both in
society and solitude.

It was a natural enough development in certain respects, yet we may still ask why he should eventually have moved to so extreme an internalisation of his emotions. How did it come about that an energetic young man, brought up on Lakeland sports, full of zest for the open air, educated in one of the great universities of the time, should have found a course which brought him finally to Rydal Mount, a settled-looking old man, brooding mildly over the scene that spread itself below the garden-walk where he walked up and down making his verses?

I have already suggested one answer. Wordsworth passed into this course because he believed that in attending to the motions of his own heart he was making a study that could be of value to all his fellow human beings. He hoped, among other things, to show by this study how the love of nature, if truly cultivated (as it was not, he believed, in his contemporary civilisation) must inevitably lead to the love of man.

Yet it is also true that *this* love of the heart was studied in default of a more direct way, and that consciousness of that default remained with him into old age. It can only be properly understood, in fact, against the failure of the revolutionary spirit of the 1790s, when he had sometimes believed that the heart of man was wakening in a more direct fashion – when, indeed, to his enraptured ears, 'The antiquated Earth, as one might say,/Beat like the heart of Man'.[30] Even in the more sober retrospect of later years he could recall moments when it had made itself manifest in a compelling manner:

> . . . as the desert hath green spots, the sea
> Small islands in the heart of stormy waves,
> So that disastrous period did not want
> Such sprinklings of all human excellence
> As were a joy to hear of.   1805 X 441 – 5

But these had proved places too precarious and isolated for him to rely upon in his quest for a true human order – still less, therefore, as a poet. It was only when he turned from hopes of revolution to consider the potencies of individual humanity that he found a field of the right proportions, by turning to all that could be learned of the heart. Within the various dimensions of that lore, ranging from the human to the metaphysical, possibilities and combinations continued to open out – particularly, I shall argue, when Coleridge's intelligence was available to suggest new areas for exploration.

In certain respects, clearly, it was a precarious enterprise. Not only were there dangers of sentimentalism, or of a quietist withdrawal; the very evidences for basing a metaphysical view of man upon the processes of the heart, being mediated through the individual human consciousness, were necessarily fallible. Yet if it has to be acknowledged that some of the limitations of Wordsworth's achievement have to do with this, it is also clear that he was enabled to achieve many things in poetry that would otherwise have remained closed to him. Among other things, the tensions and interplays resulted in a highly original use of language. Many poems that strike the reader at first as opaque spring to life once the full range of their work is glimpsed – a range which has to do, for example, with the interplay between settled forms and underlying energies.

There is another side to this concern, not altogether welcome to those who think that Romantic poetry should concern itself directly with adventures and extremes of emotional experience. For Wordsworth the heart was not only a field for exploration but a place of refuge. This status too has a basis in physiological fact, since the human heart is, among other things, a regulator. It is pre-eminent among those processes in the body which help to keep the workings of the body within certain limits. The warmth-sense – most extraordinary of them all perhaps – is directly involved, but there are many other workings of the kind, which help to maintain human beings' sense of their own worth, despite their precarious footing between the immensity of a universe above which dwarfs them and the extraordinary minuteness and proliferation of life-processes beneath which can make their professed regard for life seem absurd. Existing as they do in the midst of such extremes, there is yet opened out to their eyes a green earth and blue sky which offer a directly human appeal; even the forbidding wastes of time and space are, for that matter, greeted by a duly-paced consciousness within themselves. These facts, so basic as to be taken for granted, were for Wordsworth indications that despite the essential inhumanity of the universe a principle of mercy was also at work.

Blake took a related if different view. 'Time', he once wrote, 'is the mercy of Eternity'; he also said, however, that it was only the Space 'smaller than a Globule of Man's blood' which 'opens/Into Eternity'.[31] All larger spaces had to be made by the creating power of man.

Wordsworth, by contrast, was a poet of mediation. A full understanding of his poetry can hardly be reached, in fact, without an understanding that it is created in face of the extremes which lie beyond normal experiences, threatening humanity. Awareness of these threats, on the other hand, helps explain his constant search for a place of permanence, a search which can be traced throughout his career. When he first presented the public with an essay in the poetic sublime (his *Descriptive Sketches*), he began with a line,

Were there, below, a spot of holy ground . . .

which expressed his youthful desire to find a place of civilisation which might be adequate to human needs.

At one level, that aspiration is cognate with the one that had taken him, some years before, an orphan and schoolboy wanderer, to the verge of Grasmere, which he had seen in a moment of revelation as a place where a man might happily live and eventually die.[32] It was, he remarks, not a conscious prophecy, for at that time he foresaw no possibility of his ever living there himself; but it was none the weaker for that, and in the end he came to fulfil it.

The aspiration of that early line extends itself further, however, as we consider other things that have been said in this chapter. It expresses his desire not simply for a satisfying spot in space, a 'home', but for a place, anywhere, which was not subject to the contingencies of death, decay or fading. It was the search, one might say, for a place, other than the grave, where a man might feel himself finally composed. And what he came to learn in that quest was something which lay behind the comment of Blake just quoted. In their need to come to terms with the universe of time and space human beings were indeed furnished with an equivalent power in the mind that could measure and structure it, but the activities of that power, if undertaken in a pure form and in isolation, must end in despair. Fortunately, however, the human psyche could also sustain itself by awareness of another work – the pulse of the heart and englobulation of the blood, which were inseparable from the life-process itself. A mind that remained receptive to the work of the body of which it was a part could never be delivered into mechanical system, for even while measuring the units of time and space outside itself it would remain attentive to the pulses and englobulations of the life that was sustaining it and see that they, also, corresponded to powers in the world at large. If so conscious a poet as Wordsworth were to find a sufficient place for himself, he was likely to find in such processes a necessary guide.

There is, however, another side to the matter. The work of the heart is not restricted to the existence of man as part of nature, but includes his relationships with other animated beings. The heart can engage itself to others – and this statement, like others which we have examined, is not *simply* metaphor: the actual movements of physical heart and physical bloodstream can be intimately involved in such engagement, giving urgency to love (or for that matter to jealousy). To the extent that such centres of physical being are involved, similarly, the successful achievements of such relationships will gain in vividness and give more satisfaction. If, on the other hand, the heart commits itself to a movement or a relationship which can never be fulfilled, the looked-for englobulation will not take place: instead it will find itself caught in an unending vortex. Under the pulse of uncompleted passion all experience may be for a time more vivid, but eventually some displacement must take place, some closure, to give necessary relief.

Many of Wordsworth's greatest writings are to be seen as embodying such an experience, an involvement of vortical passion followed by displacement elsewhere – sometimes magnificently: we need think only of some of the 'spots of time' in *The Prelude*, where hardly bearable excitement is followed by an impassioned perception of the universe which is so steadily tenable as to become in his mind a permanent place. In other cases, however, where the vortex was one of impossible love or ineluctable grief, the displacement could never be more than partial. That note of 'partial displacement' is another constant feature of his poetry, taken as a whole: and it is there that we shall find one of our most constant themes.

It was not always so complicated a matter, of course. After buying Bowles's sonnets in 1789 Wordsworth read them as he walked along the street and irritated his brother by stopping in a niche of London Bridge to finish them.[33] To find a poet who could link the images of the heart so firmly and explicitly to the images of place was evidently an exhilarating experience; and an equivalent exhilaration persists to the end in his own writing. But it also follows from what we have been saying that Wordsworth's poetry particularly repays attention when he is running together his sense of the heart as seat of affections and his sense of it as centre of life. When, for instance, he speaks of truths being 'carried alive into the heart by passion'[34] the words 'alive' and 'passion', working together in complex fashion to suggest that human emotions may somehow mediate between the inmost heart of the individual and the inmost 'truth' of the universe, each demand attention, since they betray the full extent of his larger concern. The possibilities opened up by it led Wordsworth in fact into some of his most intricate adventures – whether in literature or in human relationship.

2

Towards a Pure Composure

In his Preface to the 1800 edition of *Lyrical Ballads* Wordsworth declared that valuable poetry of any range had never been produced except by a man who 'being possessed of more than usual organic sensibility, had also thought long and deeply'; he spoke of the poet as a 'man speaking to men', but went on to assert that the poet is, all the same, a man who is 'endowed with more lively sensibility, more enthusiasm and tenderness, who has a greater knowledge of human nature, and a more comprehensive soul, than are supposed to be common among mankind; a man pleased with his own passions and volitions, and who rejoices more than other men in the spirit of life that is in him.'[1]

The last clauses are particularly worthy of attention. One does not automatically think of Wordsworth as a very passionate man, and the more well-known portraits might suggest a sedate figure. Indications of a strong passionate nature survive from his earliest years, nevertheless. In a rush of boyhood mischief, he struck his whip through the petticoat of a lady in one of the family portraits, and his impetuous temperament caused his mother to say that he would be remarkable either for good or evil.[2] His love of exciting sports as a schoolboy impregnates the early books of *The Prelude*. And in spite of the firm self-control he later imposed, the sense of underlying power remained. De Quincey was emphatic:

Wordsworth's intellectual passions were fervent and strong: but they rested upon a basis of preternatural animal sensibility diffused through *all* the animal passions (or appetites); and something of that will be found to hold of all poets who have been great by

18

original force and power, not (as Virgil) by means of fine manage-
ment and exquisite artifice of composition applied to their
conceptions.[3]

There is considerable acuteness in this analysis (which might be read
as a Romantic version of 'undissociated sensibility'). And if De
Quincey's summing-up seems at variance with the initial impression
to be derived from Wordsworth's achieved poetry, that simply
indicates the extent of Wordsworth's ability to mask his own
passion; although his intellectual passions may sometimes rest ob-
servably upon the basis of a 'diffused animal sensibility' its presence
is at other times hidden, needing to be inferred in order that the
poetry may be properly understood.

Certainly Wordsworth felt the need to find a place in his poetry for
passionate experience. During his boyhood, adolescence and youth,
he had found himself subject to emotions which could not easily be
disregarded: we need think only of the excitements of skating, the
episode of the stolen boat, his ravishing of the hazel-bushes –
incidents which were among the very first to be described when he
came to draft *The Prelude*.[4x]

These and many other such experiences had shaped Wordsworth's
consciousness before he went to Cambridge and no doubt contributed to his occasional feeling that he was 'not for this hour/Or for
this place'.[5] A restraining puritanism was also at work, however,
bringing into play contrary forces such as those displayed in the
well-known incident of the Milton celebration. Having drunk well
in commemoration of Cambridge's most famous poet, he found
himself late for evening chapel and was forced to elbow his way in
haste through the outer members of the congregation, still flushed
with wine (like one of Milton's own 'sons of Belial').[6] It was an
experience to be recalled with shame by one who had often pictured
the innocence of the young Milton –

> with his rosy cheeks
> Angelical, keen eye, courageous look,
> And conscious step of purity and pride.   1805 iii 291–3

Yet Wordsworth can hardly have remained totally insensible to the
attractiveness of such experiences for a poet: was there not something to be learned in the world of passion, as well as in the school of
innocence and scholarship?

That question lurked already in some of the literature of the age, as poets became conscious of the ultimate sterility of a restrained and rational verse. It had been implicitly if mildly raised by the work of Erasmus Darwin, who, as one of the most intelligent scientists of the age, had tried in *The Botanic Garden* to create an extended poem on the behaviour of the vegetable creation, including their sexual vagaries. His success, however, had been strictly limited. No major poet was to follow in Darwin's footsteps: Coleridge, his most obvious potential follower, felt Darwin's structure to have been a brittle and precarious one, savouring of wit rather than the full play of imagination. Even if one admired its ingenuity, one would not be likely to read it more than once.

Nevertheless Wordsworth learned from Darwin's work, and not only negatively. *The Loves of the Plants*, in particular, gave him at least one memorable image. Although he distrusted that image of inspiration on a sunlit mountain-top which was a staple of traditional poetry, the image of a man standing on a mountain *at night* could be seen as a more accurate and telling emblem of the poet's condition. The mountain ascent described in the last book of *The Prelude* had several literary precedents, but these had mostly taken place elsewhere, and by day. It was Darwin who transferred the scene to Snowdon, and to the night-time:

> Where frowning Snowdon bends his dizzy brow
> O'er Conway, listening to the surge below;
> Retiring LICHEN climbs the topmost stone,
> And 'mid the airy ocean dwells alone. –
> Bright shine the stars unnumber'd *o'er her head*,
> And the cold moon-beam gilds her flinty bed;
> While round the rifted rocks hoarse whirlwinds breathe,
> And dark with thunder sail the clouds *beneath*.[7]

1791, the year in which this part of Darwin's poem was published, was probably also the year of Wordsworth's own night-ascent of Snowdon; indeed, he may have been directly incited to it by Darwin's description. The most striking feature of Darwin's lines, however, is the unusual relationship between sublimity and pathos in them. This description of a mountain-top is the very opposite of an ecstasy or a transfiguration: for all the fearfulness of the height and the general bleakness of the scene, it is the humble lichen, carrying on its own existence unharmed, that steals the scene. The survival of the delicate flower in the crevice of the fearful rock-face was to be for Wordsworth an even more telling emblem of the basic condition under which all forms of life, from the moss to the human being, had their existence.

Darwin's work contained something more than wit, then. Here was one image which succeeded, at least vestigially, in what was to be a characteristic Wordsworthian work: that of giving vibrancy to pathos by juxtaposing it with an ambiguous sublime. This might not solve the problem of creating poetry in a scientific universe; it did, however, offer a welcome relief by showing the natural mercies which could continue to operate even in that harsh dispensation. Only when the eye returned from the plant to the rock-face would it again be oppressed by a sense of the irrelevance of man to the natural creation.

Akenside had explored the dilemma of the poet in a scientific age rather differently. In *The Pleasures of Imagination* he had made much of the ways in which knowledge of scientific truth could add to the experience of beauty in nature:

> Nor ever yet
> The melting rainbow's vernal-tinctur'd hues
> To me have shone so pleasing, as when first
> The hand of science pointed out the path
> In which the sun-beams gleaming from the west
> Fall on the watry cloud, whose darksome veil
> Involves the orient; and that trickling show'r
> Piercing thro' every crystalline convex
> Of clust'ring dew-drops to their flight oppos'd,
> Recoil at length where concave all behind
> Th' internal surface of each glassy orb
> Repells their forward passage into air;
> That thence direct they seek the radiant goal
> From which their course began; and, as they strike
> In diff'rent lines the gazer's obvious eye,
> Assume a diff'rent lustre, thro' the brede
> Of colours changing from the splendid rose
> To the pale violet's dejected hue.[8]

Although this is a brave attempt to transfer into poetry the first excitements of scientific knowledge, it cannot be said to create great confidence in the further possibilities of such a mode: and it may be

Akenside's own awareness of this that caused him, within forty
lines, to pay his respects to the non-rational:

> Passion's fierce illapse
> Rouzes the mind's whole fabric; with supplies
> Of daily impulse keeps th' elastic powers
> Intensely poiz'd, and polishes anew
> By that collision all the fine machine:
> Else rust would rise, and foulness, by degrees
> Incumb'ring, choak at last what heav'n design'd
> For ceaseless motion and a round of toil.[9]

This picture of passion as a regulator for the human machine,
acting as dynamic impulse and also as a sort of oiling mechanism, is
typical of the inadequacy of the age when confronted by irrational
forces. It is not surprising, therefore, to discover that Wordsworth's
own encounters with passion seemed regularly to come as a diversion from other concerns. According to his own account, his
purposes in making the Alpine walking-tour had little to do with the
Revolution, which at the time seemed to be of little immediate
relevance to him.[10] But his glimpses of the revolutionary spirit and
enthusiasm exhibited by quite ordinary people in the villages
through which he passed bore in on him with the realisation that the
Revolution was a human fact as well as a political one – that
individual people really were, in some measure, changed by it.

His own involvement, equally, was procured only when his own
reactions were reinforced by those of his friend Beaupuy. It was
Beaupuy's depth of feeling which finally drew him – in what was
also a copybook example of an appeal to sensibility – to identify
himself with the revolutionary ideals:

> And when we chanc'd
> One day to meet a hunger-bitten Girl,
> Who crept along, fitting her languid self
> Unto a Heifer's motion, by a cord
> Tied to her arm, and picking thus from the lane
> Its sustenance, while the Girl with her two hands
> Was busy knitting, in a heartless mood
> Of solitude, and at the sight my Friend
> In agitation said, ''Tis against *that*
> Which we are fighting,' I with him believed

        Devoutly that a spirit was abroad
        Which could not be withstood. . . .   1805 ix 511–22

Wordsworth's own engagement with the Girondists was followed eventually by disillusionment, when the full terror of the Revolution became apparent. But in the meantime he had known what it was to be caught up into the infectious engagement of a common movement. He had also known passion of another kind. Annette Vallon, with whom he had fallen in love during the same period, was about to bear him a daughter.

So little is known of this relationship that any comments must include an element of speculation. It is even difficult to judge the quality of Wordsworth's feeling for her. The only direct reference to her on his part consists of a note to Dorothy many years later: 'When you are writing to France say all that is affectionate to A. and all that is fatherly to C.'[11] This shows little more than the nature of his final and settled attitude. The account in the 1805 *Prelude* (published also as 'Vaudracour and Julia') is fictionalised and not, for that reason, a fully reliable source; at least one passage, however, suggests that a general glamour may have surrounded his love, both at the time and in retrospect:

                    . . . his present mind
        Was under fascination; he beheld
        A vision, and he lov'd the thing he saw.
        Arabian Fiction never fill'd the world
        With half the wonders that were wrought for him.
        Earth liv'd in one great presence of the spring,
        Life turn'd the meanest of her implements
        Before his eyes to price above all gold,
        The house she dwelt in was a sainted shrine,
        Her chamber-window did surpass in glory
        The portals of the East, all paradise
        Could by the simple opening of a door
        Let itself in upon him, pathways, walks,
        Swarm'd with enchantment till his spirit sank
        Beneath the burthen, overbless'd for life.   1805 ix 581–95

The reminiscences of *Romeo and Juliet* here are hardly accidental; for there was a touch of Montague and Capulet in the opposition of both families to the projected marriage. In spite of this, however, Wordsworth seems to have left France on the assumption that he would eventually be returning to marry Annette; only gradually did the intention fade.

The fading may have been encouraged by a realisation that the relationship, despite the passionate attraction involved, extended no natural roots into permanence. If he married Annette he would marry a woman who belonged to a different nation and culture. Not only were their religious allegiances different but he might be forced to surrender to hers in the education of their children.[12x] And he, a Girondist, who had been offered a position in the Girondist movement, would be marrying a girl from a firm royalist family. The example of his own idol Milton hovered again before him as a warning of the likely consequences.

The most important force in discouraging him from the projected marriage, however, is likely to have been a more positive one. Early in 1794 he was reunited with Dorothy.[13] With her and with other women of their circle (notably the Hutchinson sisters) he could enjoy a relationship of affection which at once gave him a sense of security and linked him with his own background. This English version of sensibility was, as we have seen, closely linked with traditional puritan and moral values (as in the poetry of Cowper). It was restful where the more passionate relationship with Annette was restless, rooted where that was in flux.

To make this supposition is not, of course, to suggest that Wordsworth suffered a sudden change of allegiance; rather that, faced with the impossibility of marriage in the near future and with the need for emotional support in the loneliness of his new condition, he found with Dorothy a natural working relationship which could help him to survive. Only in time, on this reading of the matter, did he discover how the success of this relationship had undermined his intention of marrying Annette.

The war with France had in any case set up a barrier to an immediate reunion, forcing him to find an alternative way forward. And one important effect of the French experience had been to acquaint him further with the contradictions of passion. It was not only that passion could at one and the same time involve him in the cause of the Revolution yet also urge him to marry a girl who was opposed to it. These involvements carried further possible self-contradictions of their own. He had seen the Revolution descending from its high vision of human potentiality towards the maelstrom of anarchy and indiscriminate violence; he may also (though this is necessarily speculation) have glimpsed beneath the beauty of the woman whom he loved a structure of hardened political and religious attitudes which could in the end have proved a rock against the tides of his own more liberal and fluxile sensibility.

His return to England, by providing relief from such pressing contradictions, cannot have been altogether unwelcome, then. But the withdrawal from passionate commitment also left its effects – including, perhaps, the depressions and nervous headaches of the following period. Nor was it possible for him to slip back into the easy gentlemanly ways that he had known at Cambridge. His future mode of life must involve cognizance of what had been learned in France. The task of discovering a way of life which could be embraced with conviction was not an easy one, therefore.

Other men shared his problem. At about the same time Blake was engraving the 'Argument' to *The Marriage of Heaven and Hell* in which he complained of the perplexities now confronting an honest man. Once it had been possible for him to cultivate a wild garden in the desert – but now hypocrisy was taking over, even there.[14]

In such a situation, the publication of Godwin's *Enquiry Concerning Political Justice* was timely. It is hard to imagine that Wordsworth, whose own *An Evening Walk* and *Descriptive Sketches* had just appeared from the same publisher and were being reviewed alongside it, did not read the work at once and with avidity. Here was a work which, while facing the contemporary intellectual situation boldly, accepting the doctrine of necessitarianism, avoided its more obvious fatalistic implications by also proclaiming the necessity of disinterestedness. On a closer examination the solution might well appear less simple and all-embracing than at first sight, but the feature of the work which was likely to carry any young man through these difficulties at a first reading was the openness of the reasoning and the welcome invocation of sincerity. For Wordsworth, in whom one now senses the presence of a displaced passionate identity, working out its way, trying for some mode of direct utterance yet baffled by the complexity of the contemporary situation, the initial impact of Godwin's straightforwardness could be expected to be powerful.

A few days before the publication of *Political Justice*, however, a new turn had been given to the current complexities by the declaration of war on France. To Wordsworth, who must still have felt himself strongly identified with the cause of the revolutionaries, the news came as a considerable blow, dividing his allegiance. Nor was his feeling of betrayal altogether eased by an awareness of the growing extensiveness of the violence in France. He was at this time, as it seems, retreating quietly from the position which he had taken up in his unpublished letter to the Bishop of Llandaff, where he had argued in mitigation of earlier reports of violence that

> The animal just released from its stall will exhaust the overflow of its spirits in a round of wanton vagaries, but it will soon return to itself and enjoy its freedom in moderate and regular delight.
>
> PrW I 38

The behaviour of the revolutionaries could not by late 1793 be regarde so indulgently: Wordsworth was being forced to remember the changes in character that he had witnessed in some of his associates in France – a process of hardening which he was to explore in *The Borderers*. Yet this could not in his eyes excuse the British Government for taking measures which he believed were augmenting the violence and removing the last hope of an amelioration in France.

It was while he was brooding over these matters that Wordsworth undertook a journey which he was to remember for the rest of his life – the walk across Salisbury Plain. It was, in various ways, a turning-point for him;[15] in the context of the present discussion, its most notable features were his starting near the Isle of Wight, where he saw the preparations for war in progress, and his reflections, as he passed among the monuments of antiquity on the Plain, on the comparison between what could be known of such remote times and 'certain aspects of modern society, and . . . calamities, principally those consequent upon war, to which, more than other classes of men, the poor are subject'.[16]

The pathos of the human condition, which had already impressed itself upon him in his encounters with the solitary figures who roamed the roads of the Lake District, now struck him with greater force. Crime was to be condemned; yet the occasion of crime must often be society's neglect of the criminal – and, indeed, of true justice. So Wordsworth came to project, in the poem which he first entitled 'A Night on Salisbury Plain', a story concerning two such outcasts, acting out their parts in an unjust society against the background of a bleak and forbidding landscape like that through which he was passing.[17]

On a larger scale, meanwhile, Wordsworth was passing into a

state of moral uncertainty. For the time being at least, he was still buoyed up by the conviction that emotions such as those he had seen displayed in France must still somehow be bound to win through to victory:

> . . . in the People was my trust
> And in the virtues which mine eyes had seen,
> And to the ultimate repose of things
> I look'd with unabated confidence;
> I knew that wound eternal could not take
> Life from the young Republic, that new foes
> Would only follow in the path of shame
> Their brethren, and her triumphs be in the end
> Great, universal, irresistible.   1805 x 577–85

As he wavered in his conviction under the pressure of further events, however, he found himself increasingly forced back on an analysis of nature herself, that nature which must inevitably be deeply involved in any discussion of human nature. Here, dangers of a different kind awaited him, for the very methods which he adopted began to exert a subtle tyranny. To adopt terms of his own, he was now relying too exclusively on the analyst's scalpel, to 'probe/The living body of society/Even to the heart'.[18] The result was a process of growing perplexity (exacerbated perhaps in discussions with members of Godwin's circle during 1795):

> Thus I fared,
> Dragging all passions, notions, shapes of faith,
> Like culprits to the bar, suspiciously
> Calling the mind to establish in plain day
> Her titles and her honours, now believing,
> Now disbelieving, endlessly perplex'd
> With impulse, motive, right and wrong, the ground
> Or moral obligation, what the rule
> And what the sanction, till, demanding *proof*,
> And seeking it in everything, I lost
> All feeling of conviction, and, in fine,
> Sick, wearied out with contrarieties,
> Yielded up moral questions in despair.   1805 x 888–900

It was a unique and dour moment in Wordsworth's development, and some of the poetic products from the subsequent period diverge

significantly from the general pattern of his development. In particular, a strong sardonic streak comes to the fore. One passage is
reminiscent of Blake's indignant social criticism at the time:

> Send this man to the mine, this to the battle,
> Famish an aged beggar at your gates,
> And let him die by inches – but for worlds
> Lift not your hand against him – Live, live on,
> As if this earth owned neither steel nor arsenic,
> A rope, a river, or a standing pool.
> Live, if you dread the pains of hell, or think
> Your corpse would quarrel with a stake – alas
> Has misery then no friend? – if you would die
> By licence, call the dropsy and the stone
> And let them end you – strange it is;
> And most fantastic are the magic circles
> Drawn round the thing called life – till we have learned
> To prize it less, we ne'er shall learn to prize
> The things worth living for. –   PW I 316

Another piece, in one of the early notebooks, is so atypical of
Wordsworth's normal style that one half expects to discover it to
have been copied from another writer; yet as seen in the manuscript
it looks like an original composition:

> Away away it is the air
> That stirs among the wither'd leaves
> Away away it is not there
> Go hunt among the harvest sheaves
> There is a bed in shape as plain
> As form of hare or lions lare
> It is the bed where we have lain
> In anguish and despair.
>
> Away and take the eagles eyes,
> The tygers smell
> Ears that can hear the agonies
> And murmurings of hell
> And when you there have stood
> By that same bed of pain
> The groans are gone the tears remain

Then tell me if the thing be clear
The difference betwixt a tear
Of water & of blood.[19]

Yet another fragment, written into the notebook at about the same
time, dwells on the theme of guilt in a natural setting and reflects
Wordsworth's own disquiet at the fact that even when the guilty
mind is almost forcing a corresponding response on the scene which
it is looking at, nature seems so little to reflect the intensity of human
action:

Are there no groans in breeze or wind
Does misery leave no track behind
Why is the earth without a shape & why
Thus silent is the sky
is every glimmering of the sky
Is every loop-hole in the wood an eye
Has every star a tongue?[20]

This again has an unusual rhythmic form for Wordsworth, the
phrasing keeping closely to the contour of the emotion expressed.
Such passages, indeed, suggest something more than a gift for the
sardonic; they point to a possible path not taken – the path of a poet
who might have continued to evolve a poetry of instinctive passion.

The writer who comes to mind as an example of a man coming to
a similar point and actually choosing that path is D. H. Lawrence;
and there are, as it happens, instructive parallels between the two
men, at least in their early development, which throw further light
on the alternatives facing Wordsworth at this time. Occasionally,
indeed, the contrasts and parallels are almost incredibly pointed: one
may for example read Wordsworth's account of the ash-tree outside
the window of the cottage where he lived as a child –

　　　　　where I, so oft,
Had lain awake, on breezy nights, to watch
The moon in splendour couch'd among the leaves
Of a tall Ash, that near our Cottage stood,
Had watch'd her with fix'd eyes, while to and fro
In the dark summit of the moving Tree
She rock'd with every impulse of the wind.　　1805 iv 77–83

and then turn to Lawrence's account of the ash-tree outside *his* childhood home, described fictionally in *Sons and Lovers* (as also in the poem 'Discord in Childhood'[21]);

> ... In front of the house was a huge old ash-tree. The west wind, sweeping from Derbyshire, caught the houses with full force, and the tree shrieked again. Morel liked it.
>
> 'It's music,' he said. 'It sends me to sleep'.
>
> But Paul and Arthur and Annie hated it. To Paul it became almost a demoniacal noise. . . . Having such a great space in front of the house gave the children a feeling of night, of vastness, and of terror. The terror came in from the shrieking of the tree and the anguish of the home discord. Often Paul would wake up, after he had been asleep a long time, aware of thuds downstairs. Instantly he was wide awake. Then he heard the booming shouts of his father, come home nearly drunk, then the sharp replies of his mother, then the bang, bang of his father's fist on the table, and the nasty snarling shout as the man's voice got higher. And then the whole was drowned in a piercing medley of shrieks and cries from the great, wind-swept ash-tree.[22]

One could hardly find two passages which better encapsulate the essential likenesses and differences between the two childhoods: the instinct towards peacefulness in the one, the inescapable sense of the daemonic in the other – and the brooding sense of a strange magic over both.

Wordsworth's visit to the Isle of Wight in 1793 was paralleled by Lawrence's holiday there in 1909, when he saw the review of the fleet at Spithead.[23x] Although it was a gay occasion, he seems like Wordsworth to have felt a note of oppression as well, which found its way into his novel *The Trespasser*, where the muffled firing of guns and the sudden appearances of battleships are themes of subdued menace.

By the outbreak of war, several years later, Lawrence had become (again like Wordsworth) passionately attached to a woman of the enemy nation. He heard the news when he had been walking in the Lake District (where he had been wearing a Wordsworthian coronal of water-lilies twisted in his hat). The walking-party came down to Barrow-in-Furness to find soldiers kissing their sweethearts good-bye on the station platform and thousands of men, hastily recalled to work, streaming over the bridge to the shipyards. The sombre scene was followed by a period walking along the coast – not many miles, as it happened, from the Leven estuary where, on a day of ethereal splendour, Wordsworth heard the news of Robespierre's death and thought that the ideals of the Revolution might after all be about to triumph. This was a different sort of occasion, however, and Lawrence's sense of magic was shot through with a consciousness of pain:

> Then I went down the coast a few miles. And I think of the amazing sunsets over flat sands and the smoky sea – then of sailing in a fisherman's boat, running in the wind against a heavy sea – and a French onion boat coming in with her sails set splendidly, in the morning sunshine – and the electric suspense everywhere – and the amazing, vivid, visionary beauty of everything, heightened by the immense pain everywhere.[24]

The parallels and contrasts between the two writers do not end there; one may, for example, compare the relationship between the Wordsworths and Coleridge, making their seclusion in Dorset and Somerset a forcing-time for theories, discussion, and plans for poetry, with that of the Lawrences and Murrys, engaging in equally intense discussions in Cornwall. Again there is a contrast: the Wordsworths and Coleridge for a time achieved almost total sympathy, whereas the Murrys and Lawrences found themselves in constant contention. It is not altogether fanciful to see a ghostly likeness, however: Middleton Murry and Coleridge were both men who sometimes strove towards a state of ideal sympathy, even at the cost of self-annihilation, whereas Wordsworth and Lawrence would draw back from such a prospect – Lawrence fiercely, Wordsworth more slowly and cautiously. If we then ask why the later paths of the men should have diverged so dramatically we find ourselves proceeding to inquire further into that fierceness and that slow caution, comparing Lawrence's instinctive need for a daemonic tension between individuals (springing no doubt from his childhood experiences) with Wordsworth's need for a more straightforward and peaceful affection.[25x]

That need must, in fact, now be acknowledged as another powerful undercurrent throughout this early period. For the excursion from the Isle of Wight which was so momentous for his future development had not ended when Wordsworth left Salisbury Plain. Afterwards (spurred on, probably, by the fashion for the area instigated by William Gilpin) he had crossed into the Wye Valley and had his first sight of the landscape surrounding Tintern Abbey, a sight which, though coloured by his own restless and haunted state of mind, impressed him by its natural beauty – and particularly by the total harmony of its forms. It was in Goodrich Castle shortly afterwards that he had encountered the young girl whose inability to actualise the difference between the living and the dead inspired 'We are Seven'; it may have been in the parish church of Plas-yn-Llan (since Jones, whom he was visiting, was the incumbent there) that he experienced the sense of alienation from his fellow-countrymen as he heard prayers for war and felt himself to be the only member of the congregation not participating, which he describes in *The Pre-lude*. Either on the way there or back, also, he encountered the wild rover who told him 'strange stories' and who became the model for Peter Bell.[26]

Various strains of his thinking can be seen embryonically working in these incidents, but the immediately germinating idea at the time seems to have been that of a power in nature – at least in certain settings – which could affect the sensibility of the observer directly. (The rover's indifference to such effects presumably acted as a further challenge.)

It is his preoccupation with such directness of effect that marks off Wordsworth's attitude from that of previous nature-poets and artists of the picturesque. When William Gilpin made an expedition down the Wye some years before, he commented on the beautiful setting of Tintern Abbey:

> It occupies a gentle eminence in the middle of a circular valley, beautifully screened on all sides by woody hills, through which the river winds its course; and the hills closing on its entrance, and on its exit, leave no room for inclement blasts to enter.[27]

Gilpin also mentioned its tranquillity, 'sequestered from the com-merce of life'. The tradition of going into such places in order to indulge in moral reflections was well established at the time. But no poet or artist went so far as Wordsworth was to do in proposing the existence of a direct and *congruent* power in nature, able to affect the heart of a responsive observer.

The development of Wordsworth's view is expressed in some lines in imitation of Horace (composed in the summer of 1794)

where he found himself imagining the sort of votive offering that
would be appropriate at Rydale waterfall:

> A mind that, in a calm angelic mood
> Of happy wisdom, meditating good,
> Beholds, of all from her high powers required,
> Much done, and much designed, and more desired, –
> Harmonious thoughts, a soul by truth refined,
> Entire affection for all human kind
> A heart that vibrates evermore, awake,
> To feeling for all forms that Life can take,
> That wider still its sympathy extends
> And sees not any line where being ends;
> Sees sense, through Nature's rudest forms betrayed,
> Tremble obscure in fountain rock and shade,
> And while a secret power those forms endears
> Their social accents never vainly hears.   PW I 10–11

It is the phrase 'social accents' that is particularly striking.
Akenside had dwelt upon the mysterious associations which the
mind could discern in nature and their beneficient effect upon
conduct:

> . . . for th' attentive mind,
> By this harmonious action on her pow'rs,
> Becomes herself harmonious: wont so long
> In outward things to meditate the charm
> Of sacred order, soon she seeks at home
> To find a kindred order, to exert
> Within herself this elegance of love,
> This fair-inspir'd delight: her temper'd pow'rs
> Refine at length, and every passion wears
> A chaster, milder, more attractive mien.[28]

In this version, however, the power of nature affects only the *quality*
of action in the individual human being: the idea that the link
between nature and man might by the power of its own working
extend itself into the relationship between man and man is not
explored. Wordsworth, on the other hand, seems to be suggesting
that a vibrant response of the heart to signs of life and sense in the
landscape – even in the rocks – is rewarded by an enlarged sympathy,

which will come to include human society as well. And this in turn might suggest the existence of a connection between the responsive human sensibility and the motive power in man's moral behaviour. To one who had 'yielded up moral questions in despair', the idea of a moral *sense*, closely related to the workings – even, it might seem, the physical workings – of the human heart would be all the more welcome; I have suggested elsewhere that the development of the idea may have encouraged a critique of Godwin's philosophy, and that both Godwin and Wordsworth may have derived intellectual stimulus from the consequent discussion.[29]

The theory that this new intuition had come upon him the previous autumn at Tintern, when his harsh experiences on Salisbury Plain gave place to the intimate, fostering setting of the Wye Valley, rests largely on the importance which he ascribed to the effects of that occasion when he came to revisit the scene five years later. By then, certainly, he was willing to look back on it as a passionate experience and believe in a lasting social benefit from what had happened there. In the following spring, moreover, he had been reunited with Dorothy: the new intuition which he described in the lines just quoted would seem to have bound him more closely to her as an equally receptive and sympathetic observer of nature – and so, on our previous argument, to have further undermined the planned marriage to Annette Vallon. It was in England, among English scenes, and with certain English friends that he was most likely to find the link between nature and the moral being on which he would subsequently hope to base his philosophy.

When Wordsworth took up residence with Dorothy at Racedown in the autumn of 1795, these various currents were working together in his mind, and he seems to have looked forward to the retirement as a time mainly for reflection and study. He was no doubt also hoping that his studies might stimulate new poetry, in which he would be emboldened to 'grapple with some nobler theme'.[30x]

One immediate project, directly in line with the sardonic strain just traced, was to write a poetic translation of Juvenal: the opening pages survive.[31] But his heart was evidently not in the task. The underlying buoyancy and fixed purposes which fortify good satiric writing were lacking: he needed a time of exploratory work which would enable him to build up his own creative resources again. And his rejection of his own society was not so fierce as Lawrence's: he maintained faith in a possible renovation of the social forms. In such circumstances over-cultivation of the sardonic might be a misuse of the poetic faculty, leading towards a

> scorn and condemnation personal,
> That would profane the sanctity of Verse.
>
> 1805 x 643 – 4

Passages of a different sort (also to be found in the notebooks) voiced a stronger hope of development: they reflected the fascination, already mentioned, with the strange solitaries who sometimes passed across the landscape, mysterious in their apparent self-containment. In addition to depicting the figures of Salisbury Plain and the solitary women of *Descriptive Sketches* he wrote many drafts for a poem which eventually became *The Old Cumberland Beggar.*

His chief achievement of the time, 'The Ruined Cottage',[32] developed this theme by introducing a solitary, Margaret, who had been ruined by distant social forces, but who remained fixed to the place of her former happiness. This story, which later became a starting-point for *The Excursion*, is based once again on his sense of the impersonal way in which war bears on human beings, particularly the poor: the operations of a war which are never directly seen in the poem take away the husband who is Margaret's whole help and stay. And Wordsworth's growing interest in the phenomenon of obsession at this time manifests itself in his picture of her, listening intently for the steps of her husband, questioning any traveller who passes about the one subject that matters to her. But while she spends herself in her craving the processes of nature are performing their own patient work, so that when she dies her death comes to seem also as part of a larger change, in which her house and garden are already taking their part.

This creature of pathos was also for Wordsworth an emblem of hope. For her yearning, the yearning of a human being for its own natural kind, was one permanent human process which could surely be relied upon. Political systems might rise and fall, nations might be destroyed in war, but this power would continue to operate, like the flower growing on the storm-ridden mountain-side. Yet, as the poem suggests, any optimism fostered by such reflections was necessarily dark.

'The Ruined Cottage' marks an early climax in Wordsworth's career; in certain respects it was the best poem he ever wrote, and we shall return to it later. At the same time, it opened no immediate door to further development. And in general Wordsworth's growing preoccupation with the human heart was subject to this limiting factor. Moving to the creation of great emblematic figures of human pathos, such as Margaret, it left the reader – and the poet – to contemplate them in silence. The moral problems remained unsolved. Given these permanent facts of the human condition, what were the possibilities of alleviation? Would it ever be possible for the great mass of human beings to feel truly for one another? An even stronger element in the pathos of human isolation seemed to be the fact that most men were locked in themselves, unable even to develop the sense of others' needs which might move them to works of compassion.

In this context the experience at Tintern Abbey remained an intriguing indication of possible significance, not yet fully organised in his mind. So long as he looked for the connections between natural beauty and moral sensibility, his work would inevitably move towards evocations of human pathos in a natural setting, and this in turn would always raise the danger of sentimentalism. Tintern Abbey, after all, was only one place in the world: an experience there did not necessarily authorise statements about the whole human condition. The feelings of the heart, also, straightforwardly expressed, left his fuller personality dangerously exposed – liable, in the face of external criticisms, or his own reflections, to muster its resources to the defence of threatened identity. In the absence of other balancing forces, the only available defence would be the cool exercise of reason which he had already known, consolidating itself towards a sardonic and self-regarding detachment.

No man in fact can isolate himself in the way that Wordsworth was doing without developing some such carapace of self-defence; at the same time, as we have seen, he was perceptive enough to see that a sardonic isolation, if cultivated, would gradually, by smothering more vital impulses, lead to sterility. At Racedown he remained in dilemma, torn between his impulse to achieve something for his own society and his knowledge that Dorothy's openness of nature corresponded to an emotional resource which he would abandon at his peril. It is not altogether surprising therefore that for once in his career he turned not to poetry but to drama. In drama, at least, he could express by turns the various conflicting forces of his own nature.

The Borderers,[33] the first version of which was written during this period, is the work in which Wordsworth explores most fully the tension between man's impulses to isolation and his warmings to benevolence. Rivers, 'villain' of the play, and advocate of individual power, is drawn with a skill and insight which show the degree of Wordsworth's own engagement with such an attitude; Mortimer, who is temporarily seduced by his wiles but whose impulse to human sympathy survives precariously, expresses something of the pilgrim element in Wordsworth at this time, trying to keep alive his sense of the human heart and its significance in a world where no certainty of truth was available.

The importance of this latter motif is indicated in the course of a note which Wordsworth attached to the play many years later:

> The study of human nature suggests this awful truth, that, as in the trials to which life subjects us, sin and crime are apt to start from their very opposite qualities, so are there no limits to the hardening of the heart, and the perversion of the understanding to which they may carry their slaves.   PW I 342

In the play itself, Wordsworth is not concerned to state this directly, but to show in action the kind of transition in character involved in such a boundless hardening of the heart – a transition which, he said, he had sometimes witnessed among people he knew during his time in France.

While there is no evaluation of its workings in Wordsworth's descriptions of Rivers, the heart is invariably treated by him as a consciously accepted means and tool to action. It is a further part of the argument of the play, on the other hand, that Rivers's devotion to pure action leaves him essentially without a steady basis for existence. He can consolidate his existence only by further actions and by making converts to his way of life. It is for this reason that he hopes to set in motion the same processes of obsessive action in another man by deceiving him into an action like the one which initiated his own addiction. Once Mortimer has committed murder, for whatever reason, Rivers is sure that the same chain of consequences will ensue, transforming him into a disciple and comrade for himself and so destroying the isolation which is the Nemesis otherwise awaiting the man of pure action.

There seems to be no reason why the plot should not succeed, given Rivers's extraordinary powers of fabrication, and in one sense it does: Mortimer is eventually beguiled into abandoning the aged Herbert under the impression that he is a villain. The crucial difference between Rivers and Mortimer has already been indicated, however. Mortimer, unlike Rivers, attends to the workings of his own heart. This is shown clearly, not only in an early speech when he replies to Rivers's accusations against one of the characters (the blind man) with the words:

> Never may I own
> The heart which cannot feel for one so helpless.   I, i, 39–40

but in many similar references to the operations of his heart throughout the play; most of the other characters, including the common people who are Rivers's dupes, show the same openness. Rivers, on the other hand, never refers to his own heart in this way, though he is perfectly willing to speak of the operations of the heart in other people – particularly if he can use this as a means to work on his companions. The real extent of his contempt for the human heart as such is shown when he says, at one point,

> Benevolence that has not heart to use
> The wholesome ministry of pain and evil
> Is powerless and contemptible.   II, i, 72–4

The heart, whose 'light dancing' is elsewhere dismissed by him as 'the passion of fools',[34] is here seen in the precise rôle which he has assigned to it – to provide, that is, a mechanical support to the ends of pure action.

Rivers is by no means a contemptible figure, rather tragically deceived. The central exchange of the play is one in which he congratulates Mortimer on the murder of Herbert (not knowing that he has in fact left him abandoned to his fate instead). At this point, he shows himself to be less villainous than mistakenly noble. In lines which come as a surprise to the reader who thinks of him as devoid of any sense of human suffering, he explains the importance for him of a life of action:

> Fortitude is the child of enterprize:
> Great actions move our admiration chiefly
> Because they carry in themselves an earnest
> That we can suffer greatly.   III, v, 56–9

Mortimer agrees, to be met by the key speech of the play, again from Rivers:

> Action is transitory – a step, a blow,
> The motion of a muscle – this way or that –
> 'Tis done. And in the after-vacancy
> We wonder at ourselves like men betray'd.
> Suffering is permanent, obscure and dark,
> And has the nature of infinity.   III, v, 60–5

To this Mortimer replies: 'I do not understand you.'[35x] Rivers has, in fact, presented a truth which is greater than his own comprehension of it. Not only does the sense of suffering, in Wordsworth's eyes, create the nobility of the man of action; it is more important than action. Where the momentum of action may easily betray a man to a course which, had he foreseen it, he would not have willed, the knowledge of suffering initiates him, by means of the heart, into permanent wisdom. Rivers has inverted Wordsworth's moral universe, which begins with the wisdom of the heart and bases all action (or inaction) upon that; instead he inhabits one where the force of the heart's rhetoric is simply a spur to greater and greater self-betrayal. Nevertheless there is a splendour about him: elsewhere in the play Lennox recalls a strange incident.

> Once he headed
> A band of pirates on the Norway seas,
> And, when the King of Denmark summoned him
> To the oath of fealty, I well remember
> 'Twas a strange answer that he made; he said
> 'I hold of spirits, and the sun in heaven.'   III, iv, 27–32

This is the fierce oath of a man who has tried to achieve the nobility of a disembodied angel. But because he is not content to explore the actualities of human existence for what they are, but must use them instead as mere fuel for his fire, he has plunged into a path indistinguishable from villainy.

The shadow of a dilemma remains: how can a man know this? Is it not natural for him to live first and foremost by action? Wordsworth could suggest a final answer only by falling back on the Tintern Abbey experience, where moral understanding was seen to shade into the cultivation of natural sensibility and to be in some sense continuous with it – even as the final ruined structure of the Abbey had, in the process of time, become continuous with the surrounding landscape. Rivers himself is made to show a suspicion of the knowledge that he has missed when he recalls the moment of his isolation on the island at the time of his original crime and says

>   . . . for many days
> Beneath the burning sky on the dead sea
> I brooded o'er my injuries, deserted
> By man and nature. If a breeze had blown
> It might have found its way into my heart
> And I had been – no matter – Do you mark me?
>
> IV, ii, 15–20

Such knowledge is, of course, normally sustained by human love, but Rivers had been deprived of this by the mutiny on his ship: as Lennox remarks of him,

>   . . . restless minds,
> Such minds as find amid their fellow men
> No heart that loves them, none that they can love,
> Will turn, perforce, and seek for sympathies
> In dim relations to imagined beings.   III, iv, 33–7

Rivers has sought that relation in 'spirits, and the sun in Heaven'; it is the final clinching-point of Wordsworth's morality that if he had found it elsewhere in nature – as, say, in the blowing of a breeze – he might have received not the nourishment of pride but a more profound impulse, carried into the heart. The breeze did not blow on Rivers in his fierce isolation, but a not dissimilar experience does save Mortimer in his direst moment, when he looks up from the man whom he is about to murder. Lady Macbeth had said 'Had he not resembled/My father as he slept, I had done it'; Mortimer, coming to Herbert, sees in his face the features of his daughter Matilda, whom he loved:

> . . . It put me to my prayers. I cast my eyes upwards, and through
> a crevice in the roof I beheld a star twinkling over my head, and,
> by the living God, I could not do it.   II, iii, 298–301

This is no simple intervention by nature: Mortimer is saved also by his sense of Matilda's face in Herbert's and by the surviving religious impulse which has caused him to lift his eyes to the sky in the first place. But the sight of the star is necessary to complete the moral circle: it breaks through to his sensibility and makes the deed finally impossible.

The end of the play is not a simple victory for the human heart, however, nor is Mortimer restored to human society. That is what his followers want: they press to make him captain of their band. But Mortimer (and it is a curious oblique victory for Rivers and *his* kind of knowledge) refuses to accept their offer. Just as Rivers was impelled to a life of action which should carry within itself an under-consciousness of suffering, Mortimer will now set out on a restless life of suffering haunted by the memory of action:

> No human ear shall ever hear my voice,
> No human dwelling ever give me food,
> Or sleep, or rest . . .
> A thing by pain and thought compelled to live,
> Yet loathing life – till heaven in mercy strike me
> With blank forgetfulness, that I may die.   V, iii, 270–9

This final pilgrimage of Mortimer's suggests something of a self-projection on Wordsworth's part. Although he would not wish to dramatise his own situation in this way, he feels himself, at least in some sense, drawn to a similar course. Still haunted by that consciousness of the totality of human suffering, persisting from generation to generation, which visited him on Salisbury Plain, he feels one logical conclusion for man, as Man, to be an attitude of acknowledged guilt and self-alienation, involving also an accepted intensity of consciousness. If human beings actually faced, in their own nature, what man does to man, the driving interaction of pain and thought would overwhelm even their normal instinct for human society.

In what is perhaps the most perceptive account of the play so far written,[36] Roger Sharrock has drawn attention to the ways in which the play grapples with the issues raised for Wordsworth by his various involvements in France and draws attention to the degree of Wordsworth's self-identification with both the main characters. Mortimer, he points out, has, as a result of his engagement with Rivers, been initiated into a form of knowledge which leaves him unable to return to his old ways of thought.

Sharrock's account may be supplemented by some little-known lines of Rivers's, describing the order of knowledge into which he felt himself initiated as a result of his withdrawal from society:

— When from these forms I turned to contemplate
The opinions and the uses of the world,
I seemed a being who had passed alone
Beyond the visible barriers of the world
And travelled into things to come.   IV, ii, 141–5

Such a man is truly a 'borderer', in the ultimate sense of the word; and it is not difficult to see how closely Wordsworth's own attitude, drawn as he was into alienation from his own society after his stay in France, aligns itself with that of his hero, who claims that in his isolation he 'saw unveiled the general shapes of things'. A few years later, when he was drafting the first prospectus for *The Recluse*, he could still describe himself as a 'transitory Being' who was

In part a Fellow-citizen, in part
An outlaw, and a Borderer of his age.   PW V 6 *app. cr.*

Rivers's apartness and respect for the 'intellectual being' that he knew within himself found, it seems, at least an echo in the mind of Wordsworth, who could acknowledge an impulse of his own to stand aside from his civilisation in superior knowledge – even though his compassion cast him more nearly in the role he had ascribed to Mortimer.

The latter self-identification (which is further pointed by the fact that the poem 'The Convict' which he sent to the *Morning Post* late in 1797 was published under the pseudonym, 'Mortimer') was also strictly limited, of course. Wordsworth felt no guilt comparable to Mortimer's; instead he was searching for a position that could be validly held in the light of an equivalent knowledge. Donald E. Hayden has drawn attention to the sense of warring extremes which inhabits the play, summed up in two lines from a later version.

So meet extremes in this mysterious world,
And opposites thus melt into each other.[37]

The positive need which emerged at such points, so far as Wordsworth's own plans for himself were concerned, was for a mediant position in a world that was subject to the clash of such extreme forces. While he was condemning Mortimer to a life of suffering, he was himself, as we have seen, working in the company of Dorothy on a poetry that might express a proper role for true humanity.

Yet if he could thus sidestep the danger of hardening into a role of rationalism and emotional sterility, the mythical structure of the play continued at another level to haunt his career. The buried daemon which had lifted its head in his sardonic verse and found a vicarious voice in Rivers also felt Rivers's need for a companion in activity – a need which Dorothy could not fully supply. *The Borderers*, seen as an expressive work of art, registered the uneasy tension at this time between two impulses in himself: the impulse to glory which could find no adequate social or political context for its expression and no means of utterance beyond fitful fragments of the passionate and the sardonic, and the impulse to love of humankind which was fostered by Dorothy's quickness of sympathy, but which was always englobing itself into a static moon of contemplated pathos. In some ways this tension, and the forces which it represented, would remain basic to his career for the rest of his life; but for a few years it was to be transformed into something more like a creative dialectic. To understand how this came about, we need to look more closely at the impact upon him of Coleridge.

3

A Link of Life?

The exact point at which Wordsworth met Coleridge is not easy to determine. The evidence (based largely on reminiscences written many years later) suggests that the two men attended a public meeting on the slave trade at Bristol in the late summer of 1795, and that they met (probably with Southey and Edith Fricker) in a lodging-house, where Wordsworth read his poems, including the current version of 'Salisbury Plain'.[1] Wordsworth, writing to William Mathews in late October, said,

> Coleridge was at Bristol part of the time I was there. I saw but little of him. I wished indeed to have seen more – his talent appears to me very great.   WL (1787–1805) 153

Taken by itself this might suggest a warm but rather muted reaction on both sides. Writing in *Biographia Literaria* twenty years later, however, Coleridge was to recall that his immediate reaction to 'Salisbury Plain' had been that it was a work of poetic genius:

> It was the union of deep feeling with profound thought; the fine balance of truth in observing, with the imaginative faculty in modifying the objects observed; and above all the original gift of spreading the tone, the *atmosphere*, and with it the depth and height of the ideal world around forms, incidents, and situations, of which, for the common view, custom had bedimmed all the lustre, had dried up the sparkle and the dew-drops.   CBL I 59

A later comment by Wordsworth, furthermore, confirms that Coleridge reacted in this way and makes it clear that he, in turn, was affected by his friend's praise. Towards the end of the penultimate book of *The Prelude*, he recalls his debt:

Nor is it, Friend, unknown to thee, at least
Thyself delighted, who for my delight
Hast said, perusing some imperfect verse
Which in that lonesome journey was composed,
That also I must then have exercised
Upon the vulgar forms of present things
And actual world of our familiar days,
A higher power, have caught from them a tone,
An image, and a character, by books
Not hitherto reflected.   1805 xii 356–65

This reminiscence also sets the whole matter in a different light, so far as Wordsworth himself is concerned. For it suggests that Coleridge's flattering response was, by its very terms, directing his attention further away from the social issues involved in his poem. That poem, we suggested, was originally written out of a strong sense of the ills to which the poor are subject; but Coleridge, stressing the originality of the approach itself, as giving clear evidence of genius in the poet, offered support to Wordsworth's view of himself as a man set apart from his fellows, gifted with powers above the ordinary. We become aware once more of the emergence of two concurrent yet separable streams in his mind: his feeling for the universal bonds that unite human beings, drawing them together without account of station, and a sense that he was called to be a dedicated spirit, separated from the generality of mankind – this separation being, none the less, destined to minister ultimately to the welfare of mankind at large. Coleridge's praise evidently encouraged this second current.

What is certain is that Wordsworth's reaction to Coleridge's praise of 'A Night on Salisbury Plain' was not, as one might have expected, to offer the poem for publication, but to revise it radically. And this revision, on examination, reflects a natural development from the positions just examined, and Wordsworth's need to maintain a link between them. Whereas the first version had ended with a rousing call for action, for the 'Heroes of Truth' to act until the only vestige of tyranny left was 'that eternal pile which frowns on Sarum's plain',[2] the second stressed the need for human beings generally to develop sympathetic states of mind. In the new version it is a sign of the hero's surviving humanity that when he comes to a gibbet from which a body cased in iron is swinging he falls into a 'trance'; and the final stanza is now devoted to the similar place where he himself is later left hanging:

> They left him hung on high in iron case
> And dissolute men, unthinking and untaught
> Planted their festive booths beneath his face
> And to that spot, which idle thousands sought
> Women & children were by fathers brought
> And now some kindred sufferer driven, perchance
> That way when into storm the sky is wrought
> Upon his swinging corpse his eye may glance
> And drop as he once dropp'd in miserable trance.[3]

There is a dark undertow to this conclusion, with its presupposition that the majority of mankind consists of 'the unthinking and untaught'. Wordsworth's hopes for social change through direct action are now, it seems, waning: such actions, he is coming to believe, will always be thwarted by the masses, who cannot or will not understand what is at stake. If any hope remains it lies rather with certain solitary 'passers-by', human beings detached enough to sympathise fully with their fellows. Such sympathies, gradually communicated, may eventually leaven mankind. If so, what cannot be achieved by any immediate programme of action may finally come about as if by a natural process.

The growth of this revised conviction can readily be traced in the writing of 'The Ruined Cottage', where the presentation of Margaret, a victim of contemporary militarism through the death or disappearance of her husband, is followed by no denunciation of the social order that has brought about such happenings. Instead, her story is presented in its own, isolated pathos, the poem concluding with reflections from the Wanderer upon the final state of peace which he discovered in contemplating the scene, once it had been fully overtaken by the processes of nature.

Before either 'Salisbury Plain' or 'The Ruined Cottage' could be offered for publication, however, the presence of Coleridge was felt again, this time with longer and more far-reaching effects. 'The Ruined Cottage', newly finished, was read to him in the summer of 1797, during the course of a visit which caused Dorothy Wordsworth to write to Mary Hutchinson with enthusiasm:

> You had a great loss in not seeing Coleridge. He is a wonderful man. His conversation teems with soul, mind, and spirit. . . . At

first I thought him very plain, that is, for about three minutes: he is pale and thin, has a wide mouth, thick lips, and not very good teeth, longish loose-growing half-curling rough black hair. But if you hear him speak for five minutes you think no more of them. His eye is large and full, not dark but grey; such an eye as would receive from a heavy soul the dullest expression; but it speaks every emotion of his animated mind; it has more of the 'poet's eye in a fine frenzy rolling' than I ever witnessed. He has fine dark eyebrows, and an overhanging forehead.

WL (1787–1805) 188–9

We do not know, unfortunately, the full contents of the conversations between the poets during the months that followed. Often they have to be inferred from scattered remarks and reminiscences, and from the contents of the poetry that was produced both then and afterwards. Clearly, however, a change was overtaking both men. Wordsworth was moving from the probing but still rather staid, poetry of recent months into a more informal mode, including both personal self-analysis and the vividly dramatic writing of his contributions to *Lyrical Ballads*. Coleridge was devoting more time than before to detailed observation of the phenomena of nature about him – while also being moved to write poetry at the high imaginative level of 'Kubla Khan' and 'The Ancient Mariner'.

So uncharacteristic are these changes, in fact, that a radical appraisal of the situation is called for. The impact of Coleridge, it will be argued, was not simply that of a very intelligent fellow-poet full of wide-ranging ideas on many subjects, but of a man who was busy with certain esoteric ideas which fascinated Wordsworth by offering a new interpretation of his own earlier visionary experiences and by suggesting that the underlying unity between human beings might be more firmly founded than he had until now been willing to suppose. Coleridge, in turn, was stimulated by Wordsworth's interest and criticisms to explore his own ideas further.

I have traced elsewhere the pattern of the speculations which seem to have occupied Coleridge during these years.[4] Originally, I have argued, they were founded upon the ideas of certain Neoplatonists (whom Lamb tells us he was fond of expounding while still at school) and upon Jakob Boehme's treatise *Aurora* (which Coleridge later said that he had 'conjured over' in his schooldays). Boehme, in particular, offered a view of the universe which presupposed a set of correspondences between the deepest forces at work in it and those of the human heart. God himself was seen as the heart of the universe, the Son being in turn, as it were, the 'heart' of God. In the same way, the sun lay at the heart of the universe, with light (not heat) as its own heart. The human heart itself, therefore, being cast in the same pattern, could realise its true nature only in so far as it allowed itself to be dominated by the light that was in it; all evil resulted from a lack of that illumination. Once let that light reign, and the heart of every creature would be free to 'energise' in its own manner (to use a Neoplatonic term). For this reason, the imagery of the fountain or spring played a central part in Boehme's writings, for it offered a way of describing the role of the heart through observation of other fountainous forces in nature, including animated beings. The human heart, manifestly the spring of the human body, could then be described through imagery taken from the behaviour of springs of water, fountains of light and the instinctive behaviour of living organisms. Such a view suggested the existence of a spring-like order in the universe which was related particularly to all that is alive. In moral terms, moreover, it suggested that good conduct is created by a correspondent illumination of the heart. As Boehme put it, using his own terminology,

> When the flash is caught in the fountain of the Heart, then the Holy Ghost riseth up in the seven qualifying or fountain Spirits, into the Brain like the Daybreak, Dawning of the Day, or Morning Rednesse. . . .[5]

Encountered at the end of the eighteenth century by an English adolescent schoolboy, I have suggested, one attractive feature of this view of the heart lay in its power to draw attention away from the analytic and detached powers of the mind and remind the reader of other, spontaneous forces in the human body. At that time, moreover, it had become possible to link these phenomena in another manner, by way of all that was coming to be known about magnetism. This power had sometimes been invoked by earlier thinkers to keep in check the more sombre implications of Newton's theories by suggesting that the forces of attraction which played so great a part in them might have a matching counterpart at the human level, acting to connect individuals with each other – and to God. William Law, for example, wrote, of the under-instincts of mankind: '. . . all is *magnetism,* all is *sentiment, instinct,* and *attraction,* and the *freedom* of the will has the government of it'; and again, '. . . all things have *magnetical* effects and *instincts* both towards God and one another.'⁶ The phenomena involved had become appealing also to writers of the cult of sensibility. Rousseau's Eloisa, for instance, wrote to her lover,

> Our souls . . . touch in all points . . . and, like the magnets, of which I have heard you speak, that have the same motion, though in different places, we should have the same sensations at the two extremities of the world.⁷

In recent years all such assertions had been given a new immediacy – and possible definition – by the discovery of hypnotism, or 'animal magnetism', as it was called. This enjoyed a tremendous vogue in London during Coleridge's boyhood, three thousand people besieging the house of a well-known magnetiser on one occasion.⁸ Was there perhaps a link between the magnetism involved in the operations of gravity, the electrical magnetism which was being investigated by scientists and the animal magnetism set up between the hypnotist and his patient? If so, it suggested that the nature of the universe might be more complicated than many eighteenth-century thinkers had imagined and, in particular, that living things might not necessarily be the totally independent atomic particles that Newtonian physics suggested, being also and demonstrably linked to one another at a sub-conscious, vital level.⁹

So far as English poetry was concerned, the chief impact of Boehme's ideas and imagery was, I have argued, that they created a preliminary and embryonic language for what Keats was later to call 'the heart's imagination'. Introduced by Coleridge into poems such as 'The Ancient Mariner' and 'Frost at Midnight', that language was to be developed by Keats and others to provide for a century or more one of the great motifs of English Romantic poetry: the use of particular phenomena in nature as 'subjective correlatives' for the workings of the affections.¹⁰

So far as Coleridge was concerned, however, there was a further level to the whole enterprise. Could it be that the attractions and affinities in nature, along with the observable workings of animal instinct, gave evidence of a bond between living things which was not just a good metaphor for use in the poetry of benevolence, but an actual factor in human behaviour, working at some pre-conscious level? Such a speculation finds its way into his 1795 poem, 'The Eolian Harp':

> And what if all of animated nature
> Be but organic Harps diversely fram'd,
> That tremble into thought, as o'er them sweeps
> Plastic and vast, one intellectual breeze,
> At once the Soul of each, and God of all?   CPW I 102

Although the poet immediately checks such speculations by introducing the imagined reproof of Sara Coleridge, these were the lines which he quoted a year later to Thelwall in discussing the nature of life, and it is hard to imagine that they did not provide a part of his discussions with Wordsworth in 1797; indeed, if we suppose that not only Wordsworth, but also Southey and Coleridge read their verses aloud at the earlier meeting in Bristol, according to the custom of the time, and if we suppose that by the time they met Coleridge had written 'The Eolian Harp' (normally dated 20 August 1795), the possibility looms that Wordsworth had actually heard the lines before his departure for Racedown.

Coleridge's speculations at this time, on such a reading of the matter, rested upon a belief in the potentialities of the heart, as illuminated by the imagination, which was extending Boehme's pietistic formulations towards something approaching pantheism; preserved from it, perhaps, only by his Neoplatonic insistence that the breeze which blew upon every organism was an 'intellectual' breeze – and therefore to be related back to a divine ground of intellect subsisting beyond, as well as within, nature.

A philosophy based upon the paramountcy of the human heart would certainly have found a ready listener in Wordsworth in 1797. But there is also good reason to suppose that this further, semi-pantheistic extension of the ideas would not have fallen upon a soil that was totally unprepared. Already, at Cambridge, Wordsworth had found himself preoccupied by certain unusual states of consciousness within himself and by the light which they might shed upon the nature of reality:

> A track pursuing not untrod before
> From deep analogies by thought supplied,
> Or consciousnesses not to be subdued,
> To every natural form, rock, fruit or flower,

Even the loose stones that cover the high-way,
I gave a moral life, I saw them feel,
Or link'd them to some feeling: the great mass
Lay bedded in a quickening soul, and all
That I beheld respired with inward meaning.   1805 iii 121–9

Discussing these lines, H. W. Piper argues for the influence of various philosophers in France who had discussed the existence of an 'active principle' in nature.[11] He also draws attention to the 1794 lines, quoted earlier,[12] in which Wordsworth writes of the heart that

. . . sees not any line where being ends;
Sees sense, through Nature's rudest forms betrayed,
Tremble obscure in fountain rock and shade, . . .'   PW I 10n

That Wordsworth should not have come across theories of the active universe during his residence in France is, as Professor Piper points out, difficult to believe. At the same time, the later lines would suggest that by 1794 he had already moved into a more complex attitude. Any encouragement of pantheistic attitudes during the first flush of revolution had received a check from the Reign of Terror – a sharp reminder of nature's crueller aspects. The journey across Salisbury Plain had added a sense of history's oppressive weight. Whatever benevolent powers there might be in nature, they were not, it seemed, normally recognised by more than a few favoured individuals: the common lot of humankind through the centuries was to be enslaved by violence and fear, oppressing or oppressed.

The 1794 lines, on this argument, had been composed during a first period of recovery from this disillusionment. The last line, indeed, with its eighteenth-century elegance, might suggest a reversion to the pre-revolutionary mode of sensibility which had complemented an iron sense of law by the cultivation of tender feeling for animals, picturesque landscapes and suffering humanity. In the lines just quoted, however, one finds the familiar invocation of sympathy and sensibility being expanded towards a visionary pantheism. Within the old mode Wordsworth is trying to find a place for his own visionary experiences in youth and the agitated concern for humanity shown by men like Beaupuy.

Some clue to the intervening process may be found in another passage mentioned by Professor Piper. In *The Excursion*, Wordsworth's Solitary looks back to his feelings during the French

Revolution and remembers his enthusiasm for nature. That nature, however, he now sees as 'The Nature of the Dissolute', a false guide, as opposed to 'fostering Nature', which he had at that time rejected.[13] Wordsworth, we may assume, was wrestling with a similar distinction during the period after his return from France, his various compositions of the time spurred on by attempts to find consolation in that side of nature which answers to the sympathies of the human heart. But it was not until he came into contact with Coleridge's theories, which allowed for a work of nature at a level of consciousness below normal thinking, that he could find a framework within which the value of passionate experiences might be affirmed without risk of self-betrayal to the excesses of violent action. Once allow the existence of a primary consciousness or consciousnesses, on the other hand, and it could be argued that, at that level, mankind was in touch with a common 'link of life', running beneath all the contradictions of human events and offering a ground of human experience which was largely ignored by the more civilised. The way lay open, in fact, for the philosophy expounded by the Wanderer in the last book of *The Excursion*, which, in its first draft (composed in 1798–9), elevates Wordsworth's early visionary sense of nature to the status of revelation:

> There is an active principle alive
> In all things, in all natures, in the flowers
> And in the trees, in every pebbly stone
> That paves the brooks, the stationary rocks,
> The moving waters, and the invisible air.
> All beings have their properties which spread
> Beyond themselves, a power by which they make
> Some other being conscious of their life,
> Spirit that knows no insulated spot,
> No chasm, no solitude; from link to link
> It circulates, the Soul of all the worlds. PW V 286–7 (app.cr.)

Although the poetry composed up to 1797 contains occasional foreshadowings of this philosophy, there is little in that year that can be ascribed immediately to the impact of Coleridge's more refined speculations. *The Borderers*, however, which was much revised and not finally completed until later, contains a few images and assertions which might reflect the new influence that summer. Rivers's

oath, 'I hold of spirits, and the sun in heaven', might owe something
to Coleridge's interest in sun-religions, for example, and the incident in which Herbert's blindness was pierced for an instant by a
lightning-flash in a storm, to give a momentary physical sight of his
child ('A face, and a confused gleam of human flesh . . .') also has a
Coleridgean ring, suggesting a 'primary' faculty of vision which
might, in the absence of normal conductors, be brought into action
by the extreme stimulation of a lightning-flash.[14]

The most intriguing of these possibilities is provided by the key
incident of the play, in which Mortimer is prevented from actually
murdering Herbert by glimpsing Matilda's features in his, by feeling
an impulse to prayer and by seeing a bright star in the sky above.
Critics have understandably found this an unsatisfactory incident,
particularly since, as Enid Welsford points out,[15] he sees the whole
episode in a different light next day:

> Last night, when I would play the murderer's part,
> I did believe all things were shadows – yea,
> Living and dead, all things were bodiless –
> Till that same star summoned me back again.
> Now could I laugh till my ribs ached. Oh, fool!
> To let a creed built in the heart of things
> Dissolve before a twinkling atom.   III, ii, 72–8

John Jones argues that Mortimer's seeing of the star recalls him
from the belief (fostered by Rivers's influence) that all things are
shadows; it reminds him that they are not. He goes on to say that the
point, though characteristic of Wordsworth, is unfortunately un-
supported in the rest of the play.[16] This is true; but if we suppose
Wordsworth to have created the incident under the influence of
Coleridge's theory, it is more easily explained, at least in terms of the
play's internal consistency. It can then be supposed that Mortimer,
who in normal circumstances is under the influence of Rivers and
Rivers's version of reality (which is evidently bounded by the
general laws of time and space), is stimulated by the preternatural
arousal of his senses as he advances to the murder, first to glimpse
Matilda's features in Herbert's, and then to see the star, not, at that
moment, as the 'twinkling atom' of normal sense-perception, but as
a light which pierces the heart with palpable directness (rather like a
milder version of Blake's stars, with their 'spears'). This immediate
awareness of a 'living God' who binds all life together, makes the

murder, which would be a breaking of that bond, impossible. Next day, on the other hand, no longer hypnotised to that primal vision, he is back in Rivers's world, where the normal laws of space and time are 'a creed built in the heart of things' – a phrase which shows, incidentally, that the 'heart' has now resumed its status for him as mere metaphor.

The incident of the star did not in itself need Coleridgean prompting, since Wordsworth had from childhood been aware of the effect of looking up at the sky from a black dungeon,[17] or of seeing a star in a moment when his senses were unusually aroused,[18] and the use of the incident, with a moral link, could simply be a development of the Tintern Abbey intuition; but the difference between Mortimer's state of mind at the time and on the day after does suggest an unusual train of thought for Wordsworth, which Coleridge's speculations might have set in motion.

A clearer effect of exposure to those ideas may be traced in two shorter poems. 'The Reverie of Poor Susan' was composed, according to Wordsworth, in 1797,[19] and 'The Farmer of Tilsbury Vale' is dated some time between 1797 and 1800; the resemblance between the metres of the two poems suggests that they were both written under something of the same impulse and perhaps at the same time. Both poems involve the belief that a known and familiar landscape, particularly if impressed from an early age, will act as a permanent and powerful presence in the mind, helping to preserve the identity of its possessor against external forces which threaten its integrity. Wordsworth's adoption of this belief (which of course carried with it the implication that a country upbringing is likely to provide certain permanent advantages denied to the town-dweller) is more readily to be understood if we assume that he had been influenced by a theory of magnetism such as that outlined above. Under this, the impressed landscape becomes a permanent vehicle for the preservation of the life of the affections, since the human being's fast attachment to it also nourishes that primary consciousness which keeps alive his or her love. For Poor Susan the fact is finally tragic, however, since there is no way in which she can link the permanent landscape of her childhood and love to the loveless, shifting world of London around her. So when she hears a captive thrush singing at the corner of Wood Street, the landscape into which she is transported superimposes itself on the actual scene in front of her but makes no connection with it:

'Tis a note of enchantment; what ails her? She sees
A mountain ascending, a vision of trees;
Bright volumes of vapour through Lothbury glide,
And a river flows on through the vale of Cheapside.

The experience cannot last; it can only fade, leaving a sense of loss and abandonment:

She looks, and her heart is in Heaven: but they fade,
The mist and the river, the hill and the shade;
The stream will not flow, and the hill will not rise,
And the colours have all pass'd away from her eyes.

The primary vision cannot extend itself to unite with the world of immediate perception, and she is left a divided being.

'The Farmer of Tilsbury Vale'[20] offers a more optimistic treatment of the same phenomenon. As compared with the (probably) imaginary Susan, this farmer was an actual individual, described to Wordsworth by Coleridge's friend Tom Poole. And the picture of him is in line with some other rural vignettes, in which Wordsworth takes an unexpectedly lenient view of a man who has transgressed the rules of society, on the ground that the essential soundness of his heart has remained unaffected:

You lift up your eyes! – but I guess that you frame
A judgment too harsh of the sin and the shame;
In him it was scarcely a business of art,
For this he did all in the *ease* of his heart.

The final lines recall Poor Susan, but without any hint of her despairing longing. This man is gay and sprightly: as he goes around London he looks for things that will remind him of his life in the country, behaving exactly as if he were walking around his own farm. His favourite spots are Covent Garden and the Haymarket hill, where he will thrust his hand in a waggon and smell the hay.

'Mid coaches and chariots, a waggon of straw,
Like a magnet, the heart of old Adam can draw;
With a thousand soft pictures his memory will teem,
And his hearing is touched with the sounds of a dream.

This specific image of a magnet drawing the heart must surely be ascribed to the impact of ideas such as those described earlier.

Because this man's primary consciousness has had time to magnetise itself not just to a landscape but to a whole way of life learnt in that setting, he is possessed of an inner resource which preserves him (for all his carelessness) from losing integrity of heart among the shifting values of the town.

Discernment of this background to the two poems, with their lilting rhythms and emotional undertow, may in turn help to throw light upon the larger enterprise undertaken by Wordsworth and Coleridge at this time. The collection which came to be entitled *Lyrical Ballads* has its own, unique place in literary history: to this day, no one can open the volume after a diet of eighteenth-century verse without sensing a refreshing new power. Yet the exact nature of that power remains something of a puzzle. The advertisement, with its claim that they 'were written chiefly with a view to ascertain how far the language of conversation in the middle and lower classes of society is adapted to the purposes of poetic pleasure' has brought disappointment to readers who hoped to find in the collection an early example of 'the language of the common people' in verse. Many of the pieces are not composed in popular language at all, and those that are, are often truer to the coy idiom of the lower middle class ('And Betty's in a *sad* quandary!'; 'To go to bed for very cold/And then not sleep a wink!' – to say nothing of Simon Lee's 'poor old ankles') than to the earthy directness of the manual worker. It has been shown by R. Mayo, similarly, that so far as verse-forms are concerned, the collection contains very little that cannot be matched in the contemporary magazines.[21]

If the experiments in language seem scattered and only half successful, there is, on the other hand, by contrast with similar poems of the time, a recurrent (sometimes rather *gauche*-seeming) agitation of direct feeling, while the references to common humanity which run through the whole collection create cumulatively a new note of compassion. For many readers these qualities may emerge, not at a first reading, but as a rediscovery in the light of developing human experience. Their reaction resembles that of the heroine of Margaret Drabble's *The Garrick Year*:

> I read Wordsworth also, those selfsame poems over which I sniggered and jeered when seventeen and brilliant at school: we were taught to think them ludicrous, and at *The Idiot Boy* even Mary Scott laughed. But now I do not laugh, I weep, real wet

tears, the same tears that I shed over newspapers reports of air disasters, for they are as moving as air disasters, those poems, they have as high a content of uninflated truth. And I weep partly as an apology for my past ignorance, from which I might never have been rescued.[22x]

At this level, the *Lyrical Ballads* express over a wide range Wordsworth's vision of human suffering on Salisbury Plain and Dorothy Wordsworth's penetrating and immediate power of sympathy. But even Wordsworth did not think of his poems *simply* as moving: of 'The Idiot Boy', in fact, he said, 'I never wrote anything with so much glee'.[23] And often one feels that the dominating emotion in the village poems is not so much sympathy as relief – the liberating pleasure of the discovery that in a universe which might seem to obey no laws except those of necessity, village people do love their idiot boys and men sometimes display more gratitude than is called for by the strict balance-sheet of favours given and received.

There is another curious feature of the collection, as originally conceived. They look at first sight like a loose collocation of rather disparate poems and separate experiences. A collection which ranges from 'The Ancient Mariner', via 'Goody Blake and Harry Gill' to 'Tintern Abbey', does not immediately impress one with a sense of unity. Yet when Coleridge wrote about it to Cottle in May 1798 he said,

> We deem that the volumes offered to you are to a certain degree *one work*, in *kind tho' not in degree*, as an Ode is one work – & that our different poems are as stanzas, good relatively rather than absolutely: – Mark you, I say *in kind* tho' not in degree.   CL I 412

What common factor is it that could make one see these poems as an ode, of which the different poems are stanzas?

At this point it is useful to turn to a statement in the Preface to the 1800 edition which has puzzled some critics. An aim which is described there reaches well beyond anything said in the original Preface:

> The principal object . . . which I proposed to myself in these Poems was to make the incidents of common life interesting, by tracing in them, truly, though not ostentatiously, the primary laws of our nature: chiefly as far as regards the manner in which we associate ideas in a state of excitement.   PrW I 122–4

This psychological intention is not immediately apparent in the poems themselves, and the reader is left weighing the words 'not ostentatiously'. If one sets what is being said into a context of speculations about the link between morality and nature, and its relationship with a primary level of consciousness, on the other hand, a possible thread of consistency emerges which not only supports Coleridge's assertions of a unity in the collection as a whole, but suggests the existence of a sequential pattern of thought in the 1798 volume. 'The Ancient Mariner', the first poem in it, may be said to exhibit Coleridge's theory as mediated through a poem of the supernatural. The Mariner shows his ignorance of 'the primary laws of our nature' when he shoots the albatross, the link of life that remains to the ship in the icy wastes; by the rigorous justice of that supernatural universe, we may further suppose, the pains which he is forced to undergo are endured at the primary level of his being. For a time, indeed, he sees the world about him only as a world of death, until an unlooked-for outbreak in the fountain of his heart enables him to bless the living creatures about him and begin his long penance. That penance is still largely a torture; but it includes at least one moment of vision, in which he sees the spirits of his shipmates passing back and forth to a sun which is also a fountain of light and harmony.

The core of the poem, on this interpretation, consists of a series of experiences which are closely related to the view of humanity which we have argued Coleridge to have developed from Boehme and the Neoplatonists: a view whereby human beings find their true home in the universe only when they are able to perceive the correspondence between the spring-like heart of man and the fountainous heart of nature. The riddling nature of human experience also renders such perceptions rare, however, so that a man such as the Mariner hardly knows what to make of them. The only conviction that survives firmly in his mind is that it is desperately important for human beings to love one another and to love all other living things.[24]

Looked at from another point of view, however, the end of the poem had more topical relevance, for it may be seen to reflect a common element in the experience of those who had been drawn into a vortex of violent and passionate events such as those of the French Revolution. Any man who returned to the ordinary world of eighteenth-century England after involvement in those extremes of experience might well feel, like the Mariner, a new sense of the mercies inherent in everyday living and the goodness of the innocent ceremonies that respect the bond between life and life.[25] Considered from these points of view, 'The Ancient Mariner' provides an apt opening to a collection devoted to tales of ordinary life: it evokes vividly the sense that exposure to the primary powers of nature would leave a man in a state where even the banalities of village life would be welcome and heart-warming; it thus helps to give an underlying tone to all that follows.

The scene-setting, we may further suggest, continues in the following poems. First Coleridge's 'Foster-mother's Tale',[26] extracted from his tragedy, gives a picture of what a child might be like if his secondary consciousness had never been developed so as to link his affections to other human beings. The child of his poem has grown up in the midst of nature, so that when he learns to read, against a background of institutional religion and under the assistance of a friar, his thoughts are unlawful and heretical; he is condemned and put in a dungeon. He manages to escape, however, and goes to America, where the last thing that is known of him is that he

> set sail by silent moonlight
> Up a great river, great as any sea,
> And ne'er was heard of more: but 'tis supposed,
> He lived and died among the savage men.

The child, it seems, has found the only action which can satisfy the urgings of a primary impulse to freedom that has found no other guidance or ends.

What then of those who are forced to remain in civilisation under the same disability? This was a question which had long haunted Wordsworth in one form or another; the next poem in the collection, 'Lines left upon a Seat in a Yew-tree',[27] is one that he had apparently started years before. The underlying suggestion that emerges is that such a conflict might well result in a man's choosing to live in nature in sardonic isolation. Devoid of the large sense of human community that might have resulted from a fuller education of the heart, he would take refuge in a solitary contemplation of nature, where he could feed his mind satisfyingly, but also self-destructively, upon the beauties set before him. The hero of Wordsworth's poem is a man who returned to nature as a result of bitter experiences in the world. Having built a seat in the gloom of a tree he could sit there and view the immediate foreground, consisting of rocks with sparse herbage, as an emblem of his own unprofitable life, then lift his head to look at the loveliness of the distant scene and mourn a world which he must never know, where benevolence and loveliness went together. He (like the boy in the previous poem) is last seen in solitude – but this time dying alone, in pure bitterness of heart. By contrast, the stranger who visits the seat is invited to apply the moral to himself – to contemplate the same contrast between the gloom in the yew-tree and the lovely pathos of the distant scene beyond, but to draw a different conclusion–

> . . . that he, who feels contempt
> For any living thing, hath faculties
> Which he has never used; that thought with him
> Is in its infancy.

The fourth poem, Coleridge's 'The Nightingale',[28] portrays a 'gentle maid' who has learned to cultivate her primary consciousness more positively. Going out from her father's castle at night she listens to the nightingales who, completely magnetised to the light of the moon, sing when the moon is shining and fall silent when it passes behind a cloud–

> As if one quick and sudden Gale had swept
> An hundred airy harps!

The experience attunes her to the accents of joy in nature.

At one level, we have suggested, the early poems of the collection help focus attention upon an important feature of Wordsworth's main contributions – that they are the productions of a man whose vision of ordinary human life has been changed by his own glimpses of the agonies of desolation and who has learned to see the ordinary charities between man and man as oases in a world which would otherwise be no more than a desert of law and necessity. If they were *simply* that, however, they would hardly be the poems that we know. Many, we may argue, are brushed by the wing of Coleridge's further speculations at some point and show the effects in their structure.

'The Female Vagrant',[29] the next poem in the collection, is a special case, for in its original version it formed part of the poem 'Salisbury Plain', which had made such an impression on Coleridge when he first heard it. It told the story of a woman who, like Poor

Susan, or the Farmer of Tilsbury Vale, had grown up in attachment
to a particular landscape. She had looked after her father's flocks on
the cliffs, while she could see him fishing in his boat 'a dizzy depth
below'.[30] But when her father guarded his liberty against the
blandishments of a new landlord, trouble fell on them and they were
forced into poverty, emigration and a life of war in America. She
returned to England finally as a hopeless vagrant, who had lost
everything that made life worth living.

In this poem, the special benefit to be derived from bringing the
Coleridgean speculations into consideration is that they help to
throw into relief the nature of Wordsworth's own preoccupations.
Where Coleridge would associate the value of the child's primary
consciousness with the preservation of its sense of wonder and unity,
Wordsworth's first concern has already shown itself to be with the
importance of establishing a moral identity which is also independent. In this task also the forces of 'primary consciousness' may be
regarded as having an important part to play. The child that grew up
in the high places of nature, looking at her father 'a dizzy depth
below' was learning how to stand up, like him, in her own free
identity. But once detached from that known and familiar landscape
those powers could easily be undermined.

Since the poem was mainly in existence before he met Coleridge,
it provides us with an unusually good opportunity of seeing how far
Wordsworth's ideas had already developed in their own right. At the
end, the heroine describes her refusal to become a beggar, the
physical collapse which brought her to a hospital where she became
aware of the mental sufferings of others, 'Fretting the fever round
the languid heart', and her restoration to common life:

> again on open day I gazed,
> At houses, men, and common light, amazed.

She was now taken up by a group of wandering people but, though
moved by their kindness to her, was unwilling to join them in their
unlawful activities. So now she finds herself isolated, regretting that
she has her 'inner self abused' and looking often towards America,
'Where my poor heart lost all its fortitude'. The 'fever round the
languid heart' and its 'loss of fortitude' are touches apparently added
after the main dialogue with Coleridge began; these, therefore, may
reflect his direct influence.

The next poem 'Goody Blake and Harry Gill'[31] seems, by com-

parison with the foregoing, to reflect with peculiar intensity and
directness the excitement of Wordsworth's first exposure to Coleridge's ideas, since it stands very close to Coleridge's belief that
there was a connection between the primary consciousness and the
warmth-sense of the body. The story from which it is derived
appeared in Erasmus Darwin's *Zoönomia*, a work which (I have
elsewhere argued) stimulated Coleridge strongly.[32] Wordsworth's
anxiety to obtain it is evident from a note in the early spring of 1798
in the course of which he says,

> I write merely to request (which I have very particular reasons for
> doing) that you would contrive to send me Dr Darwin's
> Zoönomia *by the first carrier.*   WL (1787–1805) 199

The urgency of the underlining suggests that Coleridge had already
told him of the story and made him eager to read the original. It
earned its particular Wordsworthian significance, in turn, both by
Darwin's firm claim that it was true and by its support for his sense
that the common link between human beings was recognised best by
those who lived in a village community. Harry Gill, by his mean
attitude to his neighbour, depriving her of fuel which was vital to her
life but of little use to himself, had broken that bond; it was therefore
appropriate that the coldness of his heart should become physically
manifest in the uncontrollable coldness of his body.

Wordsworth himself commented on the peculiar significance of
the story if, as Darwin asserted, it was true:

> I wished to draw attention to the truth that the power of the
> human imagination is sufficient to produce such changes even in
> our physical nature as might almost appear miraculous. The truth
> is an important one; the fact (for it is a *fact*) is a valuable illustration
> of it.   PW II 401n

One further observation may be made. The fact that the story was
not merely an emblematic tale but actually recounted as true – and
psychologically explicable – at least in Coleridge's terms – evidently
gave Wordsworth the further impetus to complete his poem without
drawing an overt moral. If it was as true as that, it could be left to
take care of its own morality.

What that morality might be is, nevertheless, strongly suggested
in the next poem, the Lines beginning 'It is the first mild day of
March. . . .'[33] And as Wordsworth expounds his philosophy of

nature in its bolder form, we may once again detect signs of a continuing dialogue with his friend. In the context of Coleridge's preoccupation with springs and fountains it was natural to ask whether the etymology of the word 'spring' might not reflect some primitive awareness of a universal and vitalistic energy like that which he himself was postulating – sensed alike in the activity of springs of water, young animals, such as lambs and babies, which spring by pure instinct, the sunrise (or 'dayspring') and spring the season of the year. And all this activity, by Coleridge's theory, would bear a direct correspondence to the central 'spring' of the human body, the heart. Wordsworth takes up such ideas into his own sense of a spring morning, with its invitation to put aside other tasks and learning and take part in this universal intercourse:

> Love, now an universal birth,
> From heart to heart is stealing. . . .

The underlying powers involved, it is further suggested, are stronger than those of the normal laws by which men try to live, for they can move the springs of human action directly:

> Some silent laws our hearts may make,
> Which they shall long obey. . . .

Their inward nature realises itself in the emergence of a common harmony and joy:

> And from the blessed power that rolls
> About, below, above;
> We'll frame the measure of our souls,
> They shall be tuned to love.

The importance of preserving this 'wisdom' of human nature is explored further in 'Simon Lee',[34] where the heart is also regarded once again as a centre of fortitude. Simon, who has always been noted for his exploits in the hunting-field, his good cheer and his physical strength, now finds himself too weak even to sever an old tree-root. His fortitude shows itself in the fact that he goes on trying – until the narrator intervenes and completes the task for him with a single stroke. Yet the quality of his humanity is shown less by his greater capability in the past (or even by his fortitude in old age) than by his response to this neighbourly act:

The tears into his eyes were brought,
And thanks and praises seemed to run
So fast out of his heart, I thought
They never would have done.

Godwin had discussed the question of human gratitude in his
Political Justice and pointed out that 'gratitude . . . if by gratitude we
understand a sentiment of preference which I entertain towards
another, upon the ground of my having been the subject of his
benefits, is no part either of justice or virtue'.[35] Simon Lee's gratitude
goes further than that discussed by Godwin, however: it transcends
the very terms of the argument, since it is not even an act of 'justice
or virtue', but a flood of tears. The act of weeping manifests his
integrity. Although he formerly delighted in the rigours of the
hunting-field not as an act of willed cruelty but as a pure exercise of
joy, that exercise might have been questioned morally in terms of its
effects. It was, however, keeping alive a truth to his own heart which
now finally shows itself in his tears: they are the outward and visible
sign of a heart which remains a spring. The narrator, confronting the
fact, is drawn into its orbit, and forgets more intricate questions of
justice or virtue as he comments on the contrast with man's general
cold-heartedness that is pointed by Simon Lee's tears of gratitude:

— I've heard of hearts unkind, kind deeds
With coldness still returning.
Alas! the gratitude of men
Has oftner left me mourning.

The puzzling 'Anecdote for Fathers, shewing how the art of lying
may be taught'[36] may also have been touched by Coleridge's ideas. In
itself it relates a straightforward enough story: the narrator, taking
his young boy for a walk, begins asking whether he prefers Liswyn,
where they are walking, or Kilve, where they spent the previous
spring. When he replies 'Kilve', his father badgers him again and
again to explain why. At last, the boy, catching sight of a bright
weather-cock nearby, answers,

'At Kilve there was no weather-cock,
And that's the reason why.'

At first sight this strikes one as a common enough experience: if a
child is pestered with a question too difficult to answer he may

simply produce a silly reply. But why does this show 'how the art of lying may be taught'? Would it not have shown this rather if the child had given his father an answer which he might have believed?

A possible connection emerges, however, if we read the poem as containing an ingenious application of Coleridge's theory, resulting from further enquiry into the way into which the primary and secondary consciousnesses relate to one another – particularly in childhood. The father, by pressing the question 'why?' is forcing his child into an activity of the secondary consciousness for which it is not yet prepared. As a result the primary consciousness is turned to the defensive, a sign of this being the fact that the bright weather-cock, which would normally make a direct appeal to that conscious-ness as the most delightful feature in the landscape, becomes a point of focus for the threatening force. The child replies (with perfect truth to his own inner processes) that he preferred Kilve because there was no weather-cock there. There was no weather-cock – and no threat. But this is also a dangerous moment for his psyche, since it marks a point when his primary consciousness has momentarily ceased to have a direct relationship of delight with those things in the landscape which it normally enjoys. If this process of projection continues, it may emerge, by way of further alien fantasies, into 'the art of lying'.

The child of 'We are Seven',[37] on the other hand, is at present in no such danger. If she seems to tell an untruth when asked how many children there are in her family, this is because her primary con-sciousness is so vividly active that she is more aware of life than death. Once her secondary consciousness has developed further, she will come to deduct automatically the two dead members of her family from the total number of her brothers and sisters. She already knows that they are dead – she has played around their graves often enough. But as soon as that knowledge has been elicited from her and the firm question returned to, her primary consciousness takes over again, always more conscious of wholes than parts, of life than of death, and answers with the full total. Wordsworth no doubt liked her for sticking to her guns, even in a hopeless cause, and there is something of that too in the stubborn movement of the poem, but unless the depth of her answer, afforded by its suggestion of a primitive life-consciousness in the child, is perceived, the poem must appear slightly absurd. The possible effect of absurdity was in fact pointed out to Wordsworth by Tobin, who 'earnestly entreated'

him to cancel it from *Lyrical Ballads* on the grounds that, if published, it would make him 'everlastingly ridiculous'. Wordsworth
records his own answer: 'Nay! said I, that shall take its chance,
however, and he left me in despair.'[38]

There is one further fact about the composition of the poem,
which helps indicate the point of limitation in Wordsworth's absorption of Coleridge's ideas. He did not, according to the same account,
write the poem straightforwardly, but backwards, stanza by stanza,
moving from final expostulation and dogged reply to his first
meeting with the child. At the end, he needed an opening stanza, but
was still without this when he went in and recited it to Dorothy and
Coleridge, remarking that he would sit down to tea with more
pleasure if the poem were complete. Coleridge immediately threw
off the opening stanza as originally printed:

> A simple child, dear brother Jim,
> That lightly draws its breath,
> And feels its life in every limb,
> What should it know of death?

That Wordsworth should have required a prefatory stanza at all is
indicative of his sense that something was left unexplained in the
poem as it stood – it could, after all, have begun just as well with the
second stanza:

> I met a little cottage girl,
> She was eight years old, she said;

– and the fact that he could not phrase such a stanza may well indicate
that the primary and secondary consciousnesses, in his own version,
tended to pull apart from one another. The fact of primary consciousness, if it existed, was so important and powerful that its
functioning would need more than a four-line stanza for
Wordsworth to explain the nature of its operation in relation to the
more sober secondary function. For Coleridge, on the other hand,
there was no problem: he could put the required point simply, since
he believed that the primary consciousness expressed itself naturally
through the whole sensibility of the child. In his stanza, it is not just
the heart, but the breathing, tripping body of the child which
expresses its as yet unviolated sense of life.

Wordsworth, by contrast, was taking as his starting-point the
links between the health of the child's primary consciousness and its

sturdy independence: he could less readily perceive that the child's body itself might radiate that primary sense of life. For him, as a result, the existence of two such forms of consciousness was more likely to start a further problem and suggest a dark paradox. If there was a truth in the optimistic implications of the child's refusal to treat death as total fact, there must also be a truth in the accumulated behaviour of human beings, who had in recorded history shown little tendency to direct their behaviour by any 'life wisdom' of the primary consciousness. And in certain respects this was for him the more weighty fact, so that even when he was describing the effects of delight in nature (in the 'Lines Written in Early Spring'[39]) he found himself reverting to the fact that the pleasure, for all his faith in it, must continue proving itself to him:

> The budding twigs spread out their fan,
> To catch the breezy air;
> And I must think, do all I can,
> That there was pleasure there.

The present evidence, considered against that larger background, served only to increase his sadness about the general fate of mankind:

> If I these thoughts may not prevent,
> If such be of my creed the plan,
> Have I not reason to lament
> What man has made of man?

There is a similar elegiac note in one or two of the later ballads (such as 'The Thorn' and 'The Last of the Flock'[40]), where Wordsworth consolidates the effect of pathos hinted at in the stanza just quoted. The shepherd attached to his one remaining sheep, the bereaved mother returning to the thorn over her child's grave bear pathetic witness to the way that life cleaves defiantly and stubbornly to life (however alien the world about them) if once the magnetic bond of love has been established. In 'The Mad Mother',[41] on the other hand, the woman's forlornness and tendency to madness are mitigated by the vital magnetism induced by the act of suckling her child;

> 'Suck, little babe, oh suck again!
> It cools my blood; it cools my brain;
> Thy lips I feel them, baby! they
> Draw from my heart the pain away.'

When the baby stops its sucking and draws back, the mother is revisited by fears – this time that her child is mad; but she has now been encouraged to plunge on into the wildness of nature and find means of prolonging life for them both.

One of the most interesting examples of the way in which Coleridge's speculations seem to have intertwined with Wordsworth's preoccupations is to be found in a poem which takes the idea of the 'magnetic bond' to its extreme: 'The Complaint of a forsaken Indian Woman'.[42] Once again, the poets' different responses to the same book (in this case Hearne's *Journey . . . to the Northern Ocean*) suggests that their emphases were differing within the framework of a general agreement. Coleridge, who used the book when writing *Joan of Arc*,[43] seems to have been struck particularly by the descriptions of the Aurora Borealis 'rustling and crackling' and also, perhaps, by the accounts of the 'conjurors' who took the place of priests for the Indians (one can readily imagine how his mind would play over the report that the Indians called the Aurora Borealis 'Deer' because it corresponded to the electrical sparks produced by stroking a hanging deer-skin).[44] Wordsworth, on the other hand – and it is equally typical – was more immediately struck by Hearne's account of the Indians' callousness to their old people, whom they simply abandoned when sick, leaving them, nevertheless, some food and shelter so that they could survive for the time being and catch up again if they recovered. Hearne remarks that their custom could be ascribed to necessity and self-preservation rather than to a want of humanity and social feeling. Wordsworth seized on the idea of an Indian woman, abandoned in this way, her fire and food exhausted, lamenting her fate, as the subject for a poem. Had he simply preoccupied himself with her as a desperate figure in the snowy wastes, however, she might simply have become another of his static emblems of pathos, this time so devoid of living company that there would have been little to write about.

From this dead end Wordsworth is rescued, as it seems, by Coleridge's theory: it becomes possible to imagine that under the powerful, magnetic lights of the Aurora Borealis her primary consciousness is brought fully into play, making her vividly aware of the final issues of life and death. This interpretation is supported by the fact that when Wordsworth comes to write about the poem, he describes it as one of his attempts to 'follow the fluxes and refluxes of the mind when agitated by the great and simple affections of our nature'.[45] The phrase 'fluxes and refluxes' suggests the gravitational influence of the moon on the tides.[46x] And although, as Wordsworth says, the poem is a picture of the mind in extremity, 'the last struggles of a human being, at the approach of death, cleaving in solitude to life and society', there is something more in the poem than this might suggest. The woman's factual sense of her own weakness is dominated by yearnings of her primary consciousness, but these are not directed simply towards her companions. It might be truer to say that her condition has set up alternating magnetisms. Alone in the snowy wastes, devoid of all normal contact with the world, her basic magnetisation is to the energies of the universe, as manifested in the cracklings of the Aurora Borealis: it is as real in her dreams as in her waking perceptions, so that she is surprised to find herself alive.

> In sleep I heard the northern gleams;
> The stars they were among my dreams;
> In sleep did I behold the skies,
> I saw the crackling flashes drive;
> And yet they are upon my eyes,
> And yet I am alive.

Her first wish, therefore, is to die: in this magnetised solitude she has no fear of death, which will simply confirm her, in the waste under the stars, as a part of the living universe at large. Yet the thought of her fellows, initiated by a feeling of reproach that they did not take her further, attracts her back to her child – and this thought reminds her of the moment when her child was taken away from her:

> Through his whole body something ran,
> A most strange something did I see;
> — As if he strove to be a man,
> That he might pull the sledge for me.
> And then he stretched his arms, how wild!
> Oh mercy! like a little child.

There is here a suggestion that at the moment when the filial bond was being cut the child's primal consciousness was not only excited into action but stirred to operate at its extremes: first expanding with its own growth-impulse, trying to assume manhood in a moment in order to help her, before contracting to the helplessness of the baby in its plight and its severance. Her own adult consciousness extends the process. The urge to be with her child relapses towards a more general impulse to be with her people, and then to a recognition that she cannot even lift a limb, which gives place to a final yearning that she could have her child with her at the moment of death and so die happily, the two great magnetisms in her consciousness finally reconciled.

The same sense of double magnetism is to be found in the preceding poem – at least as it existed before Wordsworth excised its ending. In 'Old Man Travelling; Animal Tranquillity and Decay, a Sketch',[47] he depicts an old man who has in his old age become so much a part of nature that even the birds do not notice him.

> He travels on, and in his face, his step,
> His gait, is one expression; every limb,
> His look and bending figure, all bespeak
> A man who does not move with pain, but moves
> With thought.

The one expression, the one thought given out by this figure is, it seems, that the laws of nature are now speaking totally and directly through his body:

> He is by nature led
> To peace so perfect, that the young behold
> With envy, what the old man hardly feels.

But the old man's travelling is not, it turns out in the original version, so purposeless as it might seem. The narrator asks him where he is going, and why; the old man replies:

> 'Sir! I am going many miles to take
> 'A last leave of my son, a mariner,
> 'Who from a sea-fight has been brought to Falmouth,
> 'And there is dying in an hospital.'

Wordsworth altered these lines once or twice and finally omitted them altogether. In this he was no doubt assisted by his basic liking for the bare projection of a single, objective figure against a landscape; though one may doubt whether he would have felt a need to make the change had it not been for the unfortunate bathetic effect of the reference to Falmouth in the last line but one. If the reader resists that bathos, the poem gains a new dimension from the original ending, which transforms the opening picture – now visiting his imagination with the figure of a weak old man moving slowly and anonymously across the countryside in an almost superhuman effort (which must, one feels, be in vain) to reach his dying son. In the moment of extremity, again, the magnetism of human kind to its own has shown itself. The old man's travelling form at first affects one like the sight of a moving force in nature, a river or a planet, passing on its predestined way according to nature's own peaceful laws; the thought of his approaching death is softened by the atmosphere of peace, so that he impresses us with a quiet pathos. But as soon as he speaks, he reveals the operation of another law in the universe, a magnetic pull between life and life, which turns his travelling into an epic journey; his desire to see his dying son is one of human nature's sublimities.

The attempt to compare these two versions and decide which one prefers, raises a knotty critical issue, connected with the quite different effects in each case. If one uses the word 'poem' in one of its accepted senses, thinking purely in terms of verbal structure and immediate communication, one is likely to conclude that the final version, entitled simply 'Animal Tranquillity and Decay'[48] is the better. It stands in its own right in a way that the earlier version does not. But as a suggestive construct (and this is a better term for some important Romantic poems) the original version is superior.

This question is in fact crucial to *Lyrical Ballads* as a whole. It may even affect the reader's sense of the volume's dominant tone. If attention is focussed objectively upon the human beings presented there, an interesting and rewarding reading results, but it is also hard to resist a sense of sombreness. Few of the adults could be regarded as happy; most have been visited by some grievous misfortune. The reader who enters into the full process of the poems, on the other hand, is less likely to carry away an impression of gloom, since beneath the stark presentations of predicament he becomes aware of another, subtler work in progress, a groundswell of suggestions concerning the 'living universe'.

Those suggestions are particularly potent when the rôle of nature itself is in question. They range from warm descriptions of its powers of renewal (particularly in the spring) to the mercies inherent in its stability – the reliability of earth and rock, the ceremonious movement of the heavenly bodies.

Most centrally of all, perhaps, nature, from the more benevolent moments in 'The Ancient Mariner' onwards, can be seen to work in the collection as an agency of moderation. Between the fierce destructive power generated by the sun and the sterile cold and darkness of a world without light, for example, it produces the beneficent powers of the moon – which carries the further benefit that, unlike the sun, it can be scanned by the eye of man. Between the destructive power of the storm-blast and the fearfulness of a windless world it brings forth a realm of bearable winds and soft breezes. Between the terror of great movements of water in fountains and waterspouts and the equal horror of a totally still salt ocean there is found a place for stately rivers and quiet brooks which carry water to maintain human and animal life. In the human body the warmth-sense is another such mercy, along with those organising powers of consciousness that allow the human being to order its experience in patterns of time and space. Beneath these, in turn, there exists the human heart itself, with its own miraculous processes of systole and diastole which preserve the blood-system from expanding to bursting-point or congealing to solidity.

It is equally the case, however, that none of these phenomena is experienced *primarily* as a process of mediation. The miracle which each embodies is not normally, as a result, either perceived or appreciated, except on very unusual occasions. Rather, they inhabit the human consciousness so effortlessly as to be regarded as the 'ordinary' world. It was one of the avowed objects of *Lyrical Ballads*, according to Coleridge,[49] that a sense of wonder at all the marvels of nature should be reawakened. Habit (in itself a mercy) is the power which blocks such appreciation. Like ice, it forms a transparent casing for the live organism which is at once protective and deadening. As Wordsworth was shortly to put it in the 'Immortality' Ode, addressing a six-year-old child,

> Full soon thy Soul shall have her earthly freight,
> And custom lie upon thee with a weight,
> Heavy as frost, and deep almost as life!

In these circumstances it is the poet's task to dispel the 'film of familiarity and selfish solicitude', the 'lethargy of custom', and to reveal, by a process analogous to that of sunrise or spring, the loveliness that has been forgotten. But the conditions for such a reawakening will be most propitious in those who have, from childhood, had access to the sense-experiences in nature which

present the miraculous processes most directly. Coleridge puts the
case directly in a poem written while the collection was still in
progress: 'Frost at Midnight':

> But *thou*, my babe! shalt wander like a breeze
> By lakes and sandy shores, beneath the crags
> Of ancient mountain, and beneath the clouds,
> Which image in their bulk both lakes and shores
> And mountain crags: . . .

Wordsworth localises the means of renovation still more precisely in
his address to Dorothy, at the end of the 'Lines composed a few miles
above Tintern Abbey':

> Therefore let the moon
> Shine on thee in thy solitary walk;
> And let the misty mountain winds be free
> To blow against thee. . . .

To experience such immediate beauty and sensuous delight from the
chief agencies of mediation themselves is, on one reading of the
matter, to reawaken the sense of wonder at its very life-source.

   This particular line of thought in *Lyrical Ballads* reaches its culmi-
nation, in fact, in the poem just mentioned, which fittingly concludes it. 'Tintern Abbey'⁵⁰ may be regarded as Wordsworth's
greatest study of nature as mediating power. The enterprise involved demands an unusual complexity of language and diction, but
Wordsworth's growing powers prove themselves more than equal
to the task. One of the methods in the poem has been discussed by
Colin Clarke,⁵¹ who draws attention to the prevalence of a verbal
device by which the same word is used both to describe a particular
scene and to describe a state of the mind or emotions. In general, as
he points out, the echoes serve to suggest a significant correspondence between the landscape and the perceiving mind. Thus 'lofty
cliffs' are matched by 'lofty thoughts'; the 'wanderer' Wye by the
'many wanderings' of the poet; the 'lonely streams' by the 'lonely
rooms' where he meditates; the 'quiet of the sky' by 'an eye made
quiet'; the 'wild secluded scene' and 'little lines of sportive wood run
wild' by the 'Wild eyes' and 'wild ecstasies' of his sister – and, for that
matter, of his own former self. The word 'deep' works particularly
hard in the poem, the 'deep rivers' and the 'deep and gloomy wood'
being matched by 'thoughts of more deep seclusion', 'the deep

power of joy', 'far deeper zeal' and the sense of 'something far more deeply interfused'.

Clarke gives many more examples, though not all, it has to be said, necessarily work in quite the same way as these. 'Some of the more frequently used words give tonal unity, in fact, to another force in the poem, its insistence on the central power of human affection. The reiteration of such words as 'dwell' (Thy memory be as a dwelling-place . . .'; 'Whose dwelling is the light of setting suns'; 'Vagrant dwellers in the houseless woods') or 'murmur' ('With a soft inland murmur'; 'Not for this/Faint I, nor mourn, nor murmur') or 'heart' (throughout) strikes one as ministering not so much to the enforcement of an inner-outer correspondence as to the maintenance of an affective tone, which works in turn towards a limited domestication of nature. The 'vagrant dwellers in the houseless woods' are perhaps shadowy prototypes for a more ideal state of mind which, while still fully accepting the wildness of nature, would contrive to find itself not 'houseless' but at home there.

Without an awareness of these additional effects, 'Tintern Abbey' might, to an unsympathetic eye, appear a piece of clever faking, designed to conjure up the fabric of a world fitted to the mind by a process which, if examined too closely, would collapse into a series of verbal tricks. Once they are perceived, however, the rhetoric of the correspondences is seen to be supported throughout by a further and insistent stress on the power of affection, infused not merely into the repetitive use of particular words but into the tender conversational tone, the gentle even rhythm and the patient unfolding of the argument, all working expressively to reveal the persona of a poet who has learned to devote himself to the affections of the heart and who invites the reader, by participating in the same processes, to share what he has discovered.

But if the poem emerges as something more than a set of ingenious rhetorical devices, an important possible objection still remains. The reader who refuses to make the invited gesture, who argues that sympathy and affection are not the only facts of human nature that count, and that there are times when remembered beauty will not help one to greater human sympathy, may still be drawn towards a judgment that the poem is, for all its virtues, 'sentimental'.

Wordsworth himself was too stern a judge of the sentimental not to know when his own poetry might be subject to the charge. The mere thought of such a possibility seems sometimes to have inhibited him from expression. He had not even tried to write about his earlier experience at Tintern Abbey, and an important reason may well have been his meeting at that time with the rover who was to be the model for Peter Bell. The indifference to nature exhibited by such a man was quite enough to stifle, at least for the time being, any assumption that his experience, whatever its value as a personal guide to himself and a few like-minded persons, could easily be regarded as universal. During the intervening years, on the other hand, the idea (which we traced earlier in Cowper and Akenside) that the moral sensibility could be favourably affected by nature had been refined still further by some contemporary writers. J. G. Zimmermann, for example, who had written in his *On Solitude* (the English translation of which was published in 1797): 'my heart has tenaciously rooted all its fibres in this delightful SOLITUDE', had also commented, 'The view of a pleasing landscape makes the heart beat with the tenderest emotions' and described how, in response to the beauties of nature (including 'the resounding echoes of an impetuous torrent'),

> the sentiments of the mind are by the charms of the imagination instantly converted into sensations of the heart, and the softest emotions give birth to the most virtuous and worthy sentiments.'[52]

When he revisited Tintern in July 1798, moreover, Wordsworth's personal circumstances were different. He was now accompanied by the physical presence of Dorothy, with her immediacy of feeling for natural scenery, and the mental presence of Coleridge, whose theory of primary and secondary consciousness would suggest that the ability to link nature to the heart was after all available to all men, and thwarted only by the isolation and weight of habit forced upon them by the civilisation in which they grew up.

The very opening lines of his poem are touched by possible implications of Coleridge's ideas. For it is a natural consequence of a theory that associates the operation of the primary consciousness with a warmth-sense that in winter our consciousness of time should become prominent and even oppressive, while in summer it should yield to those intimations of eternity which are the prerogative of the primary consciousness, affording a sense of timelessness. Wordsworth makes the point swiftly and wittily in a reference to the lapse of time since his last visit:

> Five years have past; five summers, with the length
> Of five long winters!

The fact that return to the scene has caused an immediate revival within himself of his earlier identity, moreover, supports another element in Coleridge's theory; and that theory is also relevant to the memory of *what* he had been then:

> The sounding cataract
> Haunted me like a passion: the tall rock,
> The mountain, and the deep and gloomy wood,
> Their colours and their forms, were then to me
> An appetite. . . .

The suggestion of a kind of magnetic tension between himself and nature is even more strongly present in the previous description of himself as

> more like a man
> Flying from something that he dreads, than one
> Who sought the thing he loved.

That time, he must concede, is now past, along with the somewhat paradoxical tensions – 'aching joys' and 'dizzy raptures' – that it brought with it. But the underlying 'magnetic' force, so the poem suggests, remains active in his perception. It is this that creates the compelling sense of correspondence, between the forms of nature and the form of the mind, which still impresses itself on him – even if now as a reflective observer. It also provides the necessary link between his passionate youth and his present detachment. For it is the peculiar virtue of this power, he thinks, that because it enjoys a direct access to the human heart it can feed the springs of action immediately, encouraging those acts which link man to man, and so extend the magnetic chain within the world of civilised adults.

In this poem, therefore, Wordsworth is moving towards a provisional solution of the problem which was raised for him when the questionings of the period of the French Revolution made it impossible to continue with the simple combination of affection and established morality that had been available to poets such as Cowper. The account of his youth which he presents is that of a man who has been forced to learn his sense of the moral against another yardstick than that furnished by conventional dogmas.

So far, however, he has done no more than present a morality of affection which is still dangerously near the sentimental. To give his statement the stiffening of intellectual support some further basis is needed. Here, again, he is assisted by Coleridge's theory, which suggests that in going to nature we may in fact be renewing ourselves at one of the great fountains of life: that in moments of mystic revelation we may be seeing, quite literally, 'into the life of things'. Wordsworth both describes this kind of experience and outlines the kind of vision which it may bring, as he tries to characterise his 'sense of something far more deeply interfused'. And it is consonant with his developing ideas that the actual view of the universe which he presents is not that of nature as experienced in a moment of trance (a still evening among woodland or a calm morning over the sea, for instance) but a vision of the *whole* of nature, glimpsed momentarily as one and seen in that unity as vital, rather than dead – a concept caught masterfully in phrases such as 'the round ocean and the living air'.

At this level, there is a broadening of Wordsworth's vision to the range of the 'one life' which he shared with Coleridge (who had in turn adapted it from Boehme).[53] Yet he does not feel confident enough to present it as a final vision: it is something to be glimpsed gratefully as an intimation, rather than relied upon as a permanent and reliable resource.

At the moment when he reaches this visionary state, therefore, Wordsworth is brought also to the heart of a dilemma which, we have argued, his encounter with Coleridge's mind had rendered more acute. If such a harmony, an inner 'life of things', truly exists in nature it must in some important sense be a key to the understanding of human nature itself; for in that case there does subsist, however subterraneanly, an ultimate link of life between all animated beings, recognition of which would serve to bring human beings together in a republican sense of their common nature. If this is so, moreover, Wordsworth's sense of being set apart receives its ultimate sanction, for that which otherwise appears as a self-communing, apart from mankind, is in reality an exploration of issues which ought to be humanity's deepest concern. The poet's vocation would then be fully justified, as an enterprise which would awaken the feelings of men and women to a sense of what is deepest in their own nature. His impulse to self-elevation and his desire to serve humankind would be reconciled.

It was this implication of his current thinking, I shall argue, that governed many of Wordsworth's poetic explorations during the subsequent period – including, most importantly, the beginnings of *The Prelude*. But he needed more positive evidence that the public at large was ready to listen to such an interpretation of human nature before committing himself wholeheartedly to it. Without that further sanction, the experiences referred to in 'Tintern Abbey' could be no more than fascinating intimations, marking a field for further thought and introspection. In the total work even of that poem, therefore, he moved away again to reach his conclusion by another road – a road which provides, incidentally, an interesting parallel to that taken in the plot of *The Borderers*. There, it will be recalled, the misguided Rivers found it necessary to confirm his criminal identity by converting another to his own pattern of behaviour. Wordsworth, feeling a similar isolation, but of a quite different order, had discovered a companion in Coleridge but still felt the need of a disciple. If he had moved out of an initial wildness into a reconciliation with the rest of mankind, and if that earlier wildness nevertheless played a necessary part in the total process, he needed the reassurance of seeing a similar process enacted in a like-minded fellow human being. Accordingly he turned from his own conjectures concerning a link of life in all things to the more ready bond between himself and his sister. In Dorothy, at least, he could recognise kindred perceptions and might hope to see his solitary quest bear fruit in solid benefit. In the concluding lines, therefore, he rehearsed again the whole process he had been describing, expressing his hope that she too would be drawn into a sense of the 'one life', so finding a mainstay for her emotions in the years to come.

If that were to happen, his aim of reconciling his individual self-explorations with his desire to benefit human kind would have recorded a first and telling success, helping to vindicate the larger enterprise implicit in *Lyrical Ballads*, – at least as the work stood on its first appearance in 1798.

4

Resonances of Joy

Wordsworth afterwards remembered the occasion of the 'Lines Composed . . . above Tintern Abbey' with particular delight. He had begun it, he said, on leaving Tintern, after crossing the Wye, and concluded it just as he was entering Bristol after a ramble of four or five days with Dorothy. Not a line of it was altered, and no part written down until he reached Bristol.[1]

This unusual ease of composition is reflected in the harmonies of the achieved poem. It marks a moment of repose in Wordsworth's development, when the growth of kindliness, in response to Dorothy, and the play of mind induced by Coleridge's speculations had together lifted him from his slough of melancholia and facilitated new artistic creation. In this poetic universe, with its newly established poles of human kindliness and imaginative stimulation, he was enabled to envision a pathos and sublimity that were redeemed from the dead forms and mechanical round of a universe dominated by mechanical philosophy.

The extent to which, for the time being, this universe dominated his mind is evident from his notebooks. Here, in jottings and fragments, one finds poetic reminiscences and extended images which are closely akin to the poetry that Coleridge was producing at the same time. The Coleridgean idea that there is a strong relationship between light and sound – particularly intense in moments of entrancement – may well be reflected in one manuscript fragment:

> there would he stand
> In the still covert of some [lonesome] rock,
> Or gaze upon the moon until its light
> Fell like a strain of music on his soul
> And seem'd to sink into his very heart.   PW V 340

79

Even the language here resembles Coleridge's 'Ancient Mariner':

> This seraph-band, each waved his hand,
> No voice did they impart –
> No voice; but Oh! the silence sank
> Like music on my heart.   CPW I 205

Another fragment, describing the creative work of art, parallels Coleridge's 'Kubla Khan' (and the creation of Pandaemonium in *Paradise Lost*):

>   where truth
> Like some fair fabric in romantic glory
> Built by the charm of sounds and symphonies
> Uplifts her fair proportions at the call
> Of pleasure her best minister.   PW V 342 (PL i 710–12)

The use here of such a striking romantic image suggests how fully he had, for the time being, entered into Coleridge's fascination with the creative work of imagination.

Study of the state of trance struck further chords, prompting memories of occasions when he had temporarily felt himself initiated into a sense of the divine. Some manuscript fragments (mostly entered in a notebook which also contains an early version of 'Christabel') go further than 'Tintern Abbey' in intimating that a godlike potency can sometimes be aroused in the senses. The first describes a trance-like state in nature:

>   The leaves stir not,
> They all are steady as the cloudless sky;
> How deep the Quiet: all is motionless,
> As if the life of the vast world was hushed
> Into a breathless dream.   PW V 343

Two long subsequent passages describe the working of the state in the human being himself. The first runs as follows:

> There is creation in the eye,
> Nor less in all the other senses; powers
> They are that colour, model, and combine
> The things perceived with such an absolute
> Essential energy that we may say
> That those most godlike faculties of ours

At one and the same moment are the mind
And the mind's minister. In many a walk
At evening or by moonlight, or reclined
At midday upon beds of forest moss,
Have we to Nature and her impulses
Of our whole being made free gift, and when
Our trance had left us, oft have we, by aid
Of the impressions which it left behind,
Looked inward on ourselves, and learned, perhaps,
Something of what we are.

The second (generated perhaps by the first) tries to describe in more exact physical detail the workings of such a trance:

Long had I stood and looked into the west,
Where clouds and mountain tops and gleams of light
Children of glory all [   ]
Made one society and seemed to be
Of the same nature; long I stood and looked,
But when my thoughts began to fail, I turned
Towards a grove, a spot which well I knew,
For oftentimes its sympathies had fallen
Like a refreshing dew upon my heart;
I stretch[ed] myself beneath the shade
And soon the stirring and inquisitive mind
Was laid asleep; the godlike senses gave
Short impulses of life that seemed to tell
Of our existence, and then passed away.

These passages first affirm the creative power of the senses, and then suggest that in certain states of trance the operation of this creative power helps reveal the inner nature of human existence itself. Again one senses the influence of Coleridge, who was not only interested in the phenomenon of trance but suggested that all artists, in the act of creation, were thereby initiated into a knowledge, however finite and limited, of God's experience in creating and perceiving the universe.

This belief was usually, in Coleridge's own writings, an esoteric one. Yet it is stated without equivocation in *Biographia Literaria* and elsewhere[2x] and is arguably the controlling idea in 'Kubla Khan'. When, indeed, we set the statement that Kubla did 'a stately pleasure-dome decree' alongside the description of the world by Plotinus, as quoted by Ralph Cudworth, the seventeenth-century Platonist: 'a large and stately edifice . . . neither cut off and separated from its maker, nor yet mingled and confounded with him',[3] and recall that Coleridge was reading Cudworth late in 1796, the resemblance becomes very striking indeed, all the more so since the formula that Cudworth is producing corresponds to that which most imaginative artists would find appropriate in describing the relationship between themselves and their achieved works – a point which Cudworth himself had just made, quoting from Plutarch.

For the same reason, Coleridge could entertain the idea without too many misgivings: he was more interested in the light that such an identification might throw upon the workings of human genius than in arrogating any special status to the artist himself. (Arrogance was in any case undermined by the knowledge that in men of command-ing genius such as Kubla Khan there was also a tendency to give way to destructive urges and so in the end to hear 'ancestral voices prophesying war'.) For Wordsworth, on the other hand, who was likely to be drawn more immediately to the implications of such a belief for one's view of external nature, there were more difficult problems to be faced. In one sense it marched very closely with the belief, set out in the passages just quoted, that certain experiences in nature might be of revelatory power, for that allowed one to believe in an 'interfusion' of the divine power – which was not the same as arguing that God was *identical* with nature. Such experiences, how-ever, had to be set against his equally strong awareness of an alien power in nature, a blank face which it could turn to those who scanned it for significance.

There was one area, nevertheless, in which such speculations could be pursued with less fear of compromise. The experiences described in the notebook fragments linked themselves naturally enough with others remembered from childhood and youth. Was it possible that such experiences corresponded to the inmost principle of human growth, assisting the human being so favoured to be educated into some kind of harmony with the deepest power in the universe? Was it there that the stately growth of form was most readily seen to be encouraged by the interplay of genial powers?

This, we may argue, was one of the questions which occupied Wordsworth as he set to work on the autobiographical drafts which were eventually to be absorbed into *The Prelude*. The 1799 version of that poem begins with a sense of 'lost occasion' – a feeling that he has been prepared by his upbringing in nature for a destiny greater than is now offered by the world about him. The very form in which the question is posed, however, gives further indications of what is in his mind:

> was it for this
> That one, the fairest of all rivers, loved
> To blend his murmurs with my nurse's song
> And from his alder shades and rocky falls
> And from his fords and shallows sent a voice
> To intertwine my dreams?　　　MS JJ (1799 i 1–6)

The sense of a 'ceaseless music' in nature which can, even from earliest infancy, educate human consciousness into an awareness of 'the calm/Which Nature breathes among the fields and groves' is next expressed, to be followed shortly by an even bolder avowal:

> The soul of man is fashioned & built up
> Just like a strain of music. . . .　　　MS JJ (1799 i 67–8)

Wordsworth goes on to argue that the fashioning involved can, in certain human beings, be very simple and direct:

> I believe
> That there are spirits, which, when they would form
> A favored being, from his very dawn
> Of infancy do open out the clouds
> As at the touch of lightning, seeking him
> With gentle visitation: quiet Powers!
> Retired and seldom recognized, yet kind,
> And to the very meanest not unknown;
> With me, though rarely, in my early days
> They communed.　　　MSV (1799 i 68–77)

His own destiny he sees as having normally been shaped by more oblique processes, however:

> Others too there are who use
> Yet haply aiming at the self-same end
> Severer interventions ministry
> Of grosser kind & of their school was I.　MS JJ (1799 i 77–80)

These 'severer interventions', we discover, worked through what he was later to term the 'impressive agency of fear'.[4x] He was apparently exploring the idea that in some sense such experiences of fear provided an inroad into the primary consciousness, assisting it to see the world of sense-experience in a new light and impressing the new awareness there.

The nature of the speculations he was exploring reveals itself still more distinctly in others of these early drafts. The forms which so impress themselves are forms of stateliness and peace (seen as corresponding, perhaps, to an essential stateliness and peace in the original creation itself). The mode by which that initiation is actually gained, however, is one which intimately involves the body, including the beatings of the physical heart. Its tendency to move from fiery excitement to revelatory passiveness suggest to him the existence of some corresponding pattern of motion in the universe at large – its most violent energies being linked ultimately to a centre of silence and peace:

>   Gentle powers,
> Who give us happiness & call it peace
> When scudding on from snare to snare I plied
> My anxious visitation hurrying on,
> Still hurrying hurrying onward, how my heart
> Panted: among the lonely yewtrees & the crags
> That looked upon me how my bosom beat
> With hope & fear. – Sometimes strong desire
> Resistless overcame me & the bird
> That was the captive of another's toils
> Became my prey and then
> I heard among the solitary hills
> Low breathings coming after me and sounds
> Of undistinguishable motion steps
> Almost as silent as the turf they trod.   MS JJ (1799 i 35–49)

In this astonishing passage, Wordsworth shows himself transported by excitement, fear and guilt into a universe dominated by the movements of heart and breath, his own pantings being at once transmuted and (apparently) projected into sensed 'low breathings' by which he feels himself pursued. Yet the opening lines suggest that this silent pursuit is still linked to an underlying peace, which is thus being impressed.

One way of reading this passage, in fact, would be to see it as a reply to Dr Johnson's censure on those who followed the dictates of the heart. That censure is persuasive so long as it is taken as referring (as in the original context) to those who profess themselves unable to resist its pleadings and 'tender meltings'; Wordsworth however is concerned to recognise the full power of the heart as physical organ. Futile deliquescence of the emotions may be typical of those who have been brought up in soft luxury, but for a child brought up in nature, responsiveness to the voice of the passions, experienced among its great forms, is in Wordsworth's eyes more likely to be educative, bringing immediate reprisals of its own for any infractions of the moral law. It is through such processes, in fact, that the power of the heart to 'elevate the imagination and set the affections in right tune'[5x] is strengthened. Wordsworth speculates still more openly just afterwards:

> Ah not in vain ye beings of the hills
> And ye that walk the woods and open heaths
> By moon or starlight thus from my first dawn
> Of childhood did ye love to interweave
> The passions
> Not with the mean & vulgar works of man
> But with high objects with eternal things
> With life & nature, purifying thus
> The elements of feeling & of thought
> And sanctifying by such discipline
> Both pain & fear until we recognize
> A grandeur in the beatings of the heart   MS JJ (1799 i 130–41)

The clear implication of such a passage is that the passions and the heart flourish best where they are educated within their own element – that is, among the forms and energies of nature itself.

As the first part of the 1799 *Prelude* proceeds, this inner purport of the argument becomes more subtle. Coleridge's ideas concerning the relationship between the organic and the vital powers of man and the ways in which the human being makes his contacts with the world come more fully into play. Coleridge's original paradigm would seem to figure an organic growth at the heart (more or less literally) of the individual, which is fostered and given identity according to the disposition of his or her human energies, playing constantly between the individual and the world at large. Wordsworth is treating his own upbringing as a special case of this process, his organic and vital growth having been assisted by surroundings where organic phenomena were played upon by powers both gentle and violent (sometimes acquiring an extraordinarily subtle beauty in the process). He had thus had an unusually privileged access to forms and energies that offered models and patterns for his own development.

> [Nor, sedulous as I have been to trace]
> How Nature by collateral interest
> And by extrinsic passion peopled first
> My mind with forms, or beautiful or grand
> And made me love them may I well forget
> How other pleasures have been mine, and joys
> Of subtler origin how I have felt
> Not seldom, even in that tempestuous time
> Those hallowed and pure motions of the sense
> Which seem in their simplicity to own
> An intellectual charm, that calm delight
> Which, if I err not, surely must belong
> To those first born affinities that fit
> Our new existence to existing things
> And in our dawn of being constitute
> The bond of union betwixt life and joy.
>
> MSU and (1799 i 375-90)

In the second part of the 1799 *Prelude* he continued his speculation with a long passage about infancy, in which he described the state of the baby at its mother's breast in terms that seem to owe still more to Coleridge's speculation concerning 'primary consciousness'. On that theory, it might be argued that the child, sucking at its mother's breast, was still, as it would never be again, in a state where the two great magnetic attractions of its nature were satisfied. Its perceptions alternated between the experience of consummated infinity accompanying the act of sucking from the breast fountain (which in turn recalled the even more intimate blood relationship between heart and heart in the womb[6x]) and the experience of love which was expressed by the mother's kisses and her loving gestures and looks. The communication between life and life in the act of breast-feeding was a perfect emblem of the kind of 'gravitation' that ruled in that primary universe, while the mutual emotional dependence between mother and child were an imaged projection of the ultimate relationship that subsisted between all human beings. The first power, on

Coleridge's terms, would be the source of our feeling for wholes and for unity, the second the ultimate basis for mature love of external beings – whilst also encouraging the growth of that separating analytic power by which we must gradually learn to experience the world as object.

A similar range of thinking, developed in Wordsworth's own term, seems to underlie the whole passage:

> Bless'd the infant Babe
> (For with my best conjectures I would trace
> The progress of our Being) blest the Babe,
> Nursed in his Mother's arms, the Babe who sleeps
> Upon his Mother's breast, who when his soul
> Claims manifest kindred with an earthly soul
> Doth gather passion from his Mother's eye.
> Such feelings pass into his torpid life
> Like an awakening breeze, and hence his mind
> Even in the first trial of its powers
> Is prompt and wakeful – eager to combine
> In one appearance all the elements
> And parts of the same object, else detached
> And loth to coalesce. Thus day by day
> Subjected to the discipline of love
> His organs and recipient faculties
> Are quickened, are more vigorous, his mind spreads
> Tenacious of the forms which it receives.
> In one beloved presence, nay, and more,
> In that most apprehensive habitude
> And those sensations which have been derived
> From this beloved presence, there exists
> A virtue which irradiates and exalts
> All objects through all intercourse of sense.
> No outcast he, bewildered and depressed:
> Along his infant veins are interfused
> The gravitation and the filial bond
> Of nature that connect him with the world.
> Emphatically such a Being lives
> An inmate of this *active* universe;
> From Nature largely he receives, nor so
> Is satisfied, but largely gives again,

For feeling has to him imparted strength,
And powerful in all sentiments of grief,
Of exaltation, fear and joy, his mind,
Even as an agent of the one great mind,
Creates, creator and receiver both,
Working but in alliance with the works
Which it beholds. – Such verily is the first
Poetic spirit of our human life,
By uniform control of after years
In most abated & suppressed, in some
Through every change of growth or of decay
Preeminent till death.   MS RU and (1799 ii 267–309)

Dr Leavis has recorded how when he came to the line 'All objects through all intercourse of sense' in this passage he felt an overwhelming impulse to continue with the words 'And rolls through all things'.[7] It is not until we put the whole passage into the context of the 'primary universe', however, that we see *why* there should be this strong link between the filial bond that is interfused along the veins of the infant and the 'sense of something far more deeply interfused' in 'Tintern Abbey'. In terms of Coleridge's theory, the power which was still known to the suckling baby as its natural habitat was also present in the universe at large, sometimes to be apprehended directly in trance-like moments of revelation – and particularly available to the child that had been exposed to the forces of nature.

What then of the child as it began to grow up? Here, we may argue, the other side of Coleridge's theory – that which had to do with the relationship between vegetable growth and animal spirits – came into its own. According to that, I have suggested, the animal energies of nature were intimately related to the 'genial spirits' of the human being; the two principles, the vegetable and the animal, corresponding respectively to the two great principles involved in human growth and development. As the child turned away from its relationship of physical unity with its mother, it faced a new disposition of its energies, which must now find a way of achieving a satisfactory relationship with the world of sense; it was also, however, a matter of urgency that they should, in the course of that reorientation, retain a link with the central organic life of the child as well. The advantages of an education such as that which Wordsworth had received in nature lay, on these terms, in the fact that the 'vital' was constantly being turned back to the 'organic' and rewedded to it.

Such a presupposition may be traced through all the incidents in which Wordsworth describes how his energies, stretched to extremity in fear or exertion, would open out into revelatory experience. It emerges most explicitly of all, perhaps, in the passage where he describes how, as a child, he

> held unconscious intercourse
> With the eternal beauty drinking in
> A pure organic pleasure from the lines
> Of curling mist or from the smooth expanse
> Of waters coloured by the clouds of heaven.
>
> MS JJ (1799 i 394–8)

The term 'organic' (unusual in Wordsworth's writing) is crucial here, suggesting a direct influx of power from nature to the very roots of the primary being. And, as before, he goes on to describe how the very fact that he had nothing with which to associate the beauty that he saw actually facilitated the process of absorption:

> The sands of Westmorland the creeks & bays
> Of Cumbria's rocky limits they can tell
> How when the sea threw off his evening shade
> And to the shepherd's hut beneath the craggs
> Did send sweet notice of the rising moon
> How I have stood to images like this
> A stranger linking with the spectacle
> No body of associated forms
> And bringing with me no peculiar sense
> Of quietness and peace yet I have stood
> Even while my eye has moved oer three long leagues
> Of shining water, gathering as it seemd,
> Through the wide surface of that field of light
> New pleasure like a bee among the flowers. MS JJ (i 399–412)

The imagery of bee and flowers consolidates the link between the exertion of animal spirits on the one hand and the power of absorbing 'organic pleasure', which is best conveyed through the word 'drinks' – the bee at the flower thus providing an archetypal example of the intimate relationship between animal spirits and growing vegetative form. So Wordsworth continues by describing childhood joy in similar terms: the sense of pleasure may seem to work swiftly

and pass rapidly into the unconscious; but it in fact remains there,
creating a store of pleasures for memory to dwell on later:

> 'mid that giddy bliss
> Which like a tempest works along the blood
> And is forgotten, even then I felt
> Gleams like the flashing of a shield . . .
> — And if the vulgar joy by its own weight
> Wearied itself out of the memory
> The scenes which were a witness of that joy
> Remained, in their substantial lineaments
> Depicted on the brain and to the eye
> Were visible, a daily sight: and thus
> By the impressive agency of fear
> By pleasure and repeated happiness
> So frequently repeated, and by force
> Of obscure feelings representative
> Of joys that were forgotten these same scenes
> So beauteous and majestic in themselves
> Though yet the day was distant did at length
> Become habitually dear, and all
> Their hues and forms were by invisible links
> Allied to the affections.   1799 i 415–18; 427–42

This was a crucial piece of speculation on Wordsworth's part, for
if true it helped to describe and explain the process of maturation he
had described in 'Tintern Abbey'. The loss of vital spirits referred to
there could be regarded as set off by the fact that the sense of beauty
which was impressed through the agency of those same spirits at the
time when they were still fully active had allied itself permanently to
the general working of his affections.

In Wordsworth's later revisions of *The Prelude* other ideas would
be introduced, setting the intellectual framework of the poem a good
deal closer to conventional categories and thus making it more
readily available to his nineteenth-century readers. The passages
which we have examined still remain embedded in the text,
nevertheless, witnessing to the excitement and new direction to his
thought given by his first encounter with Coleridge's speculations –
while also leaving a series of puzzles for those who try to integrate
them too closely into the order of the final poem. Ultimately, we
come to see, *The Prelude* must be read, not only as the record of a

process but as *in itself* a process, embodying, in its various texts, stages in Wordsworth's interpretation of his own experience.

So long as Wordsworth confined his experience of the phenomena of genius to his own introspections and memories of boyhood experience, the results fell naturally into poetry. His earlier humanitarian ideals still remained strong, however; it was equally important that he should be able to continue writing a more objectively-based poetry in which, without intruding his own private experiences too openly, he could present to a contemporary audience a recognisable picture of their everyday world.

In this respect, the news of the reception of *Lyrical Ballads* which reached him in Germany was not encouraging: few reviewers seemed to understand the volume at more than a superficial level.[8x] This was not merely disappointing in itself; it was a blow to hopes that the presence of the new ideas might guarantee a wide popular audience. On an optimistic view, one might have expected that the very workings of the primary consciousness as displayed in the poems would evoke in readers a direct and popular recognition of unacknowledged and fascinating truths about their own human nature.

The apparent failure of this larger aim did not lead to a cessation of Wordsworth's attempts to link free-ranging speculations about the nature of the world with the observable facts of common life. He did, however, turn to different aspects of the 'everyday', as we may see from examining some shorter poems of the time.

One of the chief effects of Coleridge's conception of the organic, as he later described it in *The Friend*, was to change the traditional hierarchy of organic being. Instead of a series of steps, comprising the inorganic, the vegetable, the animal and the human, respectively, attention was focussed primarily upon the division between vegetable and animal. These were now to be viewed not as marking two steps in the scale of life but rather as equals, displaying respectively the dominance of different elements in all life-processes. In the vegetable world (to elaborate further) the central life-process was that of growth or subsistence according to a particular preordained form, or 'idea'. In the animal world, on the other hand, the play of energies was dominant; yet here, too, the impulse to form was powerfully felt, through active creation. Serpents, for example, could be seen to shape their energies into pure forms of movement;

birds and insects, more spectacularly, used the intricate play of their numbers to create large patterns of flight or dance.

The inner working of these energies was also instructive. They alternated between motions of 'irritability' (visible particularly in insects) and of sensibility. These could be seen, in turn, as the ground of particular human qualities. Irritability might be regarded as the physical medium for man's impulses of creative genius and aspirations to freedom; sensibility, by comparison, was associated with man's natural unity of perception and cultivation of affection.[9x]

The presence of similar ideas may be detected in several of Wordsworth's contemporary poems. Ruth, for example (in the poem of that name) displays in her final crazed state a sensibility trapped by the limits within which the stamping genius of her lover has sealed her. She remains 'innocent', but her innocence is, by its lack of freedom, pathetic.[10x]

The lower creatures, by contrast, can sometimes display the opposite phenomenon: the exercise of a 'genial' power that is quite untouched by sensibility. The theme may be discerned, for instance, in a deceptively light poem, 'Written in Germany on one of the coldest days of the century', containing the description of a fly which has mistaken the warmth of a stove for summer and emerged from its winter hiding-place to find itself caught between heat and frost, between life and death.

> His feelers methinks I can see him put forth
> To the East and the West, and the South and the North,
> But he finds neither guide-post nor guide.
> . . . Between life and death his blood freezes and thaws,
> And his two pretty pinions of blue dusky gauze
> Are glued to his sides by the frost. . . .   LB II 145–6

While he is watching with rapt attention, Wordsworth can draw a personal comfort from the fact that he himself is not in the same plight, since he has the warmth of human affection to sustain him:

> No Brother, no Friend has he near him, while I
> Can draw warmth from the cheek of my Love,
> As blest and as glad in this desolate gloom,
> As if green summer grass were the floor of my room,
> And woodbines were hanging above.

The poem concludes with the wish that he could help the insect to keep alive until summer, when it might resume its life among its myriad fellows.

In this poem Wordsworth is able to glance obliquely at the limitations of genial spirits when operating in complete freedom: as with the fly on the stove they have 'neither guide-post nor guide'. Since he himself can enjoy the interplay of genial spirits with sensibility which is fostered by an environment of affection, he finds his own lot preferable.

Preferable, at least, in the situation described, where there is a perfect correspondence between life and love. In the company of Coleridge, no doubt, it was more easy to believe the validity of that correspondence. Compelled by his enthusiasm, it was difficult not to see in the genial imagination a final clue to the real, and in affectionate vision the measure of all things. Love was exalted to dominance in the universe, and 'genial power' seen as an ultimate energy, within the play of which love could find its appropriate form.

Alone with Dorothy, on the one hand, Wordsworth was evidently reminded of the other universe that had haunted him from youth, a universe where death was the final controlling reality and where, in the final issue, all things must either dissipate or fix themselves into blank forms. Oppressed by the alienation of life in Germany, where the inhabitants often went out of their way to cheat foreigners[11] and where the scenery, though fine, had little to remind them of familiar English sights and sounds, it is not surprising that he found himself relapsing from the enchanted state in which he had often lived during the past year to awareness of the obverse human experience. Whatever one might discover about the universality of the life-sense, the fact still remained that for each individual, an individual death was waiting. And however much one might draw comfort from the affection of others, the fact that a person whom one loved could die, casually and suddenly, made all such comfort precarious. No sense of universal life could provide the resources with which to deal adequately with that situation. Lear's cry, 'Why should a dog, a horse, a rat, have life,/And thou no breath at all?' would always be ultimately unanswerable.

At the same time (and it is this that gives the poetry of the subsequent period its own, unusual quality) Wordsworth did not recoil utterly to his dreary 'Salisbury Plain' sense of humanity's inevitable sufferings and isolation. Even when the sense of death oppressed him most he could not abolish the experiences of previous months. Without forsaking those themes, however, he seems to have reversed their stress, giving more prominence to a reservation that had lurked in some of his contributions to *Lyrical Ballads*. A 'universe of life' might well exist: indeed, there was strong evidence from his own experiences in nature to suggest the existence of a primal level of consciousness within human beings which opened out to infinity – and which might in some sense be immortal. But the only fact of which we could finally be sure was that of our own necessary death and that of anyone whom we might love. Once this was fully grasped, the Coleridgean speculations ceased to give straightforward sublimity to human existence. They did indeed raise sublime overtones, but when applied to human love their result must be *to intensify pathos*, since they surrounded human mortality with a realm of other possibilities which could never be proved and which could never realise themselves in the one way that would ultimately matter – by giving an actual and permanently available knowledge of immortality. The death of an individual would always be, in the most important sense, a total loss to those who loved him or her, and any residual sense of immortality would only make the pathos of that loss correspondingly greater.

The growth of this realisation is important in Wordsworth's poetic development, since it marks off his earlier, exploratory contributions to *Lyrical Ballads* from the more straightforward poems of manliness and human pathos which he wrote for the second volume – yet also gives to that pathos a complicated structure, which is not readily grasped at first sight. It may appear sentimental until it is seen to be weighted by the double intensity of Wordsworth's new vision of the universe, and of man's place in it.

Sometimes an awareness of Wordsworth's guiding preoccupation at this time may actually help define basic contours of the text, as with the poems normally grouped together as the 'Lucy poems'; such an awareness may indeed help with the riddle of the mysterious 'Lucy' herself. It is not altogether impossible that there was a real girl who was loved by Wordsworth and who died, though if so there is no conclusive evidence as to her identity. We may be closer to the main point of the poems, therefore, if we make a less obvious connection, and associate Lucy with Lucy Gray, in his poem of that name, written about a young girl who died in the midst of nature, but whose spirit could sometimes, according to local superstition, be glimpsed there. The various Lucys are linked, we might say, not by being a single recognisable person but by a common question which hovers over each of the poems concerned. How can one properly describe the death of a young girl who has lived close to the genius of nature? What, exactly, is left – whether in the consciousness of her lover or in the place where she lived?

Wordsworth's sense of this latter question – stressing now not the possible survival of the spirit (as in 'Lucy Gray') but the sense of loss which death brings – is presented starkly in 'She dwelt among the untrodden ways'.[12] The Lucy of this poem was hardly known to anyone, and although she was naturally lovable there were few human beings available to give her the sort of love that a nature like hers called for.

The quality of her uniqueness is indicated with precision in the second stanza:

> A Violet by a mossy stone
> > Half-hidden from the Eye!
> Fair, as a star when only one
> > Is shining in the sky!

In a sensitive discussion, F. W. Bateson remarks,

> . . . it looks as though the half-hidden violet is intended to symbolise Lucy's insignificance in the public world, and the single star to represent her supreme importance in the private world. In the actual reading, however, the images behave in a much less logical way. The simplest way to put it is to say that the two images turn out to be one image. The reader begins by looking *down* at the violet and then *up* at the star, and in the process the two juxtaposed images form themselves into a single landscape – presumably a twilight one when it would be particularly difficult to distinguish the violet from the mossy stone.[13]

While the critical intuition here is sure, the logic of our previous discussion suggests that the symbolism may be still more fully organised. The landscape created by these two touches is that of Wordsworth's new 'universe of life': at one pole the flower, focus of human affection and tenderness for the particular, at the other the single star, focus of the human imagination and of wondering perception. Lucy possessed the qualities of both poles: her growth in the flesh had possessed the organic harmony of a flower's growth, while her own inward radiance had given her the quality of a star. She contained in her own self the extremes of the universe which Wordsworth had been inhabiting while in the company of the sensitive Dorothy and the imaginative Coleridge; in her, moreover, sensibility had not become separated from the 'genius' of nature.

Lucy was more than a private face in a private place, therefore – she was, while she lived, a guarantor of the 'universe of life'. And by the same token her mortality is the more significant, since it brings together two irreconcilable ideas – Lucy's beauty and the ineluctable fact of her death, all the more unthinkable if it should take place in her youth.

> But she is in her Grave, and Oh!
> The difference to me.

This is the counter to 'Lucy Gray'. No amount of dwelling on her significance as an embodiment of life-forces can reduce by one iota the dull fact of her death and the necessary loss to all who loved her.

The symbolism of violet and star, and, more particularly, the use of the word 'difference' in this poem illustrate what has been said about the increasingly private nature of Wordsworth's utterances at this time. By a curious irony Hartley Coleridge (whom Wordsworth and Coleridge had tried to bring up as an heir to the 'universe of life') probed the simplicity of its language in a later, parodying poem.[14] Though vulnerable, however, Wordsworth's poem is not a failure: Keats, indeed, spoke of the 'most perfect pathos' of the last line.[15] Yet the reader's uncertainty about the word 'difference' may not finally be dispelled until he becomes aware of the general preoccupation in these poems as a group, which justifies the amount of weight it is made to carry.

In 'Three years she grew'[16] the theme of 'Lucy Gray' (along with that of 'The Danish Boy') is reordered in a different way, to fit another facet of that preoccupation. This time Wordsworth begins with the harmonising power of nature and pictures the growth of his Lucy (rather like that of one of Blake's characters[17]) in a dell. This poem contains the most extreme version of Wordsworth's belief in nature's power to foster the growth of certain favoured individuals, very simply and directly:

'The stars of midnight shall be dear
To her, and she shall lean her ear
In many a secret place
Where rivulets dance their wayward round,
And beauty born of murmuring sound
Shall pass into her face.

'And vital feelings of delight
Shall rear her form to stately height,
Her virgin bosom swell; . . .'

These stanzas (where the use of the words 'vital' and 'stately' are as striking as that of 'organic' in the previous passage) evidently owe something to Coleridge's speculations on the relationship between the vital energies of nature and the stately growth of organic form. Anyone coming across them in isolation, however, might be justified in judging them at once beautiful and unrealistic. Yet they do not represent a belief that life among the sights and sounds of nature automatically makes people beautiful: Wordsworth had lived too long in Lakeland villages to cherish any such illusions. Although he felt that there were clear advantages to be gained from being brought up in the country, he was aware of the limitations created by small isolated communities.

Lucy, however, has been brought up not in a village but in total country solitude – just as Lucy Gray was, according to Wordsworth, sensitive, through her isolated life, to sights which a village girl would have missed. The radiance of the stars and the sound of streams, manifestations alike of the energies of nature's genius, could work directly upon her, therefore. Many are called to live in the country but few are chosen to be vehicles of nature's inward spirit; yet occasionally, he is suggesting, the miraculous process does work, producing a child such as Lucy, who can be thought of as a pure 'child of nature'. The main point of the poem lies in a further idea, however – the tragic paradox that even so pure an embodiment of nature's spirit might also die young. If so, what of her could be said to survive? Not even the ghost of Lucy Gray:

Thus Nature spake – The work was done –
How soon my Lucy's race was run!
She died, and left to me
This heath, this calm and quiet scene;

The memory of what has been,
And never more will be.

Wordsworth's rediscovered sense of death and its accompanying implications emerges strongly at this point. There is an emptiness about the depicted landscape and a resonance in the 'never more' which speak out the sense of loss. At the same time it is not a totally gloomy or pessimistic poem. The references to 'work done' and to a 'race' having been 'run' (an image to be used again in the 'Immortality' Ode) give a sense of completion – as if Lucy had fulfilled one of life's great possible patterns by growing to girlhood in complete unison with nature. To have grown up in this way is to have run one of life's races: the other (of which Lucy knew nothing) consists in learning to live with the sense of loss and of death, and so to achieve the 'seeing eye' and the 'philosophic mind'. This second race can draw sustenance from the first, nevertheless, if to 'The memory of what has been,/And never more will be' is linked that primal sympathy 'Which having been must ever be'. In dying, Lucy left a stimulus to memory at least, impressed upon the enduring forms of 'This heath, this calm, and quiet scene'; there is gain as well as loss.

In falling back on this more acceptable resource, nevertheless, Wordsworth was, necessarily, moving away from his more exploratory mode; where 'Lucy Gray', which had been written in Germany in 1799, had ended with a retailing of the local belief that Lucy was still to be seen and heard, tripping and singing over the wild, 'Three years she grew', also written during that period, draws upon the more acceptable doctrine that Lucy survives, in the places where she lived, by the renewing power of memory, which both reminds the observer of loss, and, through the work of sympathy, connecting her former presence to the present scene, helps to sustain him in that loss.

It is an oscillation which can be seen to recur continually in Wordsworth's poetic development; but the second element, we shall notice, slowly becomes more dominant. However much he may be drawn to the Coleridgean belief that 'we are all one life', he finds a surer foundation for his beliefs in the sentiment expressed in one of his own lines: 'We have all of us one human heart'. Yet that asseveration continues to draw poetic strength from – cannot indeed be fully understood without some reference to – the further possibilities opened by the earlier speculations. Certainly the idea that the common human heart might be grounded in a common link of life was too attractive to be put by quickly; for some time Wordsworth continued to be drawn by phenomena that hinted at the existence of such a deeper connection in some form – as, say, that the affections might work through mysterious processes of instinct. In 'The Brothers',[18] for example, the phenomenon of magnetisation to a particular place known from childhood plays its part, along with that of somnambulism. This latter must have seemed to offer particularly strong support to belief in the existence of a 'primary' level of consciousness. How otherwise could a sleeping human being, unconscious and not responsible for his actions, perform complicated physical manoeuvres? By drawing upon such verifiable phenomena Wordsworth could continue to explore themes such as that of interaction between genial spirits and his recently intensified consciousness of death, without straying from the verifiable human experiences.

In the case of 'The Brothers' the possible implications of somnambulism, as a manifestation of the primary consciousness and the universe of life, offer powerful reinforcement to the theme of 'localised' attachment which dominates the narrative of the whole poem. The idea that attachment to place is a rare thing is indicated in the opening, where the priest of Ennerdale, looking out of his window and commenting on the flitting, butterfly-like behaviour of the tourists, is attracted by the sight of a young man wandering in the churchyard – which has nothing to appeal to a visitor in search of the picturesque. He is, we are told, a young man who, home after long years at sea, has come to look for his brother. The priest, not knowing this, joins him and is met simply by an enquiry about a recent grave. With a little prompting he tells the story of the young man buried there, and how after long yearning for his brother Leonard, who was absent at sea, he died while sleep-walking on the fells. The visitor, who shows signs of being moved, withdraws without revealing his identity; later, however, he writes to tell the priest that he is Leonard and that the young man was his own brother.

First and foremost, the story presents a contrast between the fleeting attraction of the vale for the tourists and the deep affections that bind those who actually live there. But as we look at certain sections of the story, it becomes clear that the nature of those affections is being examined more closely, not without the aid of

Coleridgean hints. Early on, the description of Leonard's emotions at sea draws heavily on the idea of magnetism to a known and familiar landscape.[19x] Leonard heard 'in the piping shrouds . . . The tones of waterfalls',

> And, while the broad green wave and sparkling foam
> Flash'd round him images and hues, that wrought
> In union with the employment of his heart,
> He, thus by feverish passion overcome,
> Even with the organs of his bodily eye
> Below him, in the bosom of the deep,
> Saw mountains, saw the forms of sheep that graz'd
> On verdant hills, with dwellings among trees,
> And Shepherds clad in the same country grey
> Which he himself had worn.   LB II 22

In the course of the poem Leonard learns that his brother had simultaneously been experiencing this work of the magnetised heart in a more debilitating form: his pining had led to sickness. He was restored to health by the inhabitants of the vale, who looked after him each in turn; the priest declares, however,

>   . . . 'tis my belief
> His absent Brother still was at his heart.   ll. 347–8

The suspicion was fostered by a new habit which the young man had developed during those years:

> . . . often, rising from his bed at night,
> He in his sleep would walk about, and sleeping
> He sought his Brother Leonard. . . .   ll. 351–3

Eventually he died by plunging from a sheer rock called the Pillar. To Leonard's startled conjecture of suicide, the priest replies with a confident denial:

>   You recollect I mention'd
> A habit which disquietude and grief
> Had brought upon him; and we all conjectur'd
> That, as the day was warm, he had lain down
> Upon the grass, and, waiting for his comrades
> He there had fallen asleep, that in his sleep

He to the margin of the precipice
Had walk'd, and from the summit had fallen head-long:
And so no doubt he perish'd. . . .   ll. 393–401

The effect of this explanation must be to exacerbate rather than lessen Leonard's grief: in the context of the narrative, it heightens pathos. There is also, however, a covert intimation of the sublime. Sleep-walking, one of the most striking manifestations of the power of the unconscious, could, in Coleridge's theory, be associated with a primitive 'magnetism of the heart', displaying in fact its true disposition.[20x] (Lady Macbeth's revelation of guilt in her somnambulism might, for instance, be seen as springing from a source deeper than the will which governed her calm everyday appearance.) Leonard's brother, by the same token, was showing the power of his buried yearning. And the fact that he was so rapt by this magnetism that he could walk without fear into the abyss would be, on this theory, a manifestation of the power of the heart's affections to annihilate even the most basic physical fears.

This inner significance is supported by two uses of fountain-imagery. The first is the more emblematic: one of the first changes noticed by Leonard, a cleft in the hillside, is explained by the priest as marking the place where formerly two springs bubbled side by side and where one has now disappeared from a stroke of lightning. This emblem of the original bond between the brothers re-emerges later as an image of direct emotion, however. When the priest's story has reached its climax in the story of James's somnambulism, Leonard

would have thanked him, but he felt
Tears rushing in; both left the spot in silence . . .   ll. 406–7

(In versions from 1815 onwards 'Tears rushing in' became 'A gushing from the heart'.)

For him, the contrast between his brother's passionate affection and the fact of his death is matched by an equivalent tension between the corresponding powers in his own consciousness, which compound themselves into inarticulacy. His charged silence, nevertheless, is eloquent of many similar emotions and attachments which remain normally unexpressed in the locality – and are therefore overlooked by the average tourist.

Leonard's subsequent career, as related at the end of the poem, follows logically from what he has been learning in the course of it. His bond with the landscape of his childhood now finally snapped, he goes away to continue his career at sea. In that rootless element, subject to the free play of energies, he eventually becomes a 'grey-headed Mariner'. The accent is upon a figure who was originally brought up in solitude and who, now, deprived of the greatest human attachment formed in that solitude, is left as a lonely 'wanderer'.

In this poem, where the 'public' effects of pathos and dramatic irony are by themselves strong enough to sustain the general reader, no great critical problem is raised by the presence of more esoteric elements. In other poems of the time however, as we have seen, they may produce uneasy local effects of obscurity or – worse – of the commonplace, and it is here that nuclear analysis can be particularly useful, enabling the reader to descry the play of contrary elements within the atomic structure. It also helps to explain Wordsworth's bursts of fecundity. The world of life appealed to his vital energies, the experience of loss pierced his organic sensibility; and since both could find correlatives in the energies and forms, respectively, of language the possibilities for new poetry continued to open out. Whenever both sides of his nature were brought into play by a subject which brought the two worlds together he was enabled to move forward in complex creativity. We spoke earlier of Wordsworth seeking a 'place' for himself as poet; what he enjoyed on such occasions was rather a new *territory*, opened up further in dialogues with Coleridge and Dorothy, where, in a series of poetic explorations, what he knew in the world of affection could be made to move against what he knew in the world of physical life.

There was always a danger, on the other hand, that in a man where the organic sensibility counted for so much, the sense of loss might prevail, producing simple numbness. Energies and instincts were, after all, treacherous allies which could, by memory of their destructive modes, deliver human sensibility into the paralysis of grief or remorse. And it was this recognition, perhaps, that led Wordsworth during these years to place so much stress on the emotion of joy, where animal spirits flourished in freedom from such a threat. When he had first projected his character the Pedlar, picturing him as a man who had been brought up in the midst of nature and had learned his deepest lessons of wisdom from what she had to teach,[21x] he had made an explicit connection between his sense of life and his sense of joy, describing the 'transports' which he had as a result enjoyed in nature:

                          Wonder not
If such his transports were; for in all things
He saw one life, and felt that it was joy.
One song they sang, and it was audible,
Most audible then when the fleshly ear,
O'ercome by grosser prelude of that strain,
Forgot its functions, and slept undisturbed.   ll. 216–22

The experience of revelation in trance which was to be described in
the notebooks had been, in this earlier manifestation, a more vital
one, involved with the exercise of energy. The latter point is further
emphasised by his characterisation of the phenomena in nature
which best gave him this sense:

He felt the sentiment of being spread
O'er all moves, and all that seemeth still,
O'er all which, lost beyond the reach of thought
And human knowledge, to the human eye
Invisible, yet liveth to the heart;
O'er all that leaps, and runs, and shouts, and sings,
Or beats the gladsome air; or all that glides
Beneath the wave, yea, in the wave itself,
And mighty depth of waters.   ll. 208–16

There is, of course, a saving clause: these things, we read, live 'to the
heart'; yet the essential note of energetic empathy is still very
different from that described in the records of trance. And in general
it may be noted that Wordsworth's references to joy during this
period (roughly 1797 to 1802) often have an unusual charge of
meaning, manifesting itself in unusual or striking language. We have
already referred to the 'sense sublime' that 'disturbs' him with joy in
'Tintern Abbey'. Joy is a notable presence in 'The Idiot Boy' also: the
boy's lips 'burr' with joy; his mother's face 'with joy o'erflows' – and
when he returns her 'limbs are all alive with joy'. In *Peter Bell*,
similarly, joy 'knocks at' Peter's heart and later his 'staring bones all
shake with joy'. This intensified charge to the word seems finally to
burn itself out in 'Resolution and Independence', with a description
of the poet's initial elation that brings together the image of the hare
that 'raced about in joy' and of the young Burns, who 'walked in
glory and in joy'. After that, although the word remains a favourite
one in the poetry, it only occasionally (as in the sonnet that begins

'Surprised by joy, impatient as the wind . . .') flashes out with anything like the same obtrusiveness.

The reason is fairly clear. Just as the universe of death was thwarted by the fact of loss, so the universe of joy was partially negated by reminders that the free expression of instinct which sustained it could easily slip into lack of concern for others. The division between joy and 'wantonness' was traditionally a narrow one. As with the universe of life, however, there was one area of human experience where the contraries of joy and responsibility did not war so fiercely: that of childhood and early youth. And since the sense of joy survived in the memory more vividly than the sense of life, remembered childhood pleasure could provide an important point of security for the poet.

In the same way, the pleasure that children evince in their instinctive behaviour could be regarded with indulgence, and provide a theme for light verse. In 'Rural Architecture',[22] for instance, Wordsworth praises the combination of high spirits and persistence shown by some boys who build a figure of stone and then, when a storm blows it down, go up, nothing daunted, and build another. It comes out again in 'The Idle Shepherd-Boys',[23] where the pleasure of the shepherd-boys is set firmly against a landscape of natural joy. The fact that their sports lead them to neglect a lamb who is being swept away down a stream (and who has to be rescued by the poet) is rebuked – but only 'gently'. Two years later, the theme is explored still further in 'Beggars',[24] where the participants are not village lads or shepherd-boys but wilder folk, their mother like an Amazonian queen, or a Mediterranean bandit's wife. Coming along later they insist, in seeking alms, that she is dead, to be rebuked mildly by the narrator – whereupon 'Off to some other play they both together flew'.

That a serious issue lay embedded in the poem is shown by the fact that Wordsworth returned to it fifteen years later and wrote a 'Sequel to the Foregoing'[25] in which he remembered the sense of universal joy that day: a 'genial' hour, he says,

> When universal nature breathed
> As with the breath of one sweet flower . . .

He also recalled the accompanying faith which saw the two boys

> Walk through the fire with unsinged hair.

Even if that faith were too optimistic, yet still, he feels, they were 'free/From touch of *deadly* injury'.

The central image here occurs again in a passage in *The Prelude*, describing a beautiful child once seen at the theatre:

> Among the wretched and the falsely gay,
> Like one of those who walk'd with hair unsinged
> Amid the fiery furnace. 1805 vii 397–9

This closer approach to the original biblical context helps indicate the limits of Wordsworth's indulgence. Throughout his evocations of joy, in fact, the narrator is also moralist, standing apart from the scene which he describes with such loving detail. And the tendency was evidently gaining ground in Wordsworth's mind during 1802, as he considered how much his own sense of joy had declined over the years.

It was in just such a mood that he approached the writing of what is commonly regarded as the greatest of his shorter works: the 'Ode: Intimations of Immortality from Recollections of Early Childhood'.[26] This poem is written from a place of sanctuary established by linking indulgence of childhood with the exploration of personal memory: the poet, while aligning himself firmly with the main assumptions of his own society, is thus able to draw further power from recollection of childhood pleasure.

In a memorable discussion of the poem,[27] Lionel Trilling draws attention to the relationship between the statement that is being made in the Ode and Freud's discussion, in *Civilization and its Discontents*, of the development of human consciousness. After Freud had published 'The Future of an Illusion', he received from Romain Rolland a letter in which the latter claimed that Freud had overlooked the existence of what he termed an 'oceanic' consciousness in mankind, a feeling (as Freud understood it) of 'an indissoluble bond, of being one with the external world as a whole' which Rolland regarded as the root of all religious feeling. While not recognising any such emotion in himself, Freud set to work to explain such a phenomenon by referring it back to the inability of the child at the breast to distinguish its ego from the external world, and continued:

> If we may assume that there are many people in whose mental life this primary ego-feeling has persisted to a greater or lesser degree,

it would exist in them side by side with the narrower and more sharply demarcated ego-feeling of maturity, like a kind of counterpart to it.

Trilling draws attention to the resemblance between the phenomenon being described here and that in the passage beginning 'Bless'd the infant babe . . .' which we quoted earlier from *The Prelude*. He sees the Ode therefore as a poem of gain rather than loss, a poem in which the 'primal affection' which he believes to be the theme of that passage is given fuller affirmation.

This is a suggestive reading of the poem, and inasmuch as it brings it into line with later modes of discourse it is clearly valuable. At the same time it treats the poem essentially as a poem 'about growing up' – about the need, that is, to accept the loss of much of the original 'oceanic' feeling and to regard it as an adjunct of immaturity. What it ignores is the evidence in the poem, and elsewhere, that Wordsworth not only believed in such an 'oceanic' feeling, but still thought that it might have a metaphysical grounding, relating the babe at the breast not only to its own future existence but to the universe at large as well.

There are other ways in which awareness of Wordsworth's contact with Coleridge's theories – which touch Freud's at certain points, but are in important respects different – affect interpretation of the poem. Trilling's reading tends to equate the 'oceanic' sense described at some points in the poem wholly with the 'affections' which are referred to elsewhere. He therefore takes the lines in *The Prelude*'s passage about the flower which the baby points to and which has been 'beautified' by 'love/Drawn from love's purest earthly fount' as central to the sense of that whole passage: 'He does not learn about a flower but about the pretty-flower, the flower that I-want-and-that-mother-will-get-for-me.'[28x] To read the passage simply in this light, however, is inevitably to sentimentalise it. Our own investigation would direct us rather to the presence of a process of thought, even in that early passage, whereby the sense (shared at that time with Coleridge) of 'something far more deeply interfused' which is present deeply in the being, in the very heart and blood of the child, is also doomed to fade. The importance of the affection between mother and infant (which is sustained by those earlier 'first affections' but not to be identified with them) is that it lays the foundation for a similar link with the objects of nature –

a link which may survive permanently when the original vision is no more than a matter of memory and fitful revisitings. The mother's love is not simply 'oceanic', therefore: it mediates in the child's consciousness between the living world of imagination and the dead world of objects, to provide a new model for love.

One further point should be mentioned. In his letter to Freud, Rolland pointed out that his own sense of the 'oceanic' brought with it no assurance of immortality. In his various recorded discussions of the poem, on the other hand, Wordsworth made it clear that (as his subtitle might suggest) the role of imagination in the poem was indissolubly linked to the sense of immortality. 'The poem', he said, in 1815,

> rests entirely upon two recollections of childhood, one that of a splendour in the objects of sense which is passed away, and the other an indisposition to bend to the law of death as applying to our particular case. PW IV 464

When, many years later, he expounded the poem more fully to Isabella Fenwick he related his childhood sense of immortality to the sense of life exhibited by the child of 'We are Seven' and went on to say that in his own case it had been less animal vivacity than a sense of the 'indomitable spirit' in himself that had made the idea of death so hard to actualise in his mind. With a feeling congenial to this, he goes on:

> I was often unable to think of external things as having external existence, and I communed with all that I saw as something not apart from, but inherent in, my own immaterial nature. Many times while going to school have I grasped at a wall or tree to recall myself from this abyss of idealism to the reality. At that time I was afraid of such processes. PW IV 463

For Wordsworth, it seems, the shock of early human loss (his parents' deaths, for instance) may have been the more overwhelming because it broke in upon a consciousness that was unusually ill-equipped to deal with it. But it would also follow that the fading of the vision brought with it a compensatory humanising realisation of the facts of loss in others. The continuance of such a consciousness as he had in childhood might have rendered him totally self-sufficient and isolate – and so, ultimately, monstrous. It is necessary that the former total possession should accede to a gentler working of that primary force:

> . . . those first affections,
>   Those shadowy recollections,
>   Which, be they what they may,
>   Are yet the fountain light of all our day,
>   Are yet a master light of all our seeing. . . .

In his earlier *Prelude* drafts, he had been describing how his primary consciousness magnetised itself to certain great objects of sense – the very 'Fountains, Meadows, Hills and Groves' of his earliest vision. And it is they in turn that now sustain the psyche as it is displaced from its first, visionary near-solipsism to find a less vivid, but more humanly acceptable basis

> In the primal sympathy
> Which having been must ever be,
> In the soothing thoughts that spring
> Out of human suffering,
> In the faith that looks through death,
> In years that bring the philosophic mind.

'Primal sympathy', as distinct from 'primal vision', is permanent, affording a running line of sustenance through the necessary experience of loss. As the human organism begins to grow into separate existence, its privileged access to the experience of absolute vision is forfeited; but it retains a range of affections, all in various ways still related to that first and total magnetisation. So the cultivation of such affections (particularly those affections that are devoted to the unchanging forms of nature) is not simply a mercy in the face of that loss but one way of keeping alive, in however limited a fashion, the actual power itself: in the exercise of affection vision, and the loss of vision, are reconciled within a single positive force. And that force, it turns out, leads on from love of nature to love of man. Similarly with suffering. By 'the soothing thoughts that spring/Out of human suffering' Wordsworth is not suggesting that the sufferings of others can somehow be turned into an anodyne for the spectator (though this is a reading which might easily spring to mind, in view of certain familiar ideas of atonement through suffering in the Christian tradition); he is returning to his old affirmation that suffering 'shares the nature of infinity'. If the nature of infinity is revealed through *suffering* it can hardly be dismissed as a fantasy created by the pleasure-principle: for the very reason that it is 'permanent, obscure and dark', what it reveals carries more authority than any momentary revelation in a rush of joy. It also makes the 'faith that looks through death' something more than a self-gratification or a wish-fulfilment. And by its implication that infinity underlies both pleasure and suffering, it endows with permanence and sublimity the 'philosophical mind', which is able to make these reconciliations because it is possessed of a self-originating as well as a reflective power – it is, like the moon, a mediator between the finite observing mind and the infinite, unbearable source of light and energy at the heart of the universe, but it has also (and unlike the moon) an active power of its own.

The final section is pervaded by this sense of established reconciliation. The 'Fountains, Meadows, Hills, and Groves' provide the most permanent link with the earliest affections, since these objects of nature, which were seen as radiant in childhood, can still awaken an echo of the power originally created by that magnetising force:

> Yet in my heart of hearts I feel your might;
> I only have relinquish'd one delight
> To live beneath your more habitual sway.

The running brooks and the brightness of day are next seized upon – not at random, but because they are permanent reminders, respectively, of the half-irritable animation and the wondering vision which were twin characteristics of childhood. Each in its way looks back to the quality of the primal life-force:

> I love the Brooks which down their channels fret,
> Even more than when I tripp'd lightly as they;
> The innocent brightness of a new-born Day
> > Is lovely yet. . . .

(The word 'fret', recalling 'fretted by sallies of his mother's kisses', is particularly apposite.) But mention of the dawn prompts an abrupt turn in that argument:

> The Clouds that gather round the setting sun
> Do take a sober colouring from an eye
> That hath kept watch o'er man's mortality. . . .

The sun, we are made to recall, does not display its full nature as a light-fountain again until sunset. If it *then* suggests the possibility that life persists in some sense through death, the adult observer will also find such an intimation checked by his own intervening experiences of absolute loss. And yet that is not the end of the matter, either. By a final, brilliant turn, Wordsworth recalls us again to the mediating power of nature:

> Another race hath been, and other palms are won.
> Thanks to the human heart by which we live,
> Thanks to its tenderness, its joys, and fears,
> To me the meanest flower that blows can give
> Thoughts that do often lie too deep for tears.

The movement, one senses, is modelled on that by which a meditative observer might turn from his sober contemplation of a glorious sunset and notice, in the light of common day behind him, a small wild flower. The contrast would momentarily emphasise the ordinariness and simplicity of its existence, yet the physical *seeing* would still be invested with an afterglow of radiance, carried over by the eye itself from the sunset.

If the man of sensibility were to dwell on the brevity of the flower's existence, the thought might simply stir his heart and prompt a tribute from the fountain of tears. But to the 'seeing' eye the flower is something more: it stands as a close-wrought embodiment of the contradiction between mortality and immortality. Soon, we know, it will have faded, yet it holds up, in its visible heart, an infinite and active fountain of seeds, seed within seed, which are capable of continuous reproduction for ever. If the human observer chose to dwell on that, he might find an intimation that the sense of infinity to which his own heart's workings of tenderness, joy and fear deliver him extends its roots into his own 'heart of hearts'. The developed human heart, as attached to a mind that has existed in time, must always see its most natural mode to be pathos and find its most natural expression in tears; but the organic 'heart of hearts' that is at its centre carries a vitality which is in one sense immortal and in every sense sustaining. It thus gives to that sustenance the further concealed light of the ambiguous radiance that has haunted the poem as a whole.

The reconciliation afforded by these final lines, fusing the senses of mortality and immortality in the single small flower, finely sums up Wordsworth's own stance in the poem, therefore. Throughout, the central attitude which has been taken up and expressed through the rhythms and tone of the poetry is one of manly independence qualified by tender affection. His final tribute to the flower resolves any residual conflict between the two by relating the individual back to mankind and to the knowledge that 'we have all of us one human heart'. But it also, at another level, shows him still haunted by the sense that we might, beneath this, be 'one life' as well.

For his nineteenth-century readers, the more straightforward sense was enough: it chimed with their own belief in the desirability of creating a society that respected the individual while at the same time encouraging a domesticity which should foster the private affections of the heart, and they were content to glide over the more obscure points in the poem in their readiness to seize this main point. For later readers, on the other hand, aware of the failures and shortcomings of Victorian achievements, the elicitation of so simple a moral from the poem is less satisfactory and verges on the sentimental.

Lionel Trilling's fine reading helps meet the problem – at least at one level. It answers to one criterion for modern criticism set up by Richards – that of finding 'what may be made of' a poem.[29x] And for many modern readers it perhaps provides *all* that is needed to give the poem a readable content. Yet some may still feel that an attempt to read the poem purely in the light of a 'primal sympathy' which is conceived of also as 'oceanic' is not altogether satisfactory even in terms of later psychology. In such cases, a further incursion into the total process of the poem may prove rewarding by demonstrating how fully the poem as a whole dramatises movements in Wordsworth's mind that extend beyond those simple formulae – movements which are to be seen rather as corresponding to separate stages in the process whereby childhood vision may be transmuted into the sympathetic imagination of the adult.

To read the 'Immortality' Ode fully, on these terms, is, firstly, to see the heart's pathos supported and sustained by a further awareness of the power which the human heart, as physical organism, consistently displays (and an awareness of this theme in itself assists a reading of other poems of the time); it is also to perceive that his verse in the Ode owes its peculiarly rewarding and complex quality to the presence of forces which were set in motion by the impact of Coleridge's ideas. Without such radiances and excitations his verse was liable to fall into a more sober and stately march.

In some respects this is precisely what did happen in subsequent years, as the influence of Coleridge's powers faded. Yet it is also a witness to the quality of Wordsworth's poem that the *whole* achievement in it continued to exert a power over his later career as well. The mythological interpretation of human development which he had evolved there turned out, in other words, to apply to the creative vitality evinced in the poem itself: 'having been', it must in an important sense 'ever be'. In later years the re-ebullient life of nature, the spontaneous pleasures of children, along with hardly explicable personal experiences such as that of being 'surprised by joy' would continue at intervals to reawaken old trains of thought and startle him into unusual expression. He could no longer hope to base a central faith upon them; more and more he must place his trust in the positive evidences about him that certain bonds of affection were shared by all mankind. Yet he could not, in all honesty, dismiss, either, these continuing intimations that such common links might prove, after all, to be underpinned and guaranteed by the existence of a 'one life' in which all human beings were, to a degree little guessed at by most, participants – a life manifested directly in the infectious excitements of childhood and still, in adults, a hidden source of the joy which continued, against expectation, to overtake them.

5

The Isolation of the Human

While it can be argued that the surge of excitement which accompanied Wordsworth's involvement of Coleridge's ideas with his own brought an enriching complexity into his poetry, it would be wrong to suggest that his thinking about human affairs as we saw it developing earlier was seriously diverted from its natural course.

The truth seems to be rather that as the wave fell and spent itself the concerns of previous years re-emerged in greater strength and definition. Exposure to the idea that a primary life-power, sometimes directly to be apprehended in moments of trance, permeated all things had, we have argued, provided personal release at a crucial time. It had relieved Wordsworth from his dilemma concerning the status of passion by assigning it to a sphere where it could be seen to have a function of its own, linked back to a larger sense of life. It had also given him a new sense of his own relationship with the universe, suggesting that the emotions of country people, in particular, far from being the pathetic sports of creatures too deluded to see the impersonal forces which ultimately governed and ignored them, belonged to their fuller existence as human beings – to the other, equally important principle at work in the universe by which organic growth was linked with vital energy. Even his realisation that human death was a fact too stubborn to be regarded simply as a jarring note in the 'minstrelsy of life' could not abolish this fascination: instead, it gave new depth to the visitations of joy and sense of pathos experienced by the mature man.

We have already noted some preoccupations of Wordsworth's, however, which, though easily relatable to what Coleridge had offered him, were more especially his own. He had long been oppressed, for example, by a sense of the barriers between individuals, the impossibilities of communication. Even during the Wye expedition of 1793, this had been brought home to him by his encounter with the 'rover' who was to be the model of Peter Bell; and what was there a cautionary interlude during a time of revived spirits had earlier been a more common source of depression. The sense of awe that had followed his learning that in London (by contrast with his native Lakes) a man often did not even know the name of his next door neighbour, was intensified when he lived in the city and inspected the faces of the passing crowds:

> How often in the overflowing Streets,
> Have I gone forwards with the Crowd, and said
> Unto myself, the face of every one
> That passes by me is a mystery.   1805 vii 595–8

If there was an element of nightmare here, it was partly relieved by the already established psychoscape which, drawing its contours from his native Lakes, could provide from the movements and rock-faces of his native torrents and mountains a pattern within which to hold the continual crowd-fluxes of people and blank faces; but it was not easy to dismiss the sense that conurbations of this size nullified the value of the individual, or that in such societies men grew blind to the human effects of their actions. It became possible for them to set up intolerable industrial conditions, or prosecute wars, without any sense of the sufferings they were imposing on individuals whom they might be passing in the street every day.

In the city, it seemed, most men inhabited, mentally as well as physically, private cells, from which they emerged only to pursue the necessary ends of personal survival, and into which no other being could penetrate. After death, 'Each in his narrow cell for ever laid', they merely confirmed a state which had in any case been theirs through life. And it was impossible to fight this situation directly: despite occasional public events, such as the French Revolution, which brought about a temporary breaking of the partitions, the inevitable transition from revolutionary hope to public fear would always pervert the social passions to an orgy of destruction and so raise the defensive walls of each individual cell more solidly than before.

I suggested earlier, however, that this depressing reflection, which obsessed him on Salisbury Plain, had been lightened, as he passed into the Wye Valley, by an intuition that his own passionate attachment to the great and lasting forms of nature was more powerful than any sardonic attitude which might be fostered by his experiences in society. A consciousness possessed by the sublime forms of nature would automatically be redeemed from pettiness; it might also, if further cultivated, modulate into a tender feeling for the gentler manifestations of nature, and so encourage an extension of that feeling to one's fellow human beings.

Before it was given further content and definition by contact with Coleridge's speculations, this second idea had already worked deeply in Wordsworth's mind. It had caused him to give a new value to the small local community, where the solitary, or the disabled, or the simple-minded each had a part to play in the larger life of the whole. One such figure, remembered vividly from childhood, was that of the 'old Cumberland Beggar',[1] who had moved about like a natural force through the settled society of the Lakeland communities. In many ways it was easy to see this man as an object:

> Poor Traveller!
> His staff trails with him, scarcely do his feet
> Disturb the summer dust, he is so still
> In look and motion that the cottage curs,
> Ere he have pass'd the door, will turn away
> Weary of barking at him. ll. 58-63

Yet this man (who did not seem even to age) evoked respect from the old woman who opened the toll-gate for him, or the post-boy who, if he did not turn aside, passed gently to avoid disturbing him. And the charity for which he asked was, paradoxically, a source of benefit to the givers:

> the poorest poor
> Long for some moments in a weary life
> When they can know and feel that they have been
> Themselves the fathers and the dealers out
> Of some small blessings. . . . ll. 147-51

The rationale behind this and similar assertions in the poem is stated openly in a phrase which has already been quoted several times as embodying the central faith into which Wordsworth was moving:

> . . . we have all of us one human heart. l. 153

At one point in the poem, however, Wordsworth goes beyond this central statement to make an assertion which carries more

cosmic overtones. In addressing the proud and powerful of the
earth, and advising them against despising creatures such as the
Cumberland beggar, Wordsworth writes,

> 'Tis Nature's law
> That none, the meanest of created things,
> Of forms created the most vile and brute,
> The dullest or most noxious, should exist
> Divorced from good, a spirit and pulse of good,
> A life and soul to every mode of being
> Inseparably link'd.   ll. 73–9

The heart here is not simply the instrument of charity and courage
which it had been in eighteenth-century poetry, but a badge of
human equality, its workings the same in king or beggar: its pulse is
(whether actually or metaphorically) the organ through which the
true moral order of the universe most directly operates.
Wordsworth, in other words, is calling on English poets as well as
French *philosophes* to compensate for the injustices of the French
Revolution. Disillusioned as a political republican, he is proclaiming
a universal 'republic of the heart', which extends not simply to men
but to the whole of animated nature.

     The work that might most easily be read as a manifesto for this
belief is 'The Ruined Cottage', which, though eventually included in
The Excursion, was, as we saw earlier, first composed as a separate
poem. In the past, critics as diverse as Coleridge and Leavis have
praised its qualities; more recently Jonathan Wordsworth has made it
the centre of a complete study.[2x] The story of Margaret, told sparely
and with little commentary, is one of the most moving poems in
English.

     In one important respect the poem inverts a popular contempor-
ary tradition. Many eighteenth-century works of art had been
created in the shadow of ruined castles and abbeys, where Gothic
arches and evening glooms combined to provide a ready setting for
fear or pleasing melancholy. By the end of the century, also, it was
not unknown for young men to invoke the romantic genius of such
places by playing music in them. Wordsworth, seeing them as a part
of nature, was more particularly struck by their pathos. Even as a
boy he had been deeply impressed by hearing a bird singing among
the ruins of Furness Abbey,[3] while the ruins of Tintern, standing by
the river Wye and surrounded by valley and hills, had been a witness

to the power of nature to preside over and beautify the decay of man's nobler aspirations. As his sense of pathos extended to a sense of the 'one human heart', however, he came to dwell rather on the significance of the single human habitation, sending up its smoke in silence or transmitting its light at night. The sight of such a building when ruined, a human cell now finally opened to the forces of nature, could, by the same token, be more moving than that of a ruined palace or castle.

'The Ruined Cottage' is also a centrally social document: it is the story of a small family, rooted and happy in a natural setting, and its decline. The father, through a simple illness, was forced into unemployment. Restless and discontented at his lot, he joined a troop of soldiers so as to find some money for his wife and children. But with his departure, his wife, who until then had been independent, became victim to a poverty which was partly the effect of heart-sickness. The loom which could have supported her lay idle, while she became more and more obsessive in her enquiries for her husband, asking every passer-by whether he had news of him. She lost first one and then the other of her children, to be left finally alone in a house which, no longer maintained against the weather, gave little protection to her health:

> And here, my friend,
> In sickness she remained; and here she died,
> Last human tenant of these ruined walls. ll. 490–2

The narator, having heard the old man's story through, returns to the cottage with new eyes,

> and traced with milder interest,
> That secret spirit of humanity
> Which, 'mid the calm oblivious tendencies
> Of nature, 'mid her plants, her weeds and flowers,
> And silent overgrowings, still survived. ll. 502–6

The old man, seeing this, now feels bound to add a further cautionary comment. Too much grief would be wrong; now that the link between nature and humanity has been established, it is more important to maintain it:

> Be wise and chearful, and no longer read
> The forms of things with an unworthy eye. ll. 510–11

He also goes on to affirm that nature, her life surviving the death of Margaret, has herself restored a spirit of calm:

> I well remember that those very plumes,
> Those weeds, and the high spear-grass on that wall,
> By mist and silent rain-drops silvered o'er,
> As once I passed, did to my mind convey
> So still an image of tranquillity,
> So calm and still, and looked so beautiful
> Amid the uneasy thoughts which filled my mind,
> That what we feel of sorrow and despair
> From ruin and from change, and all the grief
> The passing shews of being leave behind,
> Appeared an idle dream that could not live
> Where meditation was. I turned away,
> And walked along my road in happiness.   ll. 513-25

Although the picture of Margaret's obsessive yearnings and the implied link between nature and the human heart remind one of Coleridgean theories and might reflect some influence from early conversations and 'The Eolian Harp', 'The Ruined Cottage' was composed in the period previous to their closest collaboration; in most important respects, as Jonathan Wordsworth has pointed out, it marks the high point of Wordsworth's development before Coleridge's ideas made their full impact. If there is an external influence, then, it comes rather from the direct human feeling of Dorothy Wordsworth. And indeed, the verse has a homogeneity, a nakedness to its own thought, which Wordsworth was never quite to regain. Its combination of manliness and tenderness strikes a new note in the English poetry of its time. The device of narrative within narrative further helps to express Wordsworth's own state of mind, since he could, in telling the story of Margaret, make an excursion into the heart-dominated world of Dorothy, while returning, in his narrative framework, to the mode of meditation supported by manly cheerfulness in which he was more fully at home. The story of Margaret is so finely told, in fact, that it is tempting to ask whether Wordsworth's development as a poet did not suffer positive damage from Coleridge's intervention.

The truth seems to be more complicated. Although, left to himself, Wordsworth might well have written more in the same vein, and built up a small corpus of such works, the logical end of the line he was pursuing would, I suggested earlier, have been poetic silence. There is a finality of statement, even in this poem, which is artistically inauspicious. A narrative of pathos has, through the Wanderer's telling, been placed geographically and distanced in time. What was attempted in the episode of the wandering woman in *An Evening Walk* has here been more firmly achieved. What could Wordsworth do further in this direction but repeat himself?

In terms of Wordsworth's social philosophy, moreover, a gap remained. Given the existence of a universal human pathos, as exemplified in the story of Margaret, it was still necessary to suppose the existence of a universal human eye which was capable of perceiving that pathos. A young man of sensibility might see it, but he was hardly representative of humanity in general. For this reason, an older, more representative narrator became essential – a man without Wordsworth's own educational advantages and refinements who would still see the pathos of such a history.

Having, in his boyhood, known at least one man made wise through long and solitary experience,[4x] Wordsworth felt authorised to introduce such a narrator. The fact that such figures were rare did not matter, since an education in solitude must itself be a rare phenomenon.

The description of the Pedlar which prefaces the story of Margaret in later versions of the poem became intricately involved with Wordsworth's exploration of his own early experience, as he tried to single out incidents which could be regarded as at once significant in his own experience and available to any boy brought up in the Lake District. It was written, moreover, after Racedown, when Wordsworth was already in close communication with Coleridge. Jonathan Wordsworth, who points this out in his study, regards the description of the Pedlar as an attempt to set the story of Margaret in the context of 'the one Life' which he was elaborating with Coleridge. In the light of what has been said in previous chapters, we may now ask whether it did not also contain something still more ambitious – an attempt to show, in a single and solitary individual, the nourishment and growth of the 'primary consciousness' which sustains human beings in their awareness of that 'one Life'. By describing the education of the Pedlar among the distant hills he could present a simpler and more dramatic version of his own education at Hawkshead which would at the same time give fuller authority to a 'republicanism of the heart' by showing that a

philosophy of the one Life was available not just to the sensitive, but
to every human being:

> . . . many an hour in caves forlorn
> And in the hollow depths of naked crags
> He sate, and even in their fixed lineaments,
> Or from the power of a peculiar eye,
> Or by creative feeling overborne,
> Or by predominance of thought oppressed,
> Even in their fixed and steady lineaments
> He traced an ebbing and a flowing mind,
> Expression ever varying.
>   Thus informed,
> He had small need of books; for many a tale
> Traditionary round the mountains hung,
> And many a legend peopling the dark woods
> Nourished Imagination in her growth,
> And gave the mind that apprehensive power
> By which she is made quick to recognize
> The moral properties and scope of things.
> But greedily he read and read again
> What'er the rustic Vicar's shelf supplied . . .   ll. 49–66

The remainder of the original fragment describes the Pedlar's
gradual education into the lore of universal human love. At first his
heart hardly worked in separation from his body: yet while his
thoughts and desires were made lofty, that remained lowly. He was
learning, in gratitude for the ecstasies that he had experienced,

> To look on nature with an humble heart,
> Self-questioned where it did not understand,
> And with a superstitious eye of love.   ll. 137–9

Such feelings kept him bound to the forms of nature even when he
was studying them by the most abstract of disciplines. Disquiet
arose, in fact, not from the detachment which such studies enforced,
but from an intensification of the contemplative power within:
'Accumulated feelings pressed his heart/With restless thoughts'. He
sought relief in the sound of storms; he even tried studying the laws
of light not in solitude but while looking at the rainbow thrown only
in a cloud of mist by a roaring torrent. He could find contentment,
however, only when he reached a more ecstatic state, where

He felt the sentiment of being spread
O'er all that moves, and all that seemeth still,
O'er all which, lost beyond the reach of thought
And human knowledge, to the human eye
Invisible, yet liveth to the heart . . .   ll. 208–12

It was in an attempt to escape the effects of these inward pressures
that he finally set out to become a wanderer. That enterprise carried
dangers of another kind, but what he had learnt now served him in
good stead:

    The talisman of constant thought,
And kind sensations in a gentle heart,
Preserved him.   ll. 251–3

Not only that, but the education that his heart had received made
him immediately responsive to the feelings of others:

Unoccupied by sorrow of its own,
His heart lay open; and, by nature tuned
And constant disposition of his thoughts
To sympathy with man, he was alive
To all that was enjoyed where'er he went,
And all that was endured; and in himself
Happy, and quiet in his chearfulness,
He had no painful pressure from within
Which made him turn aside from wretchedness
With coward fears. He could afford to suffer
With those whom he saw suffer.   ll. 274–84

In the final account of this man, therefore, he is to be seen as
a fine, prophet-like figure, loving towards mankind, but also
fully in possession of 'deep analogies by thought supplied,/Or
consciousnesses not to be subdued'. The same gift was to be described (in the same words) by Wordsworth as his own in *The
Prelude*: the whole passage, in fact, further extended, appeared in
Book III of that poem. The note of self-sufficiency that surrounded
the Pedlar –

He had a world about him – 'twas his own,
He made it – for it only lived to him,
And to the God who looked into his mind . . .   ll. 339–41

was also given over to the poet. In the Pedlar this self-sufficiency was to be seen – despite suspicions of madness on the part of his fellows – as admirable, since it sprang from the unremitting power of an eye that could perceive all things actively, and so

> . . . spake perpetual logic to his soul,
> And by an unrelenting agency
> Did bind his feelings even as in a chain.   ll. 354–6

It is at this point that the original 'Pedlar' fragment breaks off, however, and it is not difficult to see why. Wordsworth was once again approaching the dilemma created when an apparent perfection of love in a man was yoked together with apparent self-sufficiency. Since the Pedlar's fellows viewed his enthusiasms as signs of possible madness, his love for them could not be requited. If he achieved a reciprocal relationship of love, therefore, it was rather with 'the God who looked into his mind': however firmly established, his 'link of feelings' must remain in an essential respect unfulfilled. Although the love of nature might have led in him to the love of man, the fact that that love was not returned meant that further extension of the chain could come only from the rise of further individuals who were educated in the same radical manner as the Pedlar himself.

It was for this reason, perhaps, that Wordsworth removed the passage to *The Prelude*, where it could find its place in a much larger discussion of the relationship between love of nature and love of man. That is not to say that its appearance in the original description of the Pedlar had been totally contradictory to his purposes there. At that time, however, he had been more preoccupied with the early ecstatic experiences that the Pedlar had enjoyed, and the availability to all mankind of such total experiences, so that the main weight had fallen quite naturally upon those passages that described how 'he saw one life, and felt that it was joy' and how in his more ecstatic moments his whole being was engaged:

> Oh then what soul was his, when on the tops
> Of the high mountains he beheld the sun
> Rise up and bathe the world in light. He looked,
> The ocean and the earth beneath him lay
> In gladness and deep joy. The clouds were touched,
> And in their silent faces did he read
> Unutterable love. Sound needed none,

Nor any voice of joy: his spirit drank
The spectacle. Sensation, soul and form
All melted into him. They swallowed up
His animal being. In them did he live,
And by them did he live. They were his life.   ll. 95–106

The experience of identity with the universe in a moment of joy
was seen as having provided the basis of the Pedlar's future love, for
once such natural barriers were broken down, the barriers between
individual human beings must seem less significant. And if this
experience was indeed available to all human beings, they possessed,
whether they knew it or not, the secret of a unity stronger than
anything which separated them from one another. The memory of
such experiences was evidently what had made the French Revolution so important a memory for Wordsworth; during the period of
their first enthusiasm, all barriers between individuals seemed to be
dissolving. For a brief time, it seemed that a new age really had been
born and that the uniting life of nature was breaking through to
become the guiding force of human existence. That hope had been
lost again; but Coleridge's theory of the primary consciousness had
subsequently allowed it to flourish in a new way. Even if liberation
did not come through revolution, it might still be true that the
unifying joy which Wordsworth had sensed in nature as a boy *was* a
hidden key to the universe, was indeed the force which still bound
human beings together, preventing them from ever quite falling
apart into atomic individualism. The fact that this was not discovered by the many, even in moments of its greatest manifestation (as
in France) was simply a pathetic sign of human blindness, not a
denial of its truth. On the contrary, to anyone with eyes to see, the
warmth of the human heart, as shown in the universal phenomenon
of human affection, was a perpetual witness to the same underlying
power, which showed its presence most generally in the season of
springtime, and most intensely in human love. Under the vision of
this ultimate joy even the strife and suffering of humanity were
transformed into a 'still sad music'; by the same token the Wanderer,
though chastened by the fate of Margaret, could eventually find it
subsumed into the music of nature and turn away to walk along the
road 'in happiness'.

One problem, as we have already seen, lay in the very rarity of
men such as the Pedlar. And even if the existence of such men was

accepted, it might still be objected that this kind of vision was available only to those who had possessed themselves of it in childhood and youth, and never lost it. Any serious attempt to universalise such experiences ought also to involve a demonstration that a man who had grown up without the benefit of such rare favouring circumstances could, in later life, be brought by other means to acknowledge nature's humanising power.

In this respect the sardonic tinker whom Wordsworth had met in the Wye Valley remained a crucial figure. He, after all, had been no victim of an urban civilisation, oppressed by the artificiality which life in such society laid upon its component members, but a man often exposed to the elements and the great forms of nature. Yet even if his experiences had made him an engaging character, full of 'strange stories', nature had not wrought in *him* the further connection with humanity created by affection for her tenderer manifestations:

> A primrose by a river's brim
> A yellow primrose was to him,
> And it was nothing more.

It was in trying to meet the challenge posed by this man, evidently, that Wordsworth wrote *Peter Bell*,[5] which was conceived at about the same time as 'The Ancient Mariner', and seems at the moral level to represent a similar enterprise. Coleridge's poem shows how a man of average human upbringing might be led, through experiences of fear and physical extremity, to a vision of the universe which, however little understood, illuminates his relationship to all other living things, revealing underlying links of life and love. Wordsworth's aim is similar, but he rigorously avoids Coleridge's use of supernatural machinery. He keeps before him the actual figure of his tinker (his trade changed to that of a potter) and aims at a plausible account of his conversion in terms of events which, though apparently 'supernatural', have an everyday explanation.

Peter Bell is a wild, sensual man, not unattractive, but devoid of outgoing sympathy. On finding a lonely ass which is keeping watch over its master's body in the river, his first impulse, not seeing what the animal is doing, is to purloin it and, when it will not come with him, to beat it. When he sees what is keeping the ass there, however, he falls into a trance of horror. Unlike the youthful Wordsworth, whose education by romances and natural forms had taught him to look at such sights without fear, this Cain-like figure is himself terrified. And his fear (a mark of his inability to understand the 'ancient language of the earth') makes him afraid even of events which have a perfectly rational explanation. As he goes away with the ass now leading, he is frightened first by the shouts of the dead man's son, looking for his father, and then by the noise of a troop of miners underground.

Yet the whole turns out to be a rapid education through the ministry of fear, which prepares his heart for an influx of unaccustomed feelings. When the ass finally brings him to the cottage of the dead man's widow he breaks the news to her and in doing so finds himself initiated into the universe of life:

> And now is Peter taught to feel
> That man's heart is a holy thing;
> And Nature, through a world of death,
> Breathes into him a second breath,
> More searching than the breath of spring.   ll. 1071–5

The result of his recognition is that he sees the world as (in Wordsworth's eyes at least) it really is; and in this new sober knowledge, we are finally told, he

> Forsook his crimes, renounced his folly,
> And, after ten months' melancholy,
> Became a good and honest man.

In the reclamation of Peter Bell fear, though important, is a subordinate factor. What is more important is the 'link of life' by which he is ultimately connected back to his fellow men.[6x] In the beginning he is not totally alienated from humanity: his 'dozen wedded wives' are a sign of wildness and extravagance rather than of a deadened heart. That his wildness can emerge as open cruelty against the animal creation, however, is evident from the opening stanza of the narrative:

> All by the moonlight river-side
> Groaned the poor Beast – alas! in vain;
> The staff was raised to loftier height,
> And the blows fell with heavier weight
> As Peter struck – and struck again.

At this the narrator is forced to go back and start at the beginning, but the brief cameo has made its point, to be elaborated in a long account of Peter Bell's exposure alternately to the forms of nature and the vices of the city. He has never been intimately touched by the beauty, the silence or the tenderness of nature: as a result, his basic character has hardened, acquiring further layers of malice and cunning.

The ass is not simply a passive victim: it plays an important part in the poem by its active devotion to its dead master and its stubborn insistence on guiding Peter Bell to the dead man's home. This instinctive fidelity is a theme which occurs elsewhere in Wordsworth's poems, and seems to be linked to his discussions with Coleridge concerning the status of affection in the universe at large. In the context of discussions about the 'one human heart', it would be natural to ask whether in the animal kingdom, also, well-authenticated stories of the fidelity shown by animals to their human masters did not furnish indications of a general link from heart to heart, foreshadowing the bonds of affection to be traced more nobly – if also more fitfully – in man. A speculation of the sort occurs in the 'Two Voices' episode in 'The Ancient Mariner':

> 'The spirit who bideth by himself
> In the land of mist and snow,
> He loved the bird that loved the man
> Who shot him with his bow.'   CPW I 202

And an affection not dissimilar to this worked in Wordsworth himself as he scrutinised the asses near his house in Somerset:

> In the woods of Alfoxden I used to take great delight in noticing the habits, tricks, and physiognomy of asses; and I have no doubt that I was thus put upon writing ['Peter Bell'] out of liking for the creature that is so often dreadfully abused.   PW II 527

It is tempting to trace in this passage a residual critique of Coleridge. One can imagine Wordsworth arguing that while the figure of the albatross following a ship at sea might be a very beautiful image of universal love,[7x] it would be harder to make such an image out of nature's less elegant creatures. Yet there was something likeable about the ass, despite its unprepossessing features; and he knew of a case where one had watched over a canal where its master's drowned body lay. Its combination of uncomeliness with selfless devotion might make it a better guide than the glamorous albatross to the basic rôle of affection in the universe.

Further food for speculation was available to the poets from contemporary sources. Erasmus Darwin had discussed the growth of smiling in human beings, which he related to the suckling instinct (observing it also in young kittens and puppies).[8] Coleridge, who mentioned 'the first smile' as a subject for exploration in his notebooks, was also interested by the rather different phenomenon of grinning (which Darwin had discussed in connection with pain and epileptic attacks).[9] When he and his companion climbed Plynlimmon in 1794, they had found that the extremity of thirst made them grin – a fact which Coleridge later used in portraying the desperate thirst of the Mariner and his shipmates.[10] If the smile is a sign of growing affection, the grin expresses a more daemonic power; it is not surprising then that it should be associated with states of extremity. At one point in *Peter Bell*, the hero's reclamation is interrupted as his 'evil spirit' rises up and makes him begin to deceive himself about the nature of his previous acts. The poem proceeds:

> Let them whose voice can stop the clouds,
> Whose cunning eye can see the wind,
> Tell to a curious world the cause
> Why, making here a sudden pause,
> The Ass turned round his head and *grinned*.
>
> Appalling process! I have marked
> The like on heath, in lonely wood;
> And verily, have seldom met
> A spectacle more hideous – yet
> It suited Peter's present mood.
>
> And, grinning in his turn, his teeth
> He in jocose defiance showed. . . .   ll. 821–32

The grinning of Peter in unconscious sympathy with the ass's expression seems to indicate that he is in a daemonic state, which has rendered him unusually alive to all the fearful sights and sounds of the landscape, and so capable of an (albeit involuntary) sympathy.

This delirious state of fear leads him to remorse for some of his past misdeeds and makes him receptive to a Methodist preacher's call for repentance. The result is a softening, never before known in his nature.

> Sweet tears of hope and tenderness!
> And fast they fell, a plenteous shower!

His nerves, his sinews seemed to melt;
Through all his iron frame was felt
A gentle, a relaxing, power!

Each nerve, each fibre of his frame
And all the animal within;
Was weak, perhaps, but it was mild
And gentle as an infant child,
An infant that has known no sin.   ll. 961 – 70 and MS

The most important feature of this process is the reference to 'the animal within'. It is important to Wordsworth's argument not only that Peter Bell should not be a soft man in the beginning of the poem but that he should be possessed of a strong animal constitution. The state into which he is then to move is not unrelated to the combination of stubborn organic strength and capacity for selfless devotion found elsewhere in the animal creation – and actually cartooned in the ass's features. Peter Bell's progress to a final state of goodness and honesty is the human counterpart of a potential movement to affection in nature at large. Along this route the uncouthness and mildness of the ass stand out as a bizarre but telling landmark.

Peter Bell is one of Wordsworth's strangest productions. Undertaken alongside Coleridge's experiments with a poetry of superstition it contains many acute observations of human beings in unusual psychological states. Some of the cameos recall primitive folk-art or a medieval woodcut:

Ah, well-a-day for Peter Bell!
He will be turned to iron soon,
Meet Statue for the court of Fear!
His hat is up – and every hair
Bristles, and whitens in the moon!   ll. 521 – 5

The poem is also enlivened by touches of wit and sardonic comments on society. It is as if the act of trying to reclaim his old Wye Valley companion to the realm of nature had attracted him into a sympathetic imitation of the rover's own brand of humour.

Is it a party in a parlour?
Cramm'd just as they on earth were cramm'd –
Some sipping punch, some sipping tea,
But, as you by their faces see,
All silent and all damn'd![11]

Hazlitt, describing Wordsworth's appearance as he remembered it at
Nether Stowey, said, 'There was something of a roll, a lounge in his
gait, not unlike his own Peter Bell'.[12]

For all Wordsworth's attempts to give the tale an everyday
matter-of-factness, moreover, certain features, such as the behaviour of the ass, gave it, willy-nilly, a supernatural tone. In an
attempt to explain this curious effect, he wrote a Prologue to the
poem, imaging his refusal of sublimity by a picture of himself sitting
in a moon-shaped canoe and flying above the world:

> There's something in a flying horse,
> There's something in a huge balloon;
> But through the clouds I'll never float
> Until I have a little Boat
> Shaped like the crescent-moon.
>
> And now I *have* a little Boat,
> In shape a very crescent-moon . . .

and he describes his voyage into a region far above the storms and
discords of the world:

> Away we go – and what care we
> For treasons, tumults, and for wars?
> We are as calm in our delight
> As is the crescent-moon so bright
> Among the scattered stars.

If anything, the reader is made more, rather than less, uneasy about
Peter Bell by this strange, rather self-conscious Prologue. Its relationship to the main body of the poem emerges more clearly,
however, when we notice the full potency of the 'sky-canoe' image.

The observation that a canoe looks like a crescent moon seems a
pleasant enough piece of fantasy, but in the context of late eighteenth-century discussion of mythology and religion it had acquired
an extended significance. There had been a general recognition that
many emblems and images of ancient religion were related to the
forms of the heavenly elements. In such a context it would be natural
to regard the religion of the Red Indians as another version of these
nature religions: their feathered head-dresses representing the shining glory of the sun and their canoes being deliberately constructed
in the shape of the crescent moon.[13x] There are signs that

Wordsworth was attracted by tales of Red Indians as 'children of nature' who were uncannily sensitive to the minutest sensations in nature and filled with awe by her sublimer manifestations. From the time when he himself lived in nature.

> as if I had been born
> On Indian Plains, and from my Mother's hut
> Had run abroad in wantonness . . .   1805 i 301–3

to manhood, when he would sometimes lie down and apply his ear to the ground in the hope of hearing the wheels of an expected cart,[14] he tried to preserve this wilder side in his own nature. It was as if, while recognising the truth of all that had been said since Elizabethan times about the cruelty and degeneracy of the American Indians, he still believed their life in nature to preserve a directness of perception which was less available to the civilised. His image of the sky-canoe is a good emblem for his attempt to keep alive a similar intensity of perception and ruggedness of physique, in combination with a mildness of affection which the Indian religion seemed to shadow forth even if it did not successfully achieve it.

On these terms, the Prologue to *Peter Bell* may be seen as an attempt to explicate the poem's meaning further by suggesting the workings, in the poet himself, of an imagination that had been educated into tenderness through a profound contact with wildness. Even if this is accepted, however, the uneasiness previously referred to is not dispelled, for the real strain is brought about by the attempt to make these double strands in Wordsworth's personality therapeutic to the hero of his story. The question that he was asking was one which would confront other writers in the nineteenth century: how could a human being, once hardened into the state of experience, be brought back to a state of innocence?

And if Peter Bell's conversion fails to satisfy the reader it is because his reclaimed state seems to deny so much of his former personality. One can indeed go further and say that Wordsworth's poetic world might have been richer if he had been more ready to accept and present characters like Peter in their 'natural' form. The buried sardonic element in his own personality would no doubt have lent its weight to such characters had it been allowed freer play and his presentation of humanity would have been correspondingly wider in range.

That kind of naturalism was not what he was aiming at, however, and as a result his most memorable characters are of a different kind. They are figures such as the Old Man Travelling (more particularly as presented in the first version), the old leech-gatherer of 'Resolution and Independence' and the discharged soldier who, encountered late at night, declared quietly at parting that his trust was 'in the God of Heaven/And in the eye of him who passes me'.[15] Such figures were literally travellers, yet they were also essentially passive; the doggedness of their journeying was combined with an impressive acceptance of the world through which they passed. Upon such figures the fusion of wild impulse with developed sensibility in the poet could focus itself with less strain, therefore.

When we turn back to Wordsworth's accounts of the three figures just mentioned, in fact, we discover how firmly this passive, emblematic quality is reinforced in each case by his description, which builds them up to such a degree of 'objectivity' that one half-expects them to remain permanently silent. We feel surprise, first, that they should speak at all, and then, when they do speak, that they should say such ordinary things. By the same process, however, the 'ordinariness' is made resonant. Before the leech-gatherer speaks of his way of life, his speech is preceded by a 'flash of mild surprise'. He is so much part of nature that he transmits, rather than expresses, surprise at the narrator's suggestion that he is solitary. Nevertheless, like the discharged soldier, he is still a man who lives by a vision of himself. It is their particular virtue, we come to understand, that their vision of themselves should correspond so perfectly to their actuality; the final magical fact, beyond all others, is that inward vision should continue to exist in them at all.

For Wordsworth this is a final mercy, one which redeems the universe of human beings from the nightmare which would see every man, in the last analysis, as locked in a separate cell. The evidence of a hidden working in the heart which each man can give if one waits long enough, or approaches him under sufficiently propitious circumstances, is for him the power which rolls away the stone from the door of the human cavern. Once accept the possible existence of self-generating vision in each human being and the world is no longer a graveyard of bodies in separate compartments; it is revealed as a golden honeycomb, where each man can, in his inmost cell, work to a common music and common pattern, mediated through his own nature and through that of his fellows.

Bees and their cells are so common a presence for good in

Wordsworth's poetry as to suggest that this conception was one which ran in his mind, and there is some further support for the idea in the fact that his antagonism to Roman Catholicism did not extend to the practice of human beings inhabiting monastic or convent cells. The 'hermit' in 'Tintern Abbey'; the nuns who 'fret not at their convent's narrow room', or the 'knee-worn cells' which delight him in Catholic towns abroad[16] chime with his own conviction that solitary meditation is not necessarily an anti-social act.

In his earliest poetry Wordsworth used the cell in its fashionable, Gothic senses, writing of 'jarring monks, to gloomy cell confined' and 'the cell where the convict is laid'.[17] But in his mature poetry, he exploits the whole range of ambiguity which is opened out by the further significances of the word. At his most pessimistic he pictures the victims of political imprisonment, 'Each in his separate cell', or the

> stubborn spirit doomed to yell
> In solitary ward or cell,
> Ten thousand miles from all his brethren.[18]

In more optimistic verses he pictures tender insects sleeping in their cells, or dwells on the noise of the bee, which sounds throughout time, before and after human history,

> . . . every awful note in unison
> With that faint utterance, which tells
> Of treasure sucked from buds and bells,
> For the pure keeping of those waxen cells;

more gaily, he addresses 'Gold and Silver Fishes in a Vase':

> Type of a sunny human breast
> Is your transparent cell. . . .[19]

The last example brings into the open something which is inherent in Wordsworth's usage: when he speaks of a cell, the image of the human heart is seldom far away. Thus in a poem on a kitten he speaks of the enjoyments which dwell

> In the impenetrable cell
> Of the silent heart which Nature
> Furnishes to every Creature. . . .[20]

The early Gothic line, 'Unlocking bleeding Thought's "memorial cell"', is later softened to 'And search the affections to their inmost cell'.[21]

In Coleridgean terms, the image would be made complete only if the cell might contain a spring or fountain, and this too has its place in Wordsworth's poetry. Although precise collocation of the two images is rare, it stands out, for example, in a rather conventional poem of 1821, providing a good example of the way in which an unexpected (and apparently otiose) phrase in the later poetry may, once seen by the light of his earlier excitement, assume exactness of meaning:

> Why leap the fountains from their cells
> Where everlasting Bounty dwells? –
> That, while the Creature is sustained,
> His God may be adored.[22]

Even more striking is a poem written at Nun's Well, Brigham, in 1833. Here the unexpectedly juxtaposed image of a nun against a spring in a limestone cell evoked thoughts of the cell where Pope's Eloisa had discovered the ambiguous power of the heart's affections:

> Yet, o'er the brink, and round the limestone cell
> Of the pure spring (they call it the 'Nun's Well',
> Name that first struck by chance my startled ear)
> A tender Spirit broods – the pensive Shade
> Of ritual honours to this Fountain paid
> By hooded Votaresses with saintly cheer;
> Albeit oft the Virgin-mother mild
> Looked down with pity upon eyes beguiled
> Into the shedding of 'too soft a tear'.   PW IV 23–4

The spring or fountain in the dark cell or cavern affords one other relief, it creates music where otherwise there would be only silence. Hence, in 'Yew Trees' the particular magical effect of the conclusion, with its

> mountain flood
> Murmuring from Glaramara's inmost caves   PW II 210

– which in 'On the Power of Sound' is transferred to the fact of hearing itself:

> a Spirit aërial
> Informs the cell of Hearing, dark and blind . . .   PW II 323

Wordsworth discovered one of the best emblems for this lifelong image of human (and animal) hearts linked by a common impulse when he visited La Verna in 1837 and, hearing the cuckoo, realised that, if the spirit of St Francis was shared by his followers, some of the inmates might like himself be feeling delight –

> prompt
> To catch from Nature's humblest monitors
> Whate'er they bring of impulses sublime

and even that one of them 'Looking far forth from his aerial cell' might be tempted to apply the text, 'The Voice of One/Crying amid the wilderness' to the voice of the bird.[23] The prophecy which is proclaimed by *this* bird is that the impulsive heart's joy which it starts is as real as the more sombre work of time.

Wordsworth derived from this and other experiences, such as his never-failing delight in the sound of the cuckoo, or his invariable heart-leap at the sight of a rainbow, an intimation which ran counter to more melancholy failures of the human heart. If the individual heart was consistent with itself through time, was it not possible that all human hearts, though separated in space, might yet prove their basic consistency with one another? For all the signs to the contrary, was it not true that individual human beings sometimes gave an expression to their common human nature so powerful that it seemed like a fountain – springing perhaps, from a humanity larger than themselves?

The poem in which Wordsworth rendered his greatest example of such an intuition was, like others of the sort, based partly on actual experience, partly on an emblem in a book. 'The Solitary Reaper'[24] was stimulated by the Scottish tour of 1803, but Dorothy, who mentioned in her journal the sight of reapers in the fields, made no reference to singing. On the contrary, she gave the impression that the reapers they saw were silent, and that their impressiveness was created by the very fact that in moving quietly at work they gave an open expression to the implicit and noiseless rhythms of nature:

> It was harvest-time, and the fields were quietly (might I be allowed to say pensively?) enlivened by small companies of reapers. It is not uncommon in the more lonely parts of the Highlands to see a *single* person so employed.
>
> DWJ (De Sel) I 380

The last observation is close to the opening of 'The Solitary Reaper' but, as both Dorothy and William stated, the basic suggestion for the poem came from a sentence in Thomas Wilkinson's manuscript account of a tour of Scotland: 'Passed a Female who was reaping alone; she sung in Erse as she bended over her sickle; the sweetest human voice I ever heard: her strains were tenderly melancholy, and felt delicious, long after they were heard no more.'[25x]

As often during these years, Wordsworth's creative self finds the appropriate dimensions for his poem by taking a bearing from Dorothy and a bearing from Coleridge. The poem starts from the visual and human observation in Dorothy's journal ('Behold her, single in the field . . .') and ends with a Coleridgean extension through time, elaborating on Wilkinson's account. The song itself, which lies between, is described in lines which unobtrusively evoke the image of a great fountain:

> O Listen! for the Vale profound
> Is overflowing with the sound.

Like all fountains, the song 'shares the nature of infinity', immediately filling the whole landscape, and so redeeming it from the dreariness of spatial endlessness. In the next stanza (by a derangement of the geographical world extremely rare in Wordsworth) the song of the nightingale is heard at an oasis in the desert:

> No Nightingale did ever chaunt
> So sweetly to reposing bands
> Of Travellers in some shady haunt,
> Among Arabian Sands . . .

Finally, the song is given its full 'primal' quality, in every sense of the word, by association with the magical, sudden song of the cuckoo, heard in spring and in far isolation. In 'The Ancient Mariner' the sailors speak 'only to break/The silence of the sea'; here the cuckoo brings a more absolute relief:

> No sweeter voice was ever heard
> In spring-time from the Cuckoo-bird,
> Breaking the silence of the seas
> Among the farthest Hebrides.

(Elsewhere the cuckoo itself is described on a June evening as a song-fountain filling space: 'And the Cuckoo's sovereign cry/Fills all the hollow of the sky'.)[26]

Once the images of splendour and magic are established, Wordsworth moves, in his normal manner, to an intensification of pathos. Although the words of the song are not comprehensible to the hearer he believes that this girl, in her isolation, is singing from and for all human hearts:

Perhaps the plaintive numbers flow
For old, unhappy, far-off things,
And battles long ago:
Or is it some more humble lay,
Familiar matter of to-day?
Some natural sorrow, loss, or pain,
That has been, and may be again!

Yet if this is a song of the experience of the human heart, past, present or future, it is also, by its very quality, a song out of time, absorbed into the rhythm of her work:

Whate'er the theme, the Maiden sung
As if her song could have no ending;
I saw her singing at her work,
And o'er the sickle bending;

And it is the final triumph of the song that it becomes a self-perpetuating fountain in the heart of the hearer. Wilkinson's language of sensibility ('her strains were tenderly melancholy, and felt delicious, long after they were heard no more') is replaced by a more simple record of entrancement followed by self-renewing joy:

I listen'd till I had my fill:
And, as I mounted up the hill,
The music in my heart I bore,
Long after it was heard no more.

The only flaw in the experience, as recorded, is that it is, by its nature, a fading one. It will be recalled in the future, but never with quite the same *physical* immediacy, the same bodily fulfilment as on the original occasion. It retains enough power, however, to be the lasting emblem of a vanishing of the dykes between human beings: the voice of a single girl, singing in a field, has become eloquent of the resources of a common humanity and shared emotion which, while her song lasts, are known to be possessed fundamentally by every member of the human race.

This is no universal solution: once again the note of a common humanity has been struck not in the crowd but in solitude. Wordsworth had once known, in France, a time of universal transformation, but that had been succeeded, inexorably, by a time when the only two 'solitary greetings' which he heard as he passed through Calais in 1802 were

> *'Good morrow, Citizen!'* a hollow word,
> As if a dead Man spake it![27]

The possibility of universal reformation was still as distant as when he joked with the tinker in the Wye Valley across the barriers of vision which divided them: the 'republic of the heart' showed no signs of establishing itself in society at large.

If he himself were to create a social movement which could extend the promise of a poetry which was created out of his own experiences and offer any hope to humanity by its example, therefore, he must look not to social or political movements but nearer home, to an extension of what he himself had at times discovered in solitude. A few others who had, like himself, learned from nature an *active* response to 'the music of humanity', a group of intimate friends committed to support one another in a 'community of the heart',[28x] might in their modest manner still be able to give back to humanity a picture of the state in which it was most truly itself.

6

A Fountain Sealed

During the first years when they kept house together, Dorothy and William Wordsworth seem to have organised the business of living on the principle that they would live as cheaply as possible, in any suitable place that might offer itself. By not setting up a permanent establishment they were free to move on when they wished; and in each place where they stayed they could undertake walks and expeditions which exposed them to the forces of nature and to chance human encounters. It was also, perhaps, a post-Godwinian experiment, aimed at demonstrating the possibility of living a life not bounded by conventional ties of marriage and family.[1]

The decision to spend the winter of 1798–9 abroad was, in these circumstances, a natural one. The choice of Germany was dictated by a more direct concern. Both Wordsworth and Coleridge had been interested by the translations of German poetry which were appearing in contemporary English journals. They evidently felt that the forms which were being developed there – including the long ballad, as developed by Bürger – offered more promising models for a new kind of verse than anything then available in English.

Wordsworth's purpose was to live economically, to learn German with a view to reading German literature, and to continue writing poetry of his own. Coleridge, on the other hand, had wider needs. For him it was also essential to spend some time in a German university, in order to discover whether recent developments in science and philosophy could be related to his own intellectual preoccupations. As a result the friends soon parted, the Wordsworths wintering in Goslar and Coleridge in Göttingen.

One effect of the separation was, as we have seen, a development in Wordsworth's attitude to which may be ascribed, among other things, the Lucy poems; another was more personal. Both

Wordsworth and Coleridge found themselves unexpectedly homesick for England, Wordsworth's sense eventually finding expression in another of the 'Lucy' poems,[2] written two years later:

> I travell'd among unknown Men,
>   In Lands beyond the Sea;
> Nor England! did I know till then
>   What love I bore to thee. . . .
>
> Thy mornings shew'd – thy nights conceal'd
>   The bowers where Lucy play'd;
> And thine is, too, the last green field
>   Which Lucy's eyes survey'd!

On any theory of the general beneficence of nature, the alienation and depression to which the Wordsworths were sometimes subject in Germany was hard to explain, since the scenery around Goslar was as beautiful as that in England. In terms of Coleridge's ideas, however, the phenomenon might be more easily explained, since it could be argued that forms of nature known in childhood and youth, the scenes of one's earliest emotional experiences, had by far the most powerful magnetising effect, so that one would be closer to the springs of one's most central feelings if one continued to live one's life in sight of them – or at least near them.

Some such reasoning, I suspect, may have lain behind the sudden reversal of previous policy which led Wordsworth, on his return to England, to set up a more permanent home in the Lake District. The excursion to Germany had strained him to the very limits of his emotional orbit: life in an English village would, in an important and unobtrusive manner, provide sustenance both for himself and for his central relationship of affection with Dorothy. A life carried on in the shadow of the great forms which had haunted his boyhood imagination might, moreover, help keep alive the 'primary consciousnesses' which he had recently been evoking in his poetic reminiscences of boyhood.

That Wordsworth felt a touch of uneasiness about forsaking so abruptly his free and footloose existence is shown by some lines in 'Home at Grasmere' where he defends his decision on the grounds that it is not a final one.

> What if I floated down a pleasant stream
> And now am landed & the motion gone

> Shall I reprove myself   ah no the stream
> Is flowing, & will never cease to flow
> And I shall float upon that stream again.   PW V 324 and MS

At the same time, the way of life which was being proposed might still seem a rather relaxed mode, something nearer to the world of Jane Austen's novels than we would expect from the more uncompromising Wordsworths.

So far as Dorothy Wordsworth is concerned, indeed, the comparison with Jane Austen is not without point. Her childhood at Forncett Rectory and education according to contemporary feminine ideals had given her style a similar combination of dignity and sensibility. The major difference from her contemporary, however, lay in the intensity of feeling to which she could sometimes rise. Coleridge wrote of her in 1797:

> . . . her manners are simple, ardent, impressive –
>
> In every motion her most innocent soul
> Outbeams so brightly, that who saw would say,
> Guilt was a thing impossible in her. –
>
> Her information various – her eye watchful in minutest observation of nature – and her taste a perfect electrometer – it bends, protrudes, and draws in, at subtlest beauties & most recondite faults. . . .   CL I 330–1

De Quincey, similarly, wrote,

> The pulses of light are not more quick or more inevitable in their flow and undulation, than were the answering and echoing movements of her sympathizing attention.[3]

But De Quincey was also aware of the intensity behind this sympathy: he comments on the accuracy of Wordsworth's self-portrait in a character (in *The Excursion*)

> who, to still the tumult of his heart, when visiting the cataracts of a mountainous region, obliges himself to study the laws of light and colour, as they affect the rainbow of the stormy waters; vainly attempting to mitigate the fever which consumed him, by entangling his mind in profound speculations; raising a cross-fire of artillery from the subtilizing intellect, under the vain conceit that in this way he could silence the mighty battery of his impassioned heart. . . .

and continues,

. . . In Miss Wordsworth, every thoughtful observer might read the same self-consuming style of thought.'⁴

A similar intensity marked Wordsworth's methods of writing poetry. Hazlitt noted in 1798 that Wordsworth liked to compose while walking along a smooth gravel path; at Rydal Mount a walk was later constructed for this very purpose. But any suggestion of calmness and meditativeness is belied by De Quincey's, and other testimony: Dorothy spoke of her brother as 'kindling' when the verse-writing fit came upon him,⁵ while other accounts tell of his composing with uncontrollable gestures and exclamations. Dorothy wrote, 'He writes with so much feeling and agitation that it brings on a sense of pain and internal weakness about his left side and stomach.'⁶ The pacing up and down was often, evidently, a process of ordering, necessary to control and dampen down the effects of his emotion.

When composition was not an order imposed upon passionate emotion it was sometimes an enterprise in the opposite direction – an attempt to give life to a world which was in danger of hardening into a private prison. This alternating process (which was not, apparently, shared by Dorothy) is shown vividly in two poems composed in succession one morning. In the first, a poem which tames the whirlpool of his emotions, the scene is set by four lines describing the perpetual roar of the stream outside. Against this, Wordsworth describes the quiet of his room where he

> May lie in peace upon his bed
> Happy as they who are dead. PW IV 365

The word 'dead' suggests something more than 'peace', however; a complementary poem, written half an hour later (and taking a point of departure from Chaucer's line on death, 'Alone withouten any compaignie'⁷) mitigates such an effect, illuminating the image of his room by removing from it any imprisoning suggestion of the grave.

> I have thoughts that are fed by the sun.
>   The things which I see
>   Are welcome to me,
>   Welcome every one:
> I do not wish to lie
>   Dead, dead,
> Dead without any company;
>   Here alone on my bed,

With thoughts that are fed by the Sun,
And hopes that are welcome every one,
Happy am I.　　　　　　　　　　　　　　　PW IV 365–6

The quality of such a life is 'Sweetness and breath with the quiet of death'; the fear of death is finally replaced by a sense of reconciling peace.

Wordsworth's earlier dislike for a settled home may have been due to his distrust of the static; Grasmere, however, offered something more like the 'enlivened peace' of his second poem. So long as Dorothy was with him, moreover, it could not be a tame retreat: she herself would generate enough emotional intensity to insure him against complacency.

Dorothy was crucially important, in fact: her sensitivity and vitality were a perpetual enactment of the spontaneous movements of the heart around which her brother and Coleridge were constructing their human philosophy. Whether or not she sympathised with the general lines of Coleridge's speculation, moreover, she could subject them to the critique of appropriating to herself those images or ideas which rang true in her own emotional experience – the magic of Coleridge's feeling for the moon, for example. Her entry recording the completion of 'The Ancient Mariner' in 1798 echoes a memorable phrase in the poem:

> March 23rd. Coleridge dined with us. He brought his ballad finished. We walked with him to the Miner's house. A beautiful evening, very starry, the horned moon.

And another description of the moon there is still haunting her four years later:

> N.B. The moon came out suddenly when we were at John's Grove, and "a star or two beside".'　　　　　　DWJ 8 Feb. 1802

One notices also that a reference to Coleridge in the journals will sometimes appear in close proximity to an observation reminiscent of his own vision of nature.

Coleridge's great central image of the 'heart fountain' was vivid to her in a direct and practical form. Dorothy may not have been interested in the cosmic implications of his idea that the human heart was a spring, corresponding to other organic springs in the universe, but she knew the heart to be, literally, a fountain in the body that was immediately responsive to feeling – and also that its most powerful workings were often expressed by human tears. Without needing to follow Coleridge any further she could agree that to shed tears was to express the nobility of the heart – feeling also, perhaps, that this was man's most 'humanising' resource; indeed, when Wordsworth wrote a tribute to her, it was this use of the fountain-image that came immediately to his mind:

> She gave me eyes, she gave me ears;
> And humble cares, and delicate fears;
> A heart, the fountain of sweet tears;
> And love, and thought, and joy.[8]

There are indications that all three had, at some time in their early relationship, discussed in detail this significance of the human heart and its workings. In particular they would seem to have agreed that tears were not only the most natural outlet for its more agitated workings – but provided a positive and very necessary *relief*. It was an idea that had already appeared in Wordsworth's poem 'The Vale of Esthwaite', where he had addressed his own tears as follows:

> Flow on, in vain thou hast not flow'd,
> But eased me of a heavy load;
> For much it gives my heart relief
> To pay the mighty debt of grief,
> With sighs repeated o'er and o'er,
> I mourn because I mourned no more.   PW I 280

Coleridge, in a letter of December 1798, hearing that his child had recovered from an inoculation illness wrote, 'I must have wept, to have delivered myself of the stress and tumult of my animal sensibility'.[9] Dorothy in a journal entry of 1801 mentioned Coleridge's current unhappiness and went on 'I was melancholy and could not talk, but at last I eased my heart by weeping – nervous blubbering says William. It is not so.'[10] By the time that Wordsworth wrote the 'Immortality' Ode the idea could come naturally to his mind in a more general form:

> To me alone there came a thought of grief:
> A timely utterance gave that thought relief,
> And I again am strong.

and in his later poems he sometimes speaks again of poetry being written to give the heart 'ease', or 'relief'.[11x]

If the idea that the workings of the heart often needed to find *relief* through physical expression was a fact of familiar experience to the Wordsworths before they met Coleridge, however (it is one which has roots in previous literature[12x]), his introduction of the fountain-image gave the idea new definition and perhaps greater justification. It suggested that behind the private relief of weeping there might be a more universal and vital significance, which in turn gave a new status to pathos. We have already seen the first-fruits of this idea in 'Simon Lee',[13] where the old man's tears, excessive for the act which occasions them, speak to the narrator of a resource unknown to many of his fellows.

A more definitive statement may be found in *The Excursion*, where Wordsworth writes that the human heart can claim

> high distinction upon earth
> As the sole spring and fountain-head of tears,
> His own peculiar utterance for distress
> Or gladness. . . .   *Exc.* v 980–3

Wordsworth had discovered his most distinctive emblem in this mode some years before, however, on the very journey which was taking him with Dorothy to set up house in Grasmere. At Hart-leap Well, as we shall see later, they had experienced a form of revelation; not long afterwards, he wrote a poem about the old tradition associated with the place.

'Hart-leap Well'[14] tells the story of a knight out hunting who gave chase to a hart, and pursued it so strenuously that soon he and the animal were running alone. When he eventually reached the hart, it lay dying by a spring: he was then able to trace by its footmarks the fantastic series of leaps which it had taken. In admiration he set up pillars to mark the stages of the leap and, by the spring itself, a pleasure-house where he could come for entertainment, bringing his paramour. But now, says the narrator, visitors who pass the spot see only the three pillars ('the last . . . on the dark hill-top') and receive an impression of ruined human handiwork and natural decay. Nothing will grow properly, no animal will drink there.

A shepherd who arrives on the scene speaks of a local tradition that a murder was committed there; in his own opinion, he says, this was not some separate human murder, but simply the slaying of the hart.

The narrator of the poem, agreeing, proceeds to gloss the shepherd's superstitions with moralising of his own, supposing the existence of a 'sympathy divine' which mourned the hart. He concludes:

> One lesson, Shepherd, let us two divide,
> Taught both by what she shews, and what conceals,
> Never to blend our pleasure or our pride
> With sorrow of the meanest thing that feels.

Taken straightforwardly, the poem reads as a story followed by a pious summing-up, which moralises the shepherd's intuition by suggestion that there is something unlucky about mixing our pleasure with the suffering of others. This is a moral which human experience would hardly seem to confirm, however, and the striking parallel with 'The Ancient Mariner', where a similar concluding moral, if read in isolation, does less than justice to the full meaning of the poem, invites further exploration. Both poems, after all, involve a similar offence against life and suggest the existence of a preternatural 'sympathy' in nature.

Certain resemblances between the two plots take us further, to a poet who influenced both men. Bürger's 'Der wilde Jäger' (translated in 1796 as 'The Chase') also contains the story of a hunt. This becomes faster and faster, more and more intense, until, in a sudden breaking-off, the situation is changed. Bürger's Earl drives his quarry to a hermit's chapel which, in spite of prayers and pleas, he insists on entering for the kill. At that moment, however, everything else disappears, leaving him alone in a landscape which is not unlike some boyhood scene from *The Prelude*:

> Still dark and darker round it spreads,
>   Dark as the darkness of the grave;
> And not a sound the still invades,
>   Save what a distant torrent gave.[15]

He then hears prounced his doom, which is to go on hunting for ever, without respite.

In Wordsworth's poem the chase proceeds in a similar crescendo:

> Where is the throng, the tumult of the chace?
> The bugles that so joyfully were blown?
> —This race it looks not like an earthly race;
> Sir Walter and the Hart are left alone.

If the chase no longer looks like an earthly one, a reason may be sought in the intensity of the energies being displayed. Indeed, as with Captain Ahab in *Moby Dick*, the knight's exertion is so disproportionate as to arouse suspicion that his original decision to give chase has now been overtaken by a fiercer motivating power. And Coleridge's theory might suggest its nature: as the heart races faster in the exercise of human energy the human being is transformed into an essence of himself: he is no longer a man living by the normal needs and pleasures of every day but a man who is pursuing the ultimate desire of his heart – which is to encompass the infinite.

There is no climax to match the melodrama in Bürger, however. Instead there is a sudden transition, a single moment in which the hunter finds his own state changed from an essence of action to an essence of contemplation, and in which the infinity he sought by intensifying action towards sublimity reveals itself in pathos:

> Upon his side the Hart was lying stretch'd:
> His nose half-touched a spring beneath a hill,
> And with the last deep groan his breath had fetch'd
> The waters of the spring were trembling still.

The hart has returned to a familiar spring – perhaps the one which he knew first of all:

> 'Here on the grass perhaps asleep he sank,
> Lulled by this fountain in the summer-tide;
> This water was perhaps the first he drank
> When he had wander'd from his mother's side.'

In doing so he has presented back to the knight (if he could recognise the fact) the pathos of his own, human condition. If he truly understood himself, he might recognise his wild desire to engulf infinity as the quest for the fountain known at birth, when his heart, at one with other springs in the universe, could still feel its nature confirmed by the fountain of milk from his mother's breast. The hart lying by the spring in extremity, its mouth extended to the waters, is an emblem not only of all suffering but of all action as well: it presents back to humanity a picture of its own condition, for which the only fitting response would be a tribute paid in the tears by which humanity at once recognises and expresses its own weakness.

The knight, of course, is in no mood for tears. Flushed with triumph, he can respond only to the sensational sublimity of the leap by which the hart reached the fountain, not to the intensified pathos of its dying moments. But since the intensity of his energy has also delivered him from time, he cannot altogether escape a sense of further significance. His desire to mark the spot by pillars and a pleasure-house expresses his sense of a numinousness which he does not fully comprehend.

His gesture reminds us of another of Coleridge's poems. Kubla Khan, also, decided to build a pleasure-house by sacred waters, but (again like the knight) did not understand the full nature of the genius that he was attempting to propitiate in that place. In Coleridge's poem the mighty destructive fountain and the prophecies of war express that darker side of genius; in Wordsworth's they find their counterpart in the deathly fate of the arbour and trees which the knight had planned to last 'Till the foundations of the mountains fail'.

> The trees were grey, with neither arms nor head;
> Half-wasted the square mound of tawny green;
> So that you just might say, as then I said,
> 'Here in old time the hand of man has been.'

But just as the immense destructive energy embodied in Coleridge's fountain is very different from the dead and dreary desolation at Hart-leap Well, so the endings of the two poems stand in total contrast. 'Kubla Khan' ends with a vision of the poet himself, as inspired genius, standing radiant with godlike power in the lost paradise-garden from which the fountain of creativity flows. In Wordsworth's poem, by contrast, the poet masks himself completely. So far as he permits himself to appear at all, it is in the guise of the narrator who, trying to provide a communicable moral in reply to the shepherd's guess, frames something suitable for simple men. This is not as patronising as it might seem, since the lesson which the narrator has taken is that we are *all*, essentially, simple men: 'we have all of us one human heart'. But in order to grasp the weight of the lesson we have to turn from the ending to the larger work of the poem. By its evocation of energy, it invites the reader first to empathise with the excitement of the chase until he finds himself suddenly confronted by the still image of the hart at the spring; and then to see there what the knight could not see, through an access of the instinctive and unlearned wisdom which grasps that the infinity sought by some human beings from fiercer and fiercer movement would, if they ever reached it, reveal itself as a simple spring.

The hart at the spring gave Wordsworth an appropriate and complex image for an idea which united the speculations of Coleridge with the emotional intensity of Dorothy, and which was related to traditional wisdom by its use in the Psalms: 'As the hart panteth after the water brooks, so panteth my soul after thee, O God. My soul thirsteth for God, for the living God. . . .'[16] His account of the original visit to Hart-leap Well suggests, moreover, that as he and Dorothy contemplated the scene they had seen a further depth to the incident.

> And when the trance
> Came to us as we stood by Hart-leap Well
> The intimation of the milder day
> Which is to come the fairer world than this,
> And raised us up dejected as we were
> Among the records of that doleful place
> By sorrow for the hunted Beast who there
> Had yielded up his breath   the awful trance
> That vision of humanity, & of God
> The Mourner, God the sufferer when the heart
> Of his poor Creatures suffers wrongfully
> Both in the sadness & the joy we found
> A promise and an earnest that we twain
> A pair seceding from the common world
> Might in that hallow'd spot to which our steps
> Were tending in that individual nook
> Might even thus early for ourselves secure
> And in the midst of those unhappy times
> A portion of the blessedness which love
> And knowledge will, we trust, hereafter give
> To all the vales of earth and all mankind.
>
>   PW V 319–20 and MS

Why should the trance at Hart-leap Well have brought intimations of a 'milder day'? The evolutionary connotation of the term, striking at so early a period, suggests, once again, the intervention of a Coleridgean speculation. Coleridge knew of one rudimentary doctrine of evolution in the shape of Hartley's theory (set out in the second volume of his book) that the process of association of ideas would, properly followed, lead towards human perfection: human beings would gradually learn to concentrate such associations towards God, the source of all ideas. He had already used this notion in his poetry.[17]

During his youth, however, a more detailed theory, applying a similar set of ideas to the natural world, had been developed. In his *Zoönomia* (a book which, it will be recalled, Wordsworth was anxious to obtain in 1798) Darwin referred to Hartley's theories and then went on to argue that in nature the ultimate, primal form of life might be traced in a 'living filament', from which all other forms had evolved.[18x]

That such a belief should have been set out at so early a date is in itself surprising; even more notable is the process by which Darwin supposed the evolution to have taken place. Drawing upon contemporary physiological theory, he supposed that the original 'filament' was primarily moved by alternating processes of irritability and sensibility. These, coupled with what he called 'voluntarities and associabilities', caused the differences of form by which the whole living creation took its myriad shapes. Meditation on this led Darwin at one point to speculate still further that

> all warm-blooded animals have arisen from one living filament, which THE GREAT FIRST CAUSE endued with animality, with the power of acquiring new parts, attended with new propensities, directed by irritations, sensations, volitions, and associations; and thus possessing the faculty of continuing to improve by its own inherent activity, and of delivering down those improvements by generation to its posterity, world without end!   p.505

The latent optimism here was to be a feature of such accounts for half a century, until Erasmus's grandson came to interpret the phenomena differently; and there can be little doubt that for a time Coleridge and the Wordsworths were moved by it also. For it suggested that by submitting itself alternately to the irritations of extreme stimulus and to the sensibility of quietly developing affection the human race would continue to develop into better and better forms of itself, and sensibility come triumphantly into its own by producing greater perfections of love. The process corresponded to that which was, as we have seen,[19] identified by Wordsworth as the one by which he himself had matured; Erasmus Darwin's theory offered hope that such gains could be consolidated by humanity in successive generations, each improving on the previous one. The pattern to be

proposed, in other words, was that every time a human organism
was born, it embodied an opportunity for further refinement towards a universe of freedom and love in which all men, by developing their energies and shaping their affections more fully, would
achieve a oneness of mind which might eliminate war and finally
realise the total link of peace prophesied by the gentler organisms of
the animal creation.

If this was so it not only served as a basis of hope for the human
race, but also justified William and Dorothy in retiring to a place
where they could cultivate the affectionate side of nature, since they
could regard themselves as pioneers in this evolutionary process. So
in 'Home at Grasmere' Wordsworth goes on to recall their peaceful
arrival in Grasmere and to survey the growth of affection between
themselves and other living beings in the Vale. Where the desolate
mother of one of his early poems had said, in her bitterness, 'that
wagon does not care for us' (a statement which he had traced to a
state of mind in which 'the rebellious heart to its own will/Fashions
the laws of nature'),[20] he could write now in Grasmere,

> It loves us now, this Vale so beautiful
> Begins to love us!   PW V 320

and list the many living things which were, by familiarity, establishing links of common life and affection. One of the important
immediate effects of their settlement was in fact the series of poems
devoted to the district and the stories of common humanity which
are to be found in the second volume of *Lyrical Ballads*. The
dominant impression is of delight in rediscovering scenes known
since childhood and renewing attachment to a particular place.

At the same time, all was not perfect in the new way of life. Both
brother and sister suffered from spasms of illness, physical and
nervous, which forced them to comfort and nurse one another in
turn.

To do so involved an intensification of their affection, and the
extension of a mutual therapy, originally devised in different circumstances. At Tintern Abbey in 1798 Wordsworth had seen in
Dorothy's passionate appreciation of the landscape a reflection of his
own feelings five years earlier, and expressed his pleasure in the fact,
while also looking forward to a time

> When these wild ecstasies shall be matured
> Into a sober pleasure. . . .

He seems also to have felt an elder brother's responsibility to assist in
the process of taming this wildness, and to lead her into the paths of
reflective enjoyment where he himself had found emotional securiy.
It was not a callous attempt to shape her in his own mould so much as
a serious endeavour to lead her to a happiness for which her wilder
feelings might not be the best guide. 'Beyond any person I have
known in this world,' wrote De Quincey, 'Miss Wordsworth was
the creature of impulse':[21] and this impulse could sometimes result in
hurt. De Quincey himself tells of incidents at Nether Stowey in
which Dorothy Wordsworth, drenched from walking with
Wordsworth and Coleridge, would 'with a laughing gaiety, and
obviously unconscious of any liberty that she was taking, or any
wound that she was inflicting . . . run up to Mrs Coleridge's
wardrobe, array herself, without leave asked, in Mrs Coleridge's
dresses, and make herself merry with her own unceremoniousness
and Mrs Coleridge's gravity.'[22] He indicates that these and other
incidents wounded Mrs Coleridge's pride in the eyes of her neighbours and did a good deal to undermine the happiness of Coleridge's
marriage.

This impulsiveness of Dorothy's may explain the affectionate
rebuke to her in the first draft of 'Nutting', written in 1798:

> Thou, Lucy, art a maiden 'inland bred'
> And thou hast known 'some nurture'; but in truth
> If I had met thee here with that keen look
> Half cruel in its eagerness, those cheeks
> Thus [   ] flushed with a tempestuous bloom,
> I might have almost deem'd that I had pass'd
> A houseless being in a human shape,
> An enemy of nature, hither sent
> From regions far beyond the Indian hills–
> Come rest on this light bed of purple heath,
> And let me see thee sink into a dream
> Of gentle thoughts, protracted till thine eye
> Be calm as water when the winds are gone
> And no one can tell whither.[23x]

The transition in the last lines was evidently devised as a way of
recreating for Dorothy experiences in nature (like those which he
was simultaneously recalling for *The Prelude*), when an outburst of
excitement in the midst of natural objects was followed

by a revelation of nature's ultimate tranquillity and its correspondence with the central peace of the human being. As it stood,
however (and in spite of the indulgent quotations from *As You Like
It*[24x]), the passage did not do justice to Dorothy's normal sensitivity
in nature. Later, he removed these lines and set them in a separate
poem, explicitly addressed to her and now devoted entirely to the
experience of peaceful contemplation in a natural setting:

> This is the spot:–how mildly does the sun
> Shine in between the fading leaves! the air
> In the habitual silence of this wood
> Is more than silent; and this bed of heath–
> Where shall we find so sweet a resting-place?
> Come, let me see thee sink into a dream
> Of quiet thoughts, protracted till thine eye
> Be calm as water when the winds are gone
> And no one can tell whither. My sweet Friend,
> We two have had such happy hours together
> That my heart melts in me to think of it.[25]

The lines seem to have become a talismanic charm between brother
and sister, which they could read or recite to one another in moments
of stress, encouraging a more trance-like state. So much, at least, is
suggested by the following entry in Dorothy's journal:

> I repeated verses to William while he was in bed – he was soothed
> and I left him. 'This is the spot' over and over again.
> DWJ 4 May 1802

The incantation described, along with other endearments in
Dorothy's journals and Wordsworth's poems, marks such as intensification of the relationship, indeed, as to suggest that they were
now in love with one another. F. W. Bateson, noting entries in
Dorothy's journal such as 'William's head was bad . . . I petted him
on the carpet' went so far as to suppose that the relationship included
some sort of incestuous element.[26] Although in a second edition and
subsequent correspondence he half-denied any suggestion that
Wordsworth and his sister were ever lovers in a physical sense,[27x] he
still maintained the general form of his argument, which was that
brother and sister had gradually fallen in love with one another and
that Wordsworth, realising with horror what had happened, with-
drew sharply – perhaps at the time of the German tour. The result of
this withdrawal, following the earlier withdrawal from Annette

Vallon, had been, Bateson argued, that henceforth only one person was left for Wordsworth to love and write poetry about: himself.

That there was a gradual intensification of the relationship in these years is undeniable: the fact that Wordsworth refers to his sister as 'my Love' and she to him as 'my Beloved' is enough to suggest the fact. That he became apprehensive is also suggested by a poem of 1800[28] which relates the suicide of a girl for love and concludes.

> Ah, gentle Love! if ever thought was thine
> To store up kindred hours for me, thy face
> Turn from me, gentle Love, nor let me walk
> Within the sound of Emma's voice, or know
> Such happiness as I have known to-day.

At the same time, there is nothing to suggest either horror or withdrawal: on the contrary, many of the most tender phrases occur in poems of 1802. It is also unlikely that Wordsworth would have continued to live in the same house as Dorothy if he had been deeply disturbed by the implications of their relationship.

It is difficult, admittedly, to find the right sort of tact with which to approach the question. To look at the situation in the light of the Victorian tradition that deep affection between closely related people was acceptable and even desirable is to ignore the intensity of emotion in some important passages; to examine the evidence in post-Freudian terms, on the other hand, leads towards a diagnosis which does violence to the subtlety of the emotions involved. Either way a puzzle remains.

If there is a solution, it may perhaps be looked for along paths already followed in this study. I have suggested above that the intervention of Coleridge's theories gave an unexpected authority to the stress which Wordsworth and Dorothy had already learned to place upon the workings of the human heart, giving the heart a cosmic significance, and tracing from it a link with the whole of animated nature. If this were so, it also suggested that a love *in the heart* between human beings could never be wrong. William and Dorothy were therefore free to cultivate their affection for one another and to feel that in doing so they were not only immune from sexual danger, but were actually showing humanity its true way forward. It was, after all, a simple step from 'Nature never did betray the heart that loved her' to 'Nature never did betray the heart that loved'. Wordsworth might sometimes feel apprehensive at the intensity of his sister's feelings, but he could not feel that there was anything basically wrong in her emotion as such. The remedy was to cultivate the tranquillity, rather than the wildness, of her heart's affections.

On this reading of the situation, the language which they used to one another had a ritual significance: it expressed a belief that their binding emotion was at once intenser than affection and guarded from passion. And this interpretation may be supported by the fact that some of their expressions seem to be taken from the Song of Solomon, which had been traditionally regarded as a poem combining the language of love and the intensity of religious devotion. As early as 1798 there is a likely echo of

> My beloved spake, and said unto me, Rise up, my love, my fair one, and come away. For, lo, the winter is past, the rain is over and gone; The flowers appear on the earth; the time of the singing of birds is come, and the voice of the turtle is heard in our land . . .[29]

in the lines later entitled 'To my Sister',[30] which begin

> It is the first mild day of March:
> Each minute sweeter than before,
> The red-breast sings from the tall larch
> That stands beside our door.

and continue with an invitation to her to walk in the countryside; and when Wordsworth writes in *Tintern Abbey* of a time

> when first
> I came among these hills; when like a roe
> I bounded o'er the mountains . . .   ll.66–8

his language is reminiscent of the lines,

> The voice of my beloved! behold, he cometh leaping upon the mountains, skipping upon the hills. My beloved is like a roe or a young hart . . .[31]

If brother and sister had become accustomed to use the Canticle as a ritual form of expression for the language of strong affectionate love, their use of endearments such as 'my Love' and 'my Beloved' for each other would be explained, since these are precisely the terms used by the lovers of the poem. One of the records of Dorothy soothing her brother, also. 'After dinner we made a pillow of my shoulder – I read to him and my Beloved slept' sounds at the end like an echo from a parallel phrase in the Psalms: 'for so he giveth his beloved sleep'[32]; and there are other biblical phrases which Dorothy might have appropriated to her own affections. She could, indeed, have found a peculiarly poignant appositeness in the lines of the Canticle,

> A garden inclosed is my sister, my spouse; a spring shut up, a fountain sealed.'[33]

In the light of this deliberate and fearless cultivation of the heart's affections, one begins to see the strict accuracy of Wordsworth's description of Dorothy (in lines which she copied gratefully into her journal,[34] as

> My hope, my joy, my sister, and my friend,
> Or something dearer still, if reason knows
> A dearer thought, or in the heart of love
> There be a dearer name.

Nor is this sense diminished when one notices the apparent source of these lines in Eloisa's outburst to Abelard:

> No, make me mistress to the man I love;
> If there be yet another name more free,
> More fond than mistress, make me that to thee![35]

What Wordsworth has done is to take an acknowledged potentiality in Pope's description of the relationship ('Oh happy state,' Eloisa continues, 'when souls each other draw,/When love is liberty, and nature, law . . .') and transfer that from a love forbidden by the Church and society to the context of an unusually intense affection between brother and sister.

This type of relationship, with its strange combination of intense attachment and light playfulness, is one which was perhaps possible only during a comparatively short period of English culture. There are, however, parallel relationships during the following century or so, such as the one described in the chapter 'Lad and Girl Love' in Lawrence's *Sons and Lovers* and in Jessie Chambers's supplementary memoir, where one finds the same fierce puritanism between the lovers, the same tendency for affection to be consummated in moments of pure entrancement. Miriam Leivers, leading Paul Morel to see a wild-rose bush which she has discovered, is not altogether unlike Wordsworth leading Dorothy to see her first glow-worm:

> Almost passionately she wanted to be with him when he stood before the flowers. They were going to have a communion together – something that thrilled her, something holy . . . In bosses of ivory and in large splashed stars the roses gleamed on the darkness of foliage and stems and grass . . .. Point after point the steady roses shone out to them, seeming to kindle something in their souls. The dusk came like smoke around, and still did not put out the roses.[36]

There is a difference between this adolescent ecstasy, an experience of untested sensibilities which are still protected by a fostering parental world, and the consciously developed affections of the Wordsworths, held in a poise that comprehended larger sweeps of emotional experience. Those who equate a fierce puritanism with prudishness would, for example, be surprised to learn of Dorothy reading *The Miller's Tale* to her brother.[37x] But in both cases the cultivation of affection to such an intensity was clearly unsatisfactory. Although Chaucer's combination of a belief in human love with a humorous recognition of humanity's limitations might seem to offer a possible balance, it could not touch their basic emotional needs. In the economy of the human body, as later medicine has come to see it, over-reliance upon affection is not (as some Romantic writers thought) a value in itself but leads to a dangerous build-up of internal tension. Such tension may well have been a contributory factor to the headaches and ills which Wordsworth suffered at this time; the fact that he began to translate Chaucer as a substitute for creative work of his own is in itself suggestive.

Within these limits, then, certain elements in Bateson's diagnosis may be accepted; but it is hard to find any sign of the more melodramatic horror and withdrawal which he also postulates.[38] Wordsworth's belief in the power of affection was too great for him to draw such open conclusions, even to himself. Instead, it would seem, he responded to the facts in a more typically sober manner, recognising that his work as a poet was not prospering under the present conditions and that it might benefit from the emotional relief afforded by married life.

The decision to marry Mary Hutchinson was not reached easily. Coleridge refers to long and agonising discussions with his friend on the subject.[39] The exact nature of Wordsworth's feelings towards her is not obvious, moreover: the poetry simply expresses a lifelong affection, coupled with occasional hints of limitations. The nearest we have to an objective account of Wordsworth as lover is a remark of Coleridge's in 1811:

> . . . Wordsworth is by nature incapable of being in Love, tho' no man more tenderly attached – hence he ridicules the existence of any other passion, than a compound of Lust with Esteem & Friendship, confined to one Object, first by accidents of Association, and permanently, by the force of Habit & a sense of Duty. CL III 305

Coleridge is not at his most sympathetic towards Wordsworth here: he is pursuing his own belief that the only true form of love is one where the various forces involved flash together into a unified emotion – a belief which, according to him, Wordsworth could not share. He may also, perhaps, be recalling some assertion of Wordsworth's to the general effect that successful marriage has little to do with the emotion of 'being in love'. Such a belief would explain why he found it possible to share his affection, as such, between his wife and other women, and to see no contradiction in marrying Mary Hutchinson while inviting Dorothy ('She . . . whom I have loved/With such communion, that no place on earth/Can ever be a solitude to me'[40]) to remain a permanent member of the household.

That the Wordsworths saw no basic danger for themselves in the strength of their attachment is further supported by the fact that the decision to marry (with the concomitant recognition that Dorothy could not find a similar satisfaction in that decision) led to a new peak of affection between them and an efflorescence of poetry. In 1802 Dorothy's journal is full of undisguised emotion, while Wordsworth's poems, many of them explicitly associated with Dorothy, touch new heights in their combination of the visionary and the affectionate. During the previous period Wordsworth's inspiration had been flagging. 'Alice Fell',[41] for example, written at the request of a friend, is a rather simplistic evocation of pathos, which repeats previous effects without adding anything new of its own. Yet the next day (and perhaps in recognition of the fact) he wrote 'Beggars',[42] which restores the balance of rural life by showing the essential gaiety and resilience of children when allowed to run wild. The incident, characteristically, was one which had happened to Dorothy some years before and had been described by her in her journal. After describing how she gave bread to a beggar woman, she had continued,

> I passed on and about $\frac{1}{4}$ of a mile further I saw two boys before me, one about 10 the other about 8 years old at play chasing a butterfly. They were wild figures, not very ragged, but without shoes and stockings; the hat of the elder was wreathed round with yellow flowers, the younger whose hat was only a rimless crown, had stuck it round with laurel leaves. They continued at play till I drew very near and then they addressed me with the Beggars' cant and the whining voice of sorrow. I said I served your mother this morning. (The Boys were so like the woman who had called at the door that I could not be mistaken.) O! says the elder you could not serve my mother for she's dead and my father's on at the next town – he's a potter. I persisted in my assertion and that I would give them nothing. Says the elder, Come, let's away, and away they flew like lightning.[43]

The incident serves as a counterpoise to the dangerously indulgent pathos of 'Alice Fell'. Dorothy has recorded an occasion where the wildness of nature was preferable to the cant of human society. Her eye was not only finely attuned to the spontaneous, but mercilessly perceptive of pretence and artificiality: she saw that beggar-boys or travelling gypsies, living close to nature, often retained a unity with its freedom and vitality which was lost even to those who lived in villages. She would not, of course, have pressed the intuition to an extreme, or argued, with Lawrence, for the omnipotence of the life-principle. Despite her impulsive nature, her feelings found their most natural expression not in acting wildly but rather in an unpossessive delight in the life of free and wild things. And Wordsworth's poem 'Beggars', while lacking the immediacy of Dorothy's account, shares and emphasises this effect of delight – even in the stanza added in 1827:

> Yet *they*, so blithe of heart, seemed fit
> For finest tasks of earth or air:
> Wings let them have, and they might flit
> Precursors to Aurora's car,
> Scattering fresh flowers. . . .   PW II 224

The image is conventional but not pointless: it helps to express the effect of 'flying joy'[44x] which is given both by the butterflies and by the boys who pursue them. In another poem, 'To a Butterfly'[45], Wordsworth makes amends for any unfairness to Dorothy in the reproach of 'Nutting' by seizing this most typical response of hers and showing how, even in childhood, it held in poise her wildness of delight and her sensitivity in approach:

> Oh! pleasant, pleasant were the days,
> The time, when in our childish plays
> My Sister Emmeline and I
> Together chaced the Butterfly!
> A very hunter did I rush
> Upon the prey – with leaps and springs
> I follow'd on from brake to bush;
> But She, God love her! feared to brush
> The dust from off its wings.

In 'The Sparrow's Nest'[46] he shows the same poise of feelings, held now as a contradiction of the heart's impulses; a quivering blend of delight and unwillingness to touch:

> She look'd at it as if she fear'd it;
> Still wishing, dreading to be near it:
> Such heart was in her, being then
> A little Prattler among men. . . .

These memories in the poetry are accompanied by an intensification of feeling in Dorothy's journals – both directly, when referring to her brother, and indirectly, in her descriptions of nature. References to 'sweet and tender conversation'[47] suggest that a consciousness of the coming change was interpenetrating all their activities. On 12 April Wordsworth writes 'The Glow-Worm' on his way home from seeing Mary; on 29 April Dorothy records a visit together to John's Grove:

> Afterwards William lay, and I lay in the trench under the fence – he with his eyes shut and listening to the waterfalls and the Birds. There was no one waterfall above another – it was a sound of waters in the air – the voice of the air. William heard me breathing and rustling now and then but we both lay still, and unseen by one another. He thought that it would be as sweet thus to lie so in the grave, to hear the *peaceful* sounds of the earth and just to know that our dear friends were near.

Later in the day, she made a visionary observation of her own:

> As I lay down on the grass, I observed the glittering silver line on the ridges of the Backs of the sheep, owing to their situation respecting the Sun – which made them look beautiful but with something of strangeness, like animals of another kind – as if belonging to a more splendid world.

Dorothy was perhaps recognising that in future she must rely more fully on nature as a personal resource. On 16 March she had written:

> The moon was a good height above the mountains. She seemed far and distant in the sky there were two stars beside her, that twinkled in and out, and seemed almost like butterflies in motion and lightness. They looked to be far nearer to us than the Moon.

The following evening she had gone out by the lake in the quiet of the evening and apparently tried to compose poetry on the scene.

> I looked before me and I saw a red light upon Silver How as if coming out of the vale below,
>
>> 'There was a light of most strange birth
>> A Light that came out of the earth
>> And spread along the dark hill-side.'
>
> Thus I was going on when I saw the shape of my Beloved in the Road at a little distance.[48]

These bare statements present almost emblematically the impulse and the check, which remain inextricably intertwined. Dorothy's desire to create for herself an independent existence as writer and observer of nature cannot proceed far before an awareness of her brother obtrudes and dominates. In face of the marriage (and despite her recognition of the kindness shown to her) her love for nature will in future have something of the love of Wordsworth's 'Sailor's mother' who remains (in a poem just composed[49]) tenaciously attached to the singing-bird which is all that is left to remind her of her lost son.

Within this context of conflicting feelings it is natural to trace an undertow of personal reference in other poems of the time, such as 'The Emigrant Mother,'[50] (written the day after 'To a Butterfly'). One fact of which Dorothy must have been highly conscious as she looked forward to the marriage was that she would be forced to look on while Mary bore and raised her brother's children. In one mood she might see the situation as welcome compensation for loss of actual motherhood on her own part; in another it must exacerbate her sense of isolation. While her delight in new life must make her essentially devoted to any child, and particularly to a child of her brother's, she was too much of a Wordsworth, fierce in private identity, not to know an accompanying sense of loss. And this, for all the obvious differences, is the situation explored in 'The Emigrant Mother', where a mother who has been forced to forsake her own child tries to gain relief by looking after another. She is first drawn to the child by her own sense of loss ('An Infant's face and looks are thine;/And sure a Mother's heart is mine') then repelled by a recognition that this child has 'smiles of her own' which threaten to obliterate the memory of her own child's smile. Yet she feels a stronger link binding her to this child than to her sister's which lives near by, and finds a final reconciling bond to its likeness to her own family:

> Thou hast, I think, a look of ours,
> Thy features seem to me the same;
> His little Sister thou shalt be. . . .

This is hardly a case of Wordsworth disguising a present situation (which he rarely does); it is more likely that a matrix of current emotion enables him to write a poem on a cognate theme, and that the emotion explored in the poem then has its effect on the relationship with Dorothy – once again, almost vicariously. In the poem he makes the mother say to the child, 'Thou hast tried,/Thou know'st, the pillow of my breast'; Dorothy, after describing in her journal how her brother has written part of 'The Emigrant Mother', goes on, 'After dinner I read him to sleep – I read Spenser while he leaned on my shoulder,' and the next day, when he has completed the poem, makes an entry already quoted: 'After dinner we made a pillow of my shoulder, I read to him and my Beloved slept'.[51] The journal entries and poems of this time illuminate and interpret one another. The growing intensity of Dorothy's emotion for her brother at this time is incontestable: but it is, as before, held in agonising poise as an intensity *of the heart*, all the fiercer because every element of the more specifically sexual is denied.

The result of this tension between strength of feeling and stoic acceptance of the ordained emerges sometimes as an elegiac note, expressed most completely, perhaps, on 2 February, when she reads Milton: 'After tea I read aloud the 11th Book of Paradise Lost. We were much impressed, and also melted into tears.' The eleventh book is the one which foresees the state of life after the expulsion from Eden, when Adam and Eve will have taken on themselves the burdens and responsibilities of the human condition.[52x]

At the same time these moments of pathos alternate with much straightforward enjoyment. This is particularly true of work produced at the end of March and during April, which is full of delight in the cuckoo, the rainbow, birds and wild flowers – often, as we have seen, directly stimulated by memories of enjoyments together in childhood.

Once again, the work which brings this creative period to a climax seems to involve the supervention of Coleridgean intelligence upon a directness of feeling shared with Dorothy. On 27 March 1802, in the midst of his other poetry about the spring, Dorothy noted in her journal, 'William wrote part of an ode' – fairly clearly the famous Ode, later subtitled 'Intimations of Immortality from Recollections of Early Childhood'.

In the elaboration of the final argument to this poem, as we have seen, Wordsworth meets his sense of loss by a twofold affirmation. First he insists that the visionary attraction of nature as known in childhood never wholly fades. For this reason an unexpected visitation of the old sense may at any time link us back to our original state and a sense of fountainous infinity. And this fact, though essentially capricious and not a resource on which one may rely, surrounds with potencies of sublimity the landscape originally associated with such experiences. It reinforces the more direct magnetism of the heart which is induced by long attachment to a landscape and adds to the resonance of emotional experience. At the same time, earth also reconciles man to the loss of his total primal vision by offering him other natural objects to which his heart may attach itself and so keep alive the visionary power.

In writing the poem Wordsworth was, among other things, formulating the philosophy which allowed him to reconcile the intensity of his affection for Dorothy with the decision to marry and set up a family. The human heart is here regarded as possessing an importance which over-rides all particular individual attachments. In the light of what he was saying, in fact, it became important that as he re-established himself in his native landscape the number of persons who share that link should be enlarged: the larger the community, the greater the resources on which his affections could draw. The intense sensitivity of Dorothy and Coleridge might now be supplemented by the presence of others, such as his brother John ('the silent poet'), who had similar if quieter capacities for attachment.

It was in the logic of the situation, therefore, that Wordsworth should choose for his wife a girl characterised first by ready attachment and faithfulness. There was a further appropriateness in the fact that she embodied in her own person the very contradiction of the outer universe, as described in the Ode. The world of perception could sometimes clothe itself in glory – yet must also, and just as capriciously, fade into the 'light of common day'; Mary Hutchinson, it seems, gave the paradox outward and visible form. It is not altogether uncommon to find in a young girl (particularly one whose family has lived close to nature) a radiance which flashes out visibly at times, but which does not seem to be expressed in anything that she actually says or does. Both Mary and Sara Hutchinson evidently had something of this quality. Coleridge's attraction to Sara was based partly on his experience of an occasional visible radiance in her, which he described in his notebook lines:

> All Look or Likeness caught from Earth,
> All accident of Kin or Birth,
> Had pass'd Away: there seem'd no Trace
> Of Aught upon her brighten'd Face
> Uprais'd beneath the rifted Stone,
> Save of one Spirit, all her own
> She, she herself, and only she
> Shone in her body visibly.   CN II 2441

Wordsworth, it seems, had been conscious of a similar quality in Mary but (in consonance with the argument of his Ode) his poem about her[53] was focussed not upon that but upon their attachment of the heart, leaving himself free to comment on the paradox of her twin nature, as a being who still sometimes reflected celestial light, yet behaved in her everyday life as a part of the mechanical order. At one extreme, as remembered in youth,

> She was a Phantom of delight
> When first she gleam'd upon my sight;
> A lovely Apparition, sent

To be a moment's ornament. . . .
A dancing Shape, an Image gay,
To haunt, to startle, and way-lay.

At the other extreme, viewed as a housewife in the business of day-to-day life,

> I see with eye serene
> The very pulse of the machine;
> A Being breathing thoughtful breath;
> A Traveller betwixt life and death;
> The reason firm, the temperate will,
> Endurance, foresight, strength and skill . . .

– 'And yet', he concludes,

> a Spirit still, and bright
> With something of an angel light.

Wordsworth professes no dismay at the disparate co-existence of these two modes. It can be seen, however, that neither would have been altogether attractive to him in isolation: a totally disembodied spirit could also be totally irresponsible, a total human machine would be ultimately dreary. It was in the element between them, described in the second stanza, that he found his focus and his point of balance:

> A Creature not too bright or good
> For human nature's daily food;
> For transient sorrows, simple wiles,
> Praise, blame, love, kisses, tears, and smiles.

Such a being has contrived to find a path between two states, each in isolation insupportable: the undependable sublimity of human radiance on the one hand and the dullness of everyday duties on the other. Wordsworth's love for Dorothy, with her intensity of emotion, was now to be contained within the context of that mediating affection. By making Mary central to his future household, therefore, Wordsworth no doubt hoped that the affection between himself and Dorothy might find a continuing life within a larger mediating community of relationships where the quiet work of the mature human heart, anchored in a deeply physical love,[54x] could contain, and find a place for, more intense and extreme attachments.

7

In Face of Loss

The writing of the Immortality Ode had, as we have seen, established a large framework for Wordsworth's future career. Where 'Tintern Abbey' had created a tone, a set of sentiments, which fitted his cultivation of freedom and sensibility during the years with Dorothy, the concluding stanzas of the Ode provided authority for his new commitment to domesticity.

That domesticity involved something more than marrying and raising a family. Marriage to Mary Hutchinson might be the linchpin of the enterprise, but a true community among the 'fountains, meadows, hills and groves' of his own childhood vision ought, if it were to possess a larger human significance, to include relationships with others who shared his affection for the place. His brother John, for example, the 'silent poet' who loved to spend days in the calm of nature when he was on leave from his duties as a sea-captain and who was hoping soon to retire from the sea and settle down permanently in the neighbourhood, was one obvious member of the community; Mary's sister Sara Hutchinson another. Coleridge, naturally, must be included. If the power of the heart was strong as he and Coleridge believed, the various cross-links of affection and love (William=Mary, William=Dorothy, Coleridge=Sara, John=Sara, and so on) could all support and draw sustenance from that central nexus, so that the members of the group with their various gifts (Wordsworth and the three women as a rooted and creative household; Coleridge as visiting intelligence; John giving the world its due for the time being by serving at sea and then returning in the future to help support his relatives) would form a strong and fruitful community, an organism linked both to the ideal and the real. The interlinked initials, W.W., D.W., M.W., S.H., J.W., S.T.C., which they carved on a rock-face by Thirlmere (– significantly, on a rock by a spring), evidently formed a visual charm expressive of this shared faith.[1]

The dream proved to be short-lived, however. One of the most important links involved was that between Coleridge and Sara Hutchinson, with whom he had fallen deeply in love some years before. In one sense the love was a hopeless one, since he regarded his own marriage-bonds as indissoluble, but in the first version of his poem 'Dejection' he expressed a hope that his affection for her, particularly as she came to take her part in the Wordsworth household, might over-ride the emotional impoverishment of his marriage and give him something of the further 'genial warmth' that he needed.[2] In addition, he looked forward to the prospect that Sara would eventually marry John Wordsworth. Whether or not this was a likely match is hard to say, but it is clear that Coleridge thought so and believed that it would bring her happiness.[3x]

However fully he might convince himself of this at one level, nevertheless, the prospect evidently imposed a strain not to be removed by willed generosity of heart. When, soon afterwards, Coleridge decided to spend some time in Malta, one reason was the hope for an improvement in his health; but another may well have been his desire to be out of the way while the hoped-for marriage took place.

Whatever his expectations, Malta proved to be a place of anguish. His health deteriorated further, increasing his dependence on drugs and stimulants. And while he was there news came that John Wordsworth had been drowned at sea on his last voyage. The immediate and personal sense of loss was shattering; at the same time a subterranean and daemonic voice must have been asking whether this might not be a magical stroke in favour of his love for Sara. If so the conflict of two such emotions, both strong, but centred in different areas of his psyche, was bound to be intense and unresolvable; and this may help to explain why Coleridge lingered abroad so long and communicated so little with the Wordsworths in the meantime. When he did finally return they were shocked by his appearance, 'as if he were different from what we have expected to see; almost as much as a person of whom we have thought much and of whom we had formed an image in our own minds, without having any personal knowledge of him'.[4]

He was not the only one who had changed. If the death of John Wordsworth racked Coleridge on a bed of warring emotions, it

plunged iron into Wordsworth. 'The set is now broken,' he wrote –
meaning, not the community of the Rock of Names but the more
basic unit of the Wordsworth children. Orphaned and forced to fight
for their own interests in childhood, they had preserved their
relationship jealously, only to find it shaken to its foundations again
now. 'I am sometimes half superstitious,' Wordsworth wrote to his
brother, 'and think that as the number of us is now broken some
more of the set will be following him.'⁵

The effect upon the ideal of the 'community of the heart' was still
more undermining. John's death was a reminder that while
Wordsworth and his friends had been establishing themselves in
their Lake District home, their security was guaranteed by men who
were daily risking their lives. Most savage of all, the stroke that
killed John was a casual operation of that very nature in which
Wordsworth had put his faith – as he himself acknowledged in his
major poem on the event, the 'Elegiac Stanzas, suggested by a
picture of Peele Castle in a Storm'.⁶ It was very well to derive
intimations of immortality from visionary experiences by the sea in
youth, when the effects of light on water had seemed significant of
another fountain-light – 'the light that never was, on sea or land'⁷ –
but this idea was desperately undermined by experience of the sea's
mortal power against humanity. That light might earlier have
seemed to be the 'consecration' of a further reality, but as a 'poet's
dream' it was, like all such radiances, ambiguous and undependable.
Against the suppositious and haunting series of possibilities which it
evoked, the ability of the sea to engulf a human being in a moment of
time was actual and absolute. So Wordsworth continued (transpos-
ing his bitterness into sedateness as he did so)

> Not for a moment could I now behold
> A smiling sea and be what I have been:
> The feeling of my loss will ne'er be old;
> This, which I know, I speak with mind serene.

In a later stanza, he drew the moral of the loss more explicitly:

> Farewell, farewell the Heart that lives alone,
> Hous'd in a dream, at distance from the Kind!
> Such happiness, wherever it be known,
> Is to be pitied; for 'tis surely blind.

These words (with their echo of Othello's disenchantment), sound
the death-knell of the 'community of the heart' – at least as Coleridge

had known it. When he finally returned to the Wordsworths it was
to a situation radically changed. Things which had previously served
to support the interlinking affections of the group were now reminders of loss. 'I know it will not always be so – the time will come
when the light of the setting Sun upon these mountain tops will be as
heretofore a pure joy – not the same *gladness*, that can never be – but
yet a joy even more tender,' Dorothy had written.[8] The parenthesis
about 'gladness' is critical. When Wordsworth spoke of his brother's
immortality, similarly, it was always through the conventional idea
that a man lives on in the memory of his friends; any reference to
the power of the life-force against the fact of death was tellingly
absent.

In this atmosphere, the ferment of earlier years began to sour.
Coleridge, trying once again to draw sustenance from the
Wordsworth household and from a platonic love for Sara, so
redeeming the dreariness of his own marriage, could neither help nor
be helped. The emotional load proved even more heavy than before
and the deadening of his manner increased. He was less the ebullient
and stimulating talker that he had formerly been, and Wordsworth
commented on the fact, sadly and rather bitterly, in a poem[9x] which
turned Coleridge's fountain-image back against him in semi-
reproach:

> There is a change – and I am poor;
> Your Love hath been, nor long ago,
> A Fountain at my fond Heart's door,
> Whose only business was to flow;
> And flow it did; not taking heed
> Of its own bounty, or my need.

> What happy moments did I count!
> Bless'd was I then all bliss above!
> Now, for this consecrated Fount
> Of murmuring, sparkling, living love,
> What have I? shall I dare to tell?
> A comfortless, and hidden WELL.

> A Well of love – it may be deep –
> I trust it is, and never dry:
> What matter? if the Waters sleep
> In silence and obscurity.

— Such change, and at the very door
Of my fond Heart, hath made me poor.

Coleridge's decision to separate from his wife merely increased the strain of his relationship with Sara Hutchinson, which culminated with her withdrawal and removal to Wales in 1810. Dorothy, who had lamented the loss of the old 'divine expression of his countenance',[10] was herself declining from vivacity. In 1808 Coleridge referred to 'a decaying of genial Hope & former lightheartedness' in her.[11] And she, commenting on him in a private letter after Sara's departure used words which, from her, are unexpectedly harsh.

> We have no hope of him – none that he will ever do anything more than he has already done.[12]

The statement may be seen as conveying her disillusionment in a Coleridge who had not lived up to his own ideal of a disinterested love; a year or two later it was echoed in the words which precipitated a painful quarrel, when Basil Montagu reported to Coleridge that Wordsworth 'had no hope of him' and that he had been 'an absolute nuisance in his family'.[13] Whatever the rights and wrongs of the affair, the quarrel marked a decisive point in the relationship. The change which had taken place in Wordsworth since John Wordsworth's death was finally brought home to Coleridge, suggesting to him that he had for years past built his hopes on a delusion.

This was not altogether so, of course; it would perhaps be truer to say that Wordsworth's belief in the human heart had suffered an important modulation. Alarmed by the fate of his friend, whose ill-health and growing dependence on opium seemed partly due to the extremity of his emotional commitments, he was now pursuing some of the ideas that they had developed together in the context of more dependable affections – his wife's for example, and Dorothy's.

In their company the idea that the human race might be evolving towards a point where its own finer instincts, as exemplified at certain points in the animal creation and in the impulses of the human heart towards sympathy, would bring in the 'milder day' of universal peace and a total link between man and nature could survive – even if it now took on a more conventional tone. Coleridge's visionary and vitalistic view of the process retreated in Wordsworth's mind, giving place to a view founded on the love of husband and wife, or the affection between brother and sister. In introductory lines for *The Recluse* first drafted, probably, between 1798 and 1800, he had projected the ideal relationship between man and nature in a marriage metaphor reminiscent of George Herbert's 'bridall of the earth and skie':[14x]

> Paradise, and groves
> Elysian, Fortunate Fields – like those of old
> Sought in the Atlantic Main – why should they be
> A history only of departed things,
> Or a mere fiction of what never was?
> For the discerning intellect of Man,
> When wedded to this goodly universe
> In love and holy passion, shall find these
> A simple produce of the common day.
> – I, long before the blissful hour arrives,
> Would chant, in lonely peace, the spousal verse
> Of this great consummation . . .   PW V 4–5

The Recluse was delayed – partly because Coleridge's promised co-operation was not forthcoming; the 'blissful hour' began to seem further and further away. To write such a poem would involve projecting a view of the history and probable future of mankind and showing the recluse Wordsworth as possessor of a key that could quietly unlock many doors at which his contemporaries were battering; yet his ideal of the heart's cultivation had become so involved with that of the isolated rural community that he was already losing hope for the inhabitants of the industrial society which was growing up in contemporary England. More importantly still, the death of John Wordsworth had deeply undermined the faith in the marriage-bond between man and nature upon which *The Recluse* as a whole was to have been based.

After some years, nevertheless, Wordsworth did succeed in finding one provisional context in time and space for this new modulation in his ideas, adopting the same process as in 'Hart-leap Well' – that of taking over and adapting an existing historical tradition which presented itself as a natural vehicle. The result was his poem *The White Doe of Rylstone*, originally occasioned by a visit which he and Dorothy, accompanied by the Marshalls, made up Wharfedale, to visit Bolton Abbey, in the summer of 1807. In a copy of Whitaker's *History and Antiquities of Craven* lent to him by the

Marshalls, he found a record[15] of the tradition on which his poem was to be founded:

At this time [not long after the Dissolution] a white doe, say the aged people of the neighbourhood, long continued to make a weekly pilgrimage from [Rylstone] over the fells to Bolton, and was constantly found in the abbey church-yard during divine service; after the close of which she returned home as regularly as the rest of the congregation.

The history continued with a comment on the literary possibilities of the story:

This incident awakens the fancy. Shall we say that the soul of one of the Nortons had taken up its abode in that animal, and was condemned to do penance, for his transgressions against 'the lords' deere' among their ashes? But for such a spirit the Wild Stag would have been a fitter vehicle. Was it not then some fair and injured female, whose name and history are forgotten? Had the milk-white doe performed her mysterious pilgrimage from Ettrick Forest to the precincts of Dryburgh or Melrose, the elegant and ingenious editor of the Border Minstrelsy would have wrought it into a beautiful story.

After this, Whitaker went on to speak of other literary places where the image of the deer occurred, including Dryden's 'milk-white hind', the legend of St Hubert's conversion, and the story of Wlffade, prince of Mercia, who in hunting a stag was led to a fountain and was there baptized. Of Rylstone he went on to record, 'Norton Tower seems also to have been a sort of pleasure-house in Summer' and that 'the place is savagely wild'.

It is not difficult to see how Wordsworth's mind might have worked in reading this succession of statements. The last phrases might well arouse echoes of the 'pleasure-dome' and 'savage place' of Coleridge's 'Kubla Khan' while the legend of Wlffade was reminiscent of his own story of 'Hart-leap Well'. And this revival of a train of ideas which had led him to produce his own version of 'Kubla Khan' in the latter poem would then be an encouragement to accept Whitaker's challenge and to present the story of the white doe in a form which would rival Scott's romances yet possess a further dimension provided by his own beliefs. Such a poem would be a final version of his tribute to the 'trance' at Hart-lcap Well, with its intimations of a coming 'milder day'.

In any case, however, the image of the doe was bound to be attractive. Wordsworth had written a number of poems on the strong and disinterested attachment to human beings sometimes shown by animals – drawn on no doubt by the strong factual content in these overt instances of powerfully linking affections. *The White Doe of Rylstone*[16] is the greatest in this series; Wordsworth himself spoke of it as exhibiting 'the Apotheosis of the Animal, who gives the first of two titles to the Poem'.[17] By her faithful visitation of a place where human constancy had been proved through suffering, she becomes an emblem of the finer tone which can be glimpsed from time to time in humanity itself.

Her ancestry also, however, goes back behind the faithful animals of Wordsworth's earlier poems to display a new mutation from Coleridge's ideas about the spring and the primal consciousness. She expresses the conception that there is throughout the animal creation, wherever life manifests itself, a natural grace which is passive as well as active, which suffers as well as achieves – and which may perhaps be most itself in passivity. Most evident in spring, when animals are closest to the source of their life, it is also displayed at times throughout the animal kingdom.

The conception had been discernible in Coleridge's albatross, following the ship faithfully, hovering near the mariners and acting as a 'genial' presence; it was also a quality which might be seen in all life in moments of entranced vision. The water-snakes of 'The Ancient Mariner', blessed in a moment of spontaneous feeling, find a peaceful and static counterpart in Dorothy's journal for 1805:

> Mrs Luff's large white dog lay in the moonshine upon the round knoll under the old yew-tree, a beautiful and romantic image – the dark tree with its dark shadow, and the elegant creature as fair as a Spirit.[18]

The white doe, similarly, is a visible incarnation of the inner, passive spirit of the Nortons which is otherwise expressed clearly only in Emily (the suffering and devoted sister who is Wordsworth's own invention).

The doe's ancestry in various ideas developed in Coleridge's company is further reflected in the imagery used to describe her. Because she is associated with the 'milder day' it becomes natural to use the image of the moon (reflecting to human beings the milder essence of light which subsists at the heart of the sun). That moon is a living emblem of the 'gravitation and the filial bond' which binds all spirits together, as she moves peacefully in her course, transmitting the modified solar rays to all who are receptive; in the same way, the doe glides on her way, silently and impalpably, but still offering a significance to all who are prepared to grasp it.

The first scene of the poem is at once historically accurate and highly emblematic. Bolton Abbey is already in ruins, leaving only a chapel for worship – though the Elizabethan worship there is sincere, since it belongs to a new 'springtime' of devotion:

> For 'tis the sunrise now of zeal;
> Of a pure faith the vernal prime –
> In great Eliza's golden time.

The new devotion is confined to this smaller building in a large space where the ruined abbey and the forms of nature are the main presence and the only sound that of a river flowing nearby. Into this peaceful scene comes the doe, described in lines of a lyricism like that of the Immortality Ode:

> Comes gliding in with lovely gleam,
> Comes gliding in serene and slow,
> Soft and silent as a dream,
> A solitary Doe!
> White she is as lily of June,
> And beauteous as the silver moon
> When out of sight the clouds are driven
> And she is left alone in heaven;
> Or like a ship some gentle day
> In sunshine sailing far away,
> A glittering ship, that hath the plain
> Of ocean for her own domain. ll. 55–66

With considerable emblematising skill, Wordsworth sets his image of the lonely moon between two others, each expressing one of the complementary qualities which it reconciles in itself. The lily in June[19x] has the moon's direct, luminous purity, the ship in sunshine its ability to suggest and transmit a more active visionary – and joyous – power.

So also, at the end, the doe is seen making her faithful weekly visits to the churchyard where, amid the sculptured forms of graves

and tombs, she makes for a grave which is no more than a 'sequestered hillock green':

> There doth the gentle Creature lie
> With those adversities unmoved;
> Calm spectacle, by earth and sky
> In their benignity approved!
> And aye, methinks, this hoary Pile,
> Subdued by outrage and decay,
> Looks down upon her with a smile,
> A gracious smile, that seems to say –
> 'Thou, thou art not a Child of Time,
> But Daughter of the Eternal Prime!'   ll. 1901–10

Throughout these closing lines, the sentiments are not far removed
from those of traditional devotion: they again echo the George
Herbert of 'Sweet day, so cool, so calm, so bright', nourishing the
conception of a charity related to nature in her moments of beneficence. The final couplet, equally, echoes the words of Soul to Body
in Vaughan's 'The Evening-Watch':

> The last gasp of time
> Is thy first breath, and man's *eternall Prime*.[20]

That last word, however, also opens, momentarily, a window on to
all that Coleridge had suggested about the primal affections and their
possible link with the primary consciousness. With a touch not
uncharacteristic of his later poetry, Wordsworth uses an unobtrusive
word which can yet suggest a wealth of further significance to any
reader who picks up its fuller connotations. Such a reader, who will
already have perceived, in the earlier cluster, the thread which binds
together the lily in June, the moon in a clear sky and the distant sunlit
ship, will now also see in the image of the doe as it has been revealed
in the poem an additional quality which none of them possessed. The
lily will die, clouds will rise to obscure the moon, the ship will sail
out of sight: although they impress themselves as eternal, their
presence is temporary. But the doe, gliding in and out of the scene
with regular devotion, counterpoints her intimations of sublimity
by a faithful regularity: she becomes an image of the primal renewing itself in time, as in the seasons of the temporal universe.

For Wordsworth, the affections between human beings who are
faithful to one another have the same quality: they recreate in human

terms the spring-like freshness of vision which is revealed fitfully in the animal and vegetable creation. Despite various obvious differences of circumstances, therefore, the poem becomes the one in which his affection for Dorothy is finally sealed. Mary Moorman argues persuasively that the elder brother's words to Emily express something of his own feelings for Dorothy. The reference to 'the last leaf on a blasted tree', she points out, is reminiscent of the 'One red leaf, the last of its clan', the emblem of life-in-death in 'Christabel' which is associated with one of her journal entries.[21] If Dorothy sometimes felt herself to be keeping alive a spark of vitality which was smothered by contemporary life, moreover, she must also have feared becoming the 'wither'd branch upon a blossoming tree' of Coleridge's melancholy 'Letter to Sara Hutchinson'.[22] In Wordsworth's poem, Francis's prophecy to his sister that her fate will be similar to (if less pleasurable than) that of the white doe, feeding nearby, can therefore be viewed as offering a double source of consolation to Dorothy, also:

> '— But thou, my Sister, doomed to be
> The last leaf on a blasted tree;
> If not in vain we breathed the breath
> Together of a purer faith;
> If hand in hand we have been led,
> And thou, (O happy thought this day!)
> Not seldom foremost in the way;
> If on one thought our minds have fed,
> And we have in one meaning read;
> If, when at home our private weal
> Hath suffered from the shock of zeal,
> Together we have learned to prize
> Forbearance and self-sacrifice;
> If we like combatants have fared,
> And for this issue been prepared;
> If thou art beautiful, and youth
> And thought endue thee with all truth –
> Be strong; – be worthy of the grace
> Of God, and fill thy destined place:
> A Soul, by force of sorrows high,
> Uplifted to the purest sky
> Of undisturbed humanity!'   ll. 566–87

We need not accept the tribute as literal in all details. One does not readily think of Dorothy Wordsworth as an Emily Norton – or for that matter as a woman of sorrows. Any personal reference here must be akin to the fear expressed in 'Tintern Abbey' for her future welfare – 'If solitude, or fear, or pain, or grief,/Should be thy portion. . . .' It is the sense of having 'breathed the breath/Together of a purer faith' which strikes the recognisable note of the relationship.

The White Doe of Rylstone stands as a major product of the new phase in Wordsworth's writing, centred on a relationship shared both with Dorothy and his own household. The running thread of engagement with Coleridgean speculations is less evident, emerging only in particular passages. Instead, Wordsworth rooted his narrative more firmly in the local, the historically verifiable and the accepted doctrines of Christian love, eliciting from these the vision of a future society founded upon affection. His preoccupation with historical fact expressed itself in a hope that his own inventions would not conflict with known records: but when Scott offered to send some details which might have conflicted with the story as he was developing it he refused, voicing a fear that his composition might be disrupted.[23]

This last reaction shows a trait which emerged from time to time: his imagination was always a fragile presence, liable to abscond in face of the actual – even if the actual were no more than someone else's verbal formulations. On one occasion he found it impossible to compose when Dorothy read an associated entry in her journals: he could not escape her words, once they were in his mind.[24] In the case of this poem, however, the imagination won, enabling him to make it what it is: not a great public prophecy, but a great private emblem set against an identifiable historical tradition.

The presence of that tradition showed, nevertheless, how far Wordsworth had moved on from the earlier imaginative formulation of his attitude in the poem written near Tintern Abbey. Where that was simply a beautiful ruin which had become absorbed into and harmonised with the natural forms that surrounded it, Rylstone (a no less impressively situated ruin) retained its part in the history of the Church by the survival of worship in the one chapel. The history of the Nortons, similarly, particularised the sense of humanity which at Tintern was distanced and generalised. One notes, for example, the ingenuity of the touch by which the image of the banner with the seven wounds of Christ runs together the sense of military history with that of the Church, maintaining its milder message through human vicissitudes – while the elegiac note surrounding the emblem may also set up another echo of Othello's 'Farewell the banner . . .'.

Once Wordsworth had achieved such a construct, there was no need for him to go on wrestling with the theme of the 'milder day'. It was now firmly placed in an acceptable historical setting. Occasionally, nevertheless, it moves again in his later poetry, as in a poem of February 1816, entitled 'Invocation to the Earth' (and probably related to the end of the Napoleonic Wars). This poem (which contains some interesting parallels with Blake's 'Hear the voice of the Bard!'²⁵) is addressed by a 'Spirit' to 'the Earth'. At its primal level the Spirit recognises both a broken relationship with the Earth and a possibility of renewal:

> 'From regions where no evil thing has birth
> I come – thy stains to wash away,
> Thy cherished fetters to unbind,
> And open thy sad eyes upon a milder day. . .'   PW IV 267

The operation of the promised charm involves a complex imagery which runs together Coleridgean images of the heart and the fountain:

> I sprinkle thee with soft celestial dews,
> Thy lost, maternal heart to re-infuse!
> Scattering this far-fetched moisture from my wings,
> Upon the act a blessing I implore,
> Of which the rivers in their secret springs,
> The rivers stained so oft with human gore,
> Are conscious. . . .

With this recurrence of his earlier vision of nature as possessing an inner 'heart' which will ultimately be revealed at the coming of the 'milder day', the riddling quality of all such visionary ideas for Wordsworth also re-emerges, however, and the poem ends on a note of mystery:

> The Spirit ended his mysterious rite,
> And the pure vision closed in darkness infinite.

The poem is an indication of the power which the theme of a mildness at nature's heart continued to exercise over his later thinking – and more particularly over his intimate relationships, since there, if anywhere, he could look for some foreshadowing of the larger process.

So powerful, indeed, in earlier years, had been this belief in the prophetic 'moment of affection', the moment when a sense of nature's self-renewing life led on to an experience of trance, that one is led on to ask whether cultivation of it did not, at a more immediate level, result in some psychic damage to his sister. Did not this deliberate cultivation of affection undermine the spontaneity and directness of feeling which were Dorothy's distinctive gifts?

In one sense, it could be argued, the whole relationship involved such a betrayal. The attempt to guide emotional experiences toward a moment of entrancement might be a logical continuation from occasions when, as at Hart-leap Well, the trance had come unsought, but by bringing in an element of conscious control it became a form of emotional indulgence and diversion, consonant with Wordsworth's philosophy of central peace, perhaps, but not with Dorothy's lively sensibility.

The history of Lawrence and Jessie Chambers is again briefly relevant. Jessie's attempt to give permanence to some of the moments which she had enjoyed in nature with Lawrence was accompanied by a recognition of a power in him which she evidently responded to intensely and which we can see as having no necessary or permanent connection with the more tranquil experiences:

> With wild things, flowers and birds, a rabbit in a snare, the speckled eggs in a hole in the ground he was in primal sympathy – a living vibration passed between him and them. . . .[26]

Wordsworth does not say quite this of Dorothy, but he does mention the mixture of fearfulness and attraction which she felt in the presence of such objects, and when he came to write a poem for her (in the series 'On the Naming of Places') the place which he chose for her was a dell in Easedale which enclosed a brook there for part of its descent. In that place he had on one occasion heard all the voices of wild nature creating a consort of natural joy:

> . . . where down a rock
> The Stream, so ardent in its course before,
> Sent forth such sallies of glad sound, that all
> Which I till then had heard, appeared the voice
> Of common pleasure: beast and bird, the lamb,
> The shepherd's dog, the linnet and the thrush,

Vied with this waterfall, and made a song,
Which, while I listened, seemed like the wild growth
Or like some natural produce of the air,
That could not cease to be.   PW II III–I2

The sense recorded here has no necessary connection with habits
of meditative contemplation or of trance: it would be just as natural
to make it central, and to accept contemplation and trance as
occasional by-products. This, one suspects, was Dorothy's own
inclination. For her brother, on the other hand, as his preface to *The
Recluse* shows, the relation between the heart and the 'discerning
intellect of man' must dominate; it was only through that operation
that the paradisal experience of joy would be found to be 'a simple
produce of the common day'.

In this sense it could be argued that he was guilty of having given
Dorothy a false orientation; one might even go on to trace a parallel
between the mental breakdown which eventually overtook Jessie
Chambers and that which Dorothy Wordsworth suffered in her later
years. In each case, it might be said, though in very different
circumstances, a natural spring of vitality had been repressed, and
nature's laws had taken their inexorable course.

If this is so, Wordsworth himself could not have recognised the
fact: to do so would have been to turn his back on an important part
of the faith to which he had devoted his whole life. That he did
recognise a tragic irony in the fate of his sister is clear from a
reminiscence of the Duke of Argyle, who on one occasion heard
Wordsworth in old age reading from 'Tintern Abbey':

> The strong emphasis that he put on the words addressed personal-
> ly to the person to whom the poem is addressed struck me as
> almost unnatural at the time – 'My dear, *dear* friend' ran the
> words, – 'in thy wild eyes'. It was not till after the reading was
> over that we found out that the old paralytic and *doited* woman we
> had seen in the morning was the sister to whom *T.A.* was
> addressed, and her condition accounted for the fervour with
> which the old Poet read lines which reminded him of their better
> days.[27]

It would be easy to charge Wordsworth with veiled hypocrisy
here; to do so, however, would not only be over-melodramatic – it
would be to ignore the fact that when Wordsworth originally wrote
his poem Dorothy was already twenty-six, and perfectly responsible

for her own actions. If there had been an emotional misdirection she, as much as her brother, was to blame; and indeed the misdirection could better be ascribed to the contours of the map which they alike shared. Both were equal heirs to the dislike and fear of passionate involvement which their forbears had received from the puritan tradition and which now seemed to them, in turn, to have been confirmed in the excesses of the French Revolution. Given this mistrust, it was natural to channel their attitudes towards a concentration on those elements in nature that made for peace and tranquillity, and to accept, at least to this extent, all that the eighteenth century had taught concerning the necessity of bridling one's feelings.

On this score De Quincey is again telling. At one point he declares that Dorothy's impulsiveness was 'under the continual restraint of severe good sense'; at another he dwells on the effects of this in her everyday behaviour:

> Her manner was warm and even ardent; her sensibility seemed constitutionally deep; and some subtle fire of impassioned intellect apparently burned within her, which, being alternately pushed forward into a conspicuous expression by the irrepressible instincts of her temperament, and then immediately checked, in obedience to the decorum of her sex and age, and her maidenly condition, gave to her whole demeanour, and to her conversation, an air of embarrassment, and even of self-conflict, that was almost distressing to witness.[28]

In so far as there is a betrayal here, it can be laid at the door of a whole civilisation, which could check the impulsiveness of women ruthlessly through all the media of deportment and convention. Wordsworth himself was too much a child of his own culture to rebel against its dictates on that score. What his poetry permanently owed to his sister, however, was a more limited but highly valuable gift, also picked upon by De Quincey:

> . . . the exceeding sympathy, always ready and always profound, by which she made all that one could tell her, all that one could describe . . . reverberate, as it were, *à plusieurs reprises*, to one's own feelings, by the manifest impression it made upon *hers*.[29]

When one retires to this level of discourse, on the other hand, the relationship between brother and sister ceases to be a matter for posthumous recrimination and regains the note of quixotic enterprise which it had for its original participants. One finds oneself being drawn back from the intricate achievement of poems like 'Hart-leap Well' and *The White Doe of Rylstone* to those which express more directly his co-operation with Dorothy's feelings and sympathies, acting respectively as impulse and guide for his more reflective sense, and stimulating him to express, in stately form, the pathos of the human condition.

As one looks further into this 'stateliness', moreover, one glimpses their access to a resource which was hardly available to later figures such as Lawrence and Jessie Chambers. Both could fall back on a tradition of dignified speech and conduct which they found surviving even among very simple figures of their own culture, such as the leech-gatherer. The resort to such a tradition might not resolve the emotional tensions which they suffered, but it provided a place of refuge which at least guarded them from excesses of sentimentality. It is a point which no sensitive reader of Dorothy Wordsworth's journals is likely to miss: and it is true of Wordsworth's poetry throughout his life, providing an important note in 'The Ruined Cottage' and reaching what is perhaps its finest expression in 'Michael'.

An examination of Wordsworth's achievement in the latter poem[30] reveals much, in fact, about the very precise and delicate poise by which the relationship between brother and sister was sustained. Already, in 1801, he is cultivating a mixture of intense feeling, direct expression and dignity of diction which moves beyond even that of 'The Ruined Cottage', since the use of a separate narrator is avoided: the story is related with the bareness and simplicity of the Old Testament at its best. There is much in the narrative also to remind the reader of biblical themes: the simplicity of life among flocks of sheep, the ability to commune alone with the divine power behind the universe, the covenant between father and son. Yet it is, in terms of orthodox Christianity, a strikingly sceptical poem: the prayers of Michael and his wife and their neighbours for Luke as he leaves home for the town are completely ineffective. Only Michael remains (rather like God the father as seen by some of the later biblical prophets), faithful to his covenant of love whatever the breaches committed by the erring child over whom he is yearning.

Insofar as one can generalise at a social level from the story (and there is something about the air of inevitability with which the cursory account of Luke's downfall is given that encourages generalisation) it can be seen to foreshadow the conservatism of Wordsworth's later political thinking. The small family, united by love (a love which in the old man has emerged as purified from its earlier form of 'instinctive tenderness, the same/Fond spirit that blindly works in the blood of all' to an individual and less self-oriented emotion associated with the desire to perpetuate his own way of life), is a perfect form of the 'community of the heart', its significance effortlessly emblematised in the lamp which is hung in the cottage each evening and known to their neighbours far and wide as 'The Evening Star'. But the whole weight of the story suggests that such a state is precarious, attainable only by those who have remained fully attached to a wild landscape known from childhood:

> Fields, where with chearful spirits he had breath'd
> The common air; the hills, which he so oft
> Had climb'd with vigorous steps; which had impress'd
> So many incidents upon his mind
> Of hardship, skill or courage, joy or fear;
> Which like a book preserv'd the memory
> Of the dumb animals, whom he had sav'd,
> Had fed or shelter'd, linking to such acts,
> So grateful in themselves, the certainty
> Of honourable gains; these fields, these hills
> Which were his living Being, even more
> Than his own Blood – what could they less? had laid
> Strong hold on his affections, were to him
> A pleasurable feeling of blind love,
> The pleasure which there is in life itself.   LB II 202–3

The attachment described here is powerful in origin and rein-forced through time; for the young Luke, on the other hand, it is still so fragile that it cannot long survive his displacement into city life. And if this potency and fragility are interpreted logically they become the cue for a deeply conservative attitude to society, since it follows that the whole civilisation of the town is not only monst-rously irrelevant to the basic human resources of attachment to a wild and familiar landscape, but an enemy, able to destroy them with redoubtable speed.

In the beginning, one feels, this was not what Wordsworth had in mind as he set up his own community in Grasmere – he was intent on the more straightforward task of showing his fellow-men how, in a rural setting, the universal workings of the heart could be both expressed and studied in a pure form, and he no doubt expected his family and friends to prove exemplary participants. But as his own community wilted under various stresses and strains it was natural for him to revert to the more conservative values suggested by his tale. Indeed, the very success of poems such as 'Michael', as compared with the less sympathetic reception given to other early writings, may well have helped to set his feet more firmly on the road.

The continuing popularity of 'Michael' in the Victorian age is a commonplace of literary history. And if its success was not necessarily beneficial to Wordsworth's development, since it encouraged the weighty presentation of commonplaces which mars some of his later work, it was on its own account, thoroughly deserved: he had achieved a new maturity and homogeneity of style, matching Dorothy's combination of dignity and sensibility with a manly elegance and simple pathos of his own.

'Michael' also shows the extent to which Wordsworth was, by contrast with the excesses of contemporary sentimentalism, perfecting a new restraint in rendering the workings of human emotion. His more esoteric beliefs sometimes emerge into the open – particularly in the passage beginning 'There is a comfort in the strength of love. . . .' Love is the power which has been created in the shepherd through his long attachment to a particular wild place; and love sustains him there, even in the collapse of hopes which love itself had nurtured. But the character and pathos of the shepherd's life are independent of this doctrine: they are communicated through a bare recital of the facts of his life.

Nothing, in fact, indicates Wordsworth's restraint in this poem better than the fact that he did *not* mention one fact about the original sheepfold which, one suspects, helped to give significance to the story as he had heard it in Grasmere – and which might stand as an emblem for much more in his own career. He describes with some exactitude the setting of the ruined sheepfold, on its lonely site near the boisterous brook of Greenhead Ghyll, and gives directions for reaching it which are gracefully matter-of-fact. But he makes no use at all of the feature of its appearance which struck Dorothy, and which she recorded faithfully in her journal[31] – that the original builder, in forming its stone walls, had sealed it into the rough shape of a human heart.

8

Centres of Concord

Despite Wordsworth's growing conviction that the common workings of the heart revealed themselves more surely against the experience of loss than in the motions of unthinking joy, there was one
important area where the 'one human heart' must retain its continuity with the sense of the 'one life': that of childhood.

The fact that that delight must forfeit some of its immediacy in
future years did not in the least detract from its value in childhood.
On the contrary, it was all the more important that the child should
develop all those faculties which enhanced its links with nature.
Children who were exposed to the forces of romance and to the
wildness of nature were in Wordsworth's view building up resources which would serve them well when they had to face the
sobering experiences of adulthood.

His own early experiences, he felt, had initiated him into an
anterior realm of childhood magic which was immediate and direct.
He was particularly fascinated by those experiences which could still
reproduce the magic with uncanny force. In one of his most famous
poems he had described the leap of the heart which he continued to
feel whenever he saw a rainbow – an experience which suggested
that the workings of the heart and the sense of wonder were at some
level inextricably linked. He was equally fascinated by the glow-
worm, the mysterious and isolated cell of glowing life to which he
took delight in introducing Dorothy.[ix]

The cuckoo's song, another wonder, could reorganise perception
of the world in a more radical way. Where the form of the rainbow,
fully present to the observer, yet changing according to his point of
view, moving as he moved, created a spatial correspondence which
did not fully acknowledge the stability of the substantial world, the
voice of the cuckoo refused to be organised in spatial terms at all:

While I am lying on the grass,
I hear thy restless shout:
From hill to hill it seems to pass,
About, and all about!²ˣ

This sense of disturbance, a derangement of perception which assists the rebegetting of the visionary experience, leads Wordsworth to relocate the point of union between the isolated delight of the visionary and the world of space and time. Each self-isolating wonder has the quality of a self-originating spring, to which the human heart, at least, may respond directly, since it belongs to the same order. So the cuckoo reminds the poet of the 'visionary hours' of his childhood, when it was

No Bird; but an invisible Thing,
A voice, a mystery. . . .

To listen to the bird is not simply to remember that 'golden time' but to recreate it – or in Wordsworth's stronger word, 'beget' it – afresh:

O blessed Bird! the earth we pace
Again appears to be
An unsubstantial, faery place;
That is fit home for Thee!

When, on one occasion, Wordsworth tried to give an extended account of such phenomena,³ he placed them as part of a long process necessary to educate human beings into habits of 'admiration' on the one hand and 'love' on the other. Both feelings were with us from the first, he argued, but the process by which they evolved were completely different:

Our sympathies of tender love are slow
Diffused by motions scarcely visible
Not so our admiration – that is near
And sudden & spreads fast; how long it is,
To pass things nearer by, ere the delight
Abate or with less eagerness return
Which flashes from the eyes of babes in arms
When they have caught, held up for that extent,
A prospect of the Moon. . . .   ll. 3–11 and MS

After suggesting other objects of immediate delight ('A little rill/ Of water sparkling down a rocky slope/By the way-side, a beast, a bird,

a flower') he goes on to describe an 'after transport' which from time
to time seizes the growing child:

> Brac'd, startled into notice, lifted up
> As if on plumes, with sudden gift of fan,
> By things of Nature's rarer workmanship,
> Her scatter'd accidents of sight and sound –
> The peacock's fan with all its [   ] eyes
> Unfurl'd, the rainbow, or the Cuckoo's shout,
> An echo, or the glow-worm's faery lamp,
> Or some amazement and surprize of sense,
> When it hath pass'd away, returns again
> In later days, – the fluid element
> That yields not when we touch it, lake or pool,
> Or stream transparent as the liquid deep
> And safe with all its dangers underfoot. . . .   ll. 24–36

The wonder that first accompanies this experience of waters frozen
into ice then spreads itself to other apparent impossibilities:

>   a ship that sails
> The seas, the lifeless arch of stones in air
> Suspended, the cerulean firmament
> And what it is; the River that flows on
> Perpetually, whence comes it, whither tends,
> Going and never gone; the fish that moves
> And lives as in an element of death;
> Or aught of more refin'd astonishment,
> Such as the Skylark breeds, singing aloft
> As if the Bird were native to the heavens,
> There planted like a Star. . . .   ll. 41–51

As these wonders begin to stale by repetition, the needs which they
fulfil are, he continues, met by the more artificial wonders of fable
and romance:

> Trees that bear gems for fruit, rocks spouting milk,
> And diamond palaces, and birds that sing
> With human voices, formidable hills,
> Or magnets which, leagues off, can witch away
> Iron, disjointing in a moment's space
> The unhappy ship that comes within their reach. . . . ll. 85–90

In due time, the child, growing more *blasé*, yet also 'haunted oft/By what has been his life at every turn,' is visited by

> Another soul, spring, centre of his being,
> And that is Nature.   ll. 138–9

Nature thus encourages a belief that whatever grandeur he senses in his own mind is matched by a secret centre of grandeur in the universe, which helps establish her superiority to the world of men.

>   If upon mankind
> He looks, and on the human maladies
> Before his eyes, what finds he there to this
> Fram'd answerably? What but sordid men,
> And transient occupations, and desires
> Ignoble and deprav'd? Therefore he cleaves
> Exclusively to Nature as in her
> Finding his image, what he has, what lacks,
> His rest and his perfection. From mankind,
> Like earlier monk or priest, as if by birth
> He is sequester'd: to her altar's laws
> Bound by an irrefutable decree;
> No fellow labourer of the brotherhood,
> Single he is in state, monarch and king;
> Or like an Indian, when, in solitude
> And individual glory, he looks out
> From some high eminence upon a tract
> Boundless of unappropriated earth;
> So doth he measure the vast universe,
> His own by right of spiritual sovereignty.   ll. 194–213

While this is going on, he concludes, a parallel work of nature is keeping alive the tender sympathies, so that another range of images, such as a taper in the night, smoke from a cottage by day, a garden, 'a churchyard, and the bell that tolls to church' – even the roaring ocean and wild wilderness – conspire to give him a sense of union with and love for the world, and so, eventually, for his fellows.

Wordsworth's omission from all completed versions of *The Prelude* of the disquisition on childhood imagination must be a matter for surprise and conjecture. Perhaps on later reflection he felt less sure that the world of fantasy was so positive a blessing. In one of his addresses to Coleridge he suggested that his friend's troubles might have been due to a childhood and youth too much given over to works of imagination and too little exposed to the forces of nature. Even in his own case he could not be sure that the experiences of wonder had always led to the love of humanity: there was some evidence that, in his youth, cultivation of the wonderful in nature had led to an isolating aestheticism.

Despite the attractiveness of the later marvels described, moreover, they relied partly upon the writings of the reflective or book-fed mind, and so did not have the immediate natural power of the rainbow or glow-worm to start a movement of delight. In time, their magic might fail. For an effect more readily and surely available, therefore, he must look rather to certain experiences in which the opposing forces of his mind had been caught and resolved in a single vivid and memorable landscape. Among other unused drafts for the last book of *The Prelude* (devoted to scenes that, like the view from Snowdon, served as remembrancers of the 'analogy betwixt/The mind of man and nature') two such experiences are recorded. The first took place on a stormy autumn day when

> The wind blew through the hills of Coniston
> Compress'd as in a tunnel, from the lake
> Bodies of foam took flight, and the whole vale
> Was wrought into commotion high and low –
> Mist flying up and down, bewilder'd showers,
> Ten thousand thousand waves, mountains and crags,
> And darkness, and the sun's tumultuous light.

Yet, in the middle of the chaos,

> A large unmutilated rainbow stood
> Immoveable in heav'n, kept standing there
> With a colossal stride bridging the vale,
> The substance thin as dreams, lovelier than day, –
> Amid the deafening uproar stood unmov'd,
> Sustain'd itself through many minutes space;
> As if it were pinn'd down by adamant.   *Prel.* pp. 623–4

It was with 'pins of adamant' that Satan and his fellow-daemons constructed their causeway through Chaos in *Paradise Lost*;[4] in the case of the rainbow's bridge, however, effortlessly imposing its prismatic colours (a notable, if precarious, grace of the Newtonian universe) across a scene of total disorder, any such daemonic element is to be seen not as fallen, but as a surviving link with the original, unfallen, divine creativity.

This scene in nature emblematises one great area of tension in Wordsworth's mind, creating into actuality an otherwise unimaginable opposition between vision and chaos, between an imposing projection of radiance and a possible totality of vortex. The next description belongs to his other world, that world of trance where such opposites are harmonised. In this case it was a horse, pointed out to him by his companion ('a Peasant of the valley where I dwelt') that arrested his attention:

> 'Twas a horse, that stood
> Alone upon a little breast of ground
> With a clear silver moonlight sky behind.
> With one leg from the ground the creature stood
> Insensible and still, – breath, motion gone,
> Hairs, colour, all but shape and substance gone,
> Mane, ears, and tail, as lifeless as the trunk
> That had no stir of breath; we paused awhile
> In pleasure of the sight, and left him there
> With all his functions silently sealed up,
> Like an amphibious work of Nature's hand,
> A Borderer dwelling betwixt life and death,
> A living Statue or a statued Life.   *Prel.* p. 624

An experienced 'mental traveller', Wordsworth here recognises familiar border country. The trance-like effect created when a particular form of life, arrested in the moonlight, imposes a simultaneous sense of permanence and light, gives an effect of death without death's bleakness, of life without life's disorders.

Such moments in nature provide a correlative for his mature attempts to blend 'finite' with 'infinite' vision. They reconcile opposing forces (and so, incidentally, guard against the nightmare extremes of each) while manifesting a unique and positive beauty of their own.

The mediating power of the moon has already been mentioned in this connection; the breeze, a similar phenomenon, mediating between the extremes of violent gale and dead calm, is possessed of a positive quality by reason of its ability to caress and sustain the human being around which it rolls. So the agonised question 'Was it for this . . .' that originally opened *The Prelude* can in the complete version be replaced by a delight in nature's mediating power:

> O there is blessing in this gentle breeze,
> A visitant that while it fans my cheek
> Doth seem half-conscious of the joy it brings
> From the green fields, and from yon azure sky.

The greenness of the fields and blueness of the sky themselves extend the area of consolation: in a universe designed on economical principles, the mid-tones between black and white would be varying shades of grey, not bright colours, each making their individual and direct appeal to the primary chemical senses.

In landscape, similarly, even the wildest country may conceal a scene of unexpected reconciliation. In the poem[5] which begins with the Druidic line,

> Our walk was far among the ancient trees . . .

Wordsworth describes the discovery of a small paradisal spot unapproached by any path, in the midst of wild, thickly wooded country:

>   . . . a slip of lawn,
> And a small bed of water in the woods,
> All round this pool both flocks and herds might drink
> On its firm margin, even as from a well
> Or some stone-bason which the Herdsman's hand
> Had shap'd for their refreshment, nor did sun
> Or wind from any quarter ever come
> But as a blessing to this calm recess,
> This glade of water and this one green field.
> The spot was made by Nature for herself:
> The travellers know it not. . . .

This simple scene, again illustrative of nature's power to reach beyond the confines of her simpler laws to create unpredictable graces of her own, is a milder form of Coleridge's notebook dream:

> – some wilderness-plot, green and fountainous and unviolated by Man.[6]

In Wordsworth's poem it is used as an emblem for Mary Hutchinson, and the particular qualities which only someone who lived with her regularly could know and value.

The lake or mere, fed by a spring and discharging itself into a stream, was another reconciling image, a mediator between the deadness of stagnant water and the energy of uncontrollable torrent. This form had the further virtue of reflecting the surrounding scenery: it could stand, indeed, as an unusually close image for a correspondence between certain forms in the universe and the inward nature of the developed, meditative heart.

Wordsworth creates a more complex (and consequently more private) image of this kind in an episode near the end of *The Excursion*, where those who have been listening to an inspired discourse from the Pastor go out to the lake at sunset.

> . . . by happy chance we saw
> A twofold image; on a grassy bank
> A snow-white ram, and in the crystal flood
> Another and the same! Most beautiful,
> On the green turf, with his imperial front
> Shaggy and bold, and wreathèd horns superb,
> The breathing creature stood; as beautiful,
> Beneath him, showed his shadowy counterpart.
> Each had his glowing mountains, each his sky,
> And each seemed centre of his own fair world:
> Antipodes unconscious of each other,
> Yet, in partition, with their several spheres,
> Blended in perfect stillness, to our sight! *Exc.* ix 439–51

As the walkers pause, entranced, the lady who has proposed the walk whispers to the narrator that the sight is for her an emblem of the state of mind created in her by the old man's eloquence. She also hints at an important limitation:

> 'While he is speaking, I have power to see
> Even as he sees; but when his voice hath ceased,
> Then, with a sigh, sometimes I feel, as now,
> That combinations so serene and bright
> Cannot be lasting in a world like ours,
> Whose highest beauty, beautiful as it is,
> Like that reflected in yon quiet pool,
> Seems but a fleeting sunbeam's gift, whose peace
> The sufferance only of a breath of air!' *Exc.* ix 465–73

The other images which we have mentioned might be open to the same objection: as the product of a particular set of favouring circumstances in time and space, each is transient. At the same time, they have one important feature making for permanence: the reconciliation they effect can be carried in the mind and recalled at any time with full force – which even the magnetising power of more beautiful scenes cannot.

There is a further ground on which these emblems might be criticised, however: they all presuppose that the central truths of the universe will inevitably, when discovered, prove pleasing. For all their success in reconciling finite and infinite, it might be objected, they themselves have potential opposites: the fact of suffering encountered in a place of sublimity, for example.

This sense has always been hard to render in poetry; it was particularly so in the teeth of the Augustan tradition that one of the poet's primary obligations was to give pleasure. One attempt of the sort (also in *The Excursion*) aroused the contempt of reviewers. In Book Four, the Solitary has been comparing the soul's aspirations after immortality to an eagle rising to look at the sun after it has set when he is arrested by a sound –

> '. . . a solemn bleat;
> Sent forth as if it were the Mountain's voice,
> Again!' – The effect upon the soul was such
> As he expressed: for, from the mountain's heart
> The solemn bleat appeared to come; there was
> No other – and the region all around
> Stood silent, empty of all shape of life.
> – It was a Lamb – left somewhere to itself,
> The plaintive spirit of the solitude!　　*Exc.* iv 403–12 (app. cr.)

It was not until 1845 that Wordsworth capitulated to the ridicule that had greeted that 'solemn bleat' and altered it: his stubbornness was perhaps associated with the importance which he attached to the experience, which had actually happened to him.[7x] The Sage's soaring sublimity has been checked by a sense of 'sad dependence upon time, and all/The trepidations of mortality';[8] the resonating bleat, heard in this sublime and mountainous setting, has given a voice to the intensified pathos of the animal creation and its sufferings in a world where, even in childhood, the 'gravitation and the filial bond' may easily seem to fail.

The sense is expressed less controversially elsewhere. Among the 'Poems on the Naming of Places' there is one[9] which describes a September morning when Wordsworth, Dorothy and Coleridge were walking along the shore of Grasmere, filled with pleasure by the play of nature around them and the noise of harvesting in the nearby fields. In this general scene of movement and happiness the only hint of any other emotion is buried in the mention of occasional moments when they paused to

> watch some tuft
> Of dandelion seed or thistle's beard,
> Which, seeming lifeless half, and half impell'd
> By some internal feeling, skimm'd along
> Close to the surface of the lake that lay
> Asleep in a dead calm, ran closely on
> Along the dead calm lake, now here, now there,
> In all its sportive wanderings all the while,
> Making report of an invisible breeze
> That was its wings, its chariot, and its horse,
> Its very playmate, and its moving soul.[10x]

In their mood any suggestions of 'dead calm' and lifelessness were apprehended only as stillnesses, providing a background for the general motion and vitality which more naturally attracted their attention. While they were chatting, they saw a man fishing by the lake and exclaimed that he must be improvident and reckless to spend a day fishing when he could be drawing good pay in the harvest field.

> Thus talking of that Peasant, we approach'd
> Close to the spot where with his rod and line
> He stood alone; whereat he turn'd his head
> To greet us – and we saw a man worn down
> By sickness, gaunt and lean, with sunken cheeks
> And wasted limbs, his legs so long and lean
> That for my single self I look'd at them,
> Forgetful of the body they sustain'd. –
> Too weak to labour in the harvest field,
> The man was using his best skill to gain
> A pittance from the dead unfeeling lake
> That knew not of his wants.

The silent answer to their hasty comments provides the poem with its title and concluding moral: for them the promontory will now always be 'Point Rash-Judgment'. But the appearance of the figure in the narrative has an effect beyond local rebuke. The man himself has opened out a hollow place in the world of life that they have been cheerfully taking for granted. One is reminded of other figures in Wordsworth, such as the woman who said 'That wagon does not care for us'[11] – inhabitants of a negative universe who introduce a discontinuity into the sense of life and joy, victims of a waxing sickness which seems possessed by a silent force of its own. After the man has been seen, the lake, which was previously a reflecting surface for sporting tufts of seed to skim across, is seen as 'the dead unfeeling lake/That knew not of his wants'. And although in every other respect the scene is the same, the mood of the walkers is transformed.

The poem 'Point Rash-Judgment' is unlike all the other 'Poems on the Naming of Places' in not identifying a particular member or members of Wordsworth's 'community of the heart' with a place. This is not, perhaps, accidental. His larger sense of things demanded the introduction of a poem which would give depth to his sense of pathos by a reminder that his community could not expect to exist totally in pleasure, but must include in its communal consciousness an awareness of the intractability – and the impersonality – of suffering.

In summing up the incident, Wordsworth uses a word which carries a strong private charge: all three friends, he says, received the same 'admonishment'. In this context, the word conveys something more than prompt reproof of an over-hasty judgment. The sight of the man has broken in upon their life-centred mood by presenting them with a human exemplar of the death-principle that is always present in the universe: it has reminded them that mortality is not simply an ambiguous darkness or gulf which man faces at the end of his life, but a process which is perceptible around him wherever he looks. When presented suddenly, and vividly, as in the peasant on the shore, a sick man for whom the lake is little more than dead void which may, if he is lucky, provide food to stave off his privations, it can appear as a state which operates with an ungraspable process of its own, a silent blank whirlpool which has neither the peace of silence not the energy of moving water, but into which the living organism is impotently absorbed.

Something of this sense is often present in Wordsworth's use of the word 'admonish'. There is the incident in *The Prelude* where, walking in the streets of London, he came across a blind beggar wearing a label to tell his story:

And, on the shape of the unmoving man,
His fixèd face and sightless eyes, I look'd
As if admonish'd from another world. [12x]

The sick peasant and the blind beggar strike the note of Keats's
Moneta in 'The Fall of Hyperion': each suggests a face that is, like
hers, bleak and wasted by privation. They remind the observer that
the 'pathos' of humanity is, at its most intense, not a subject for
pleasurable art, but very literally a 'suffering', resisting attempts to
make it over to a fashionable audience.

Wordsworth's poetry allows no more than glimpses of this extremity. Just as in Book Six of *The Prelude* he moves swiftly back to
the ordinary world from his description of a snake-like moon on the
waters of Como which had expressed a core of fear in the beautiful
but unorganisable night scene, [13] so he does not linger over images
which suggest a core of intractable suffering in the human face of
pathos. Even in the most sensitive reader, words such as 'monitor'
and 'admonishment' are unlikely to evoke more than an oblique
contraction of the heart before he moves on. It was left to Keats to
present Moneta as a priestess-like presence, and to expose her
significance more fully.

That Wordsworth proceeded no further along this line is perhaps a
sign of the intensity of feeling which the idea always started in him; it
may also suggest that he could see in advance the inevitable logic of
the idea as developed by Keats – that it would make poetry impossible – and therefore foreclosed the discussion. But it should be
recognised that the withdrawal could also be justified for him by the
observation that nature herself, by her own rhythms, was perpetual-
ly mitigating the intensity of such experience.

The point can be made succinctly in terms of one of Wordsworth's
favourite images. The moon can (as at Como) be a compulsive focus
of fear; for the dejected or deprived man, equally, it may stand in the
sky as a blank disk, a starved light that emblematises the world's
indifference to his needs. In either case, it is a nightmare image. But
when it is viewed against larger dimensions of time and space (by
those who can afford such contemplation) another order comes into
play, a waning and waxing which ultimately contains all these
images as phases in a fuller process. The ordinary universe comes to
the rescue of such a meditative observer, by suggesting that if it
cannot resolve man's dilemma about the status of his nightmare

experiences, it can at least take up his impotence into its own merciful rhythms.

At such a point, it will be seen, the cycle of Wordsworth's intellectual universe is rounding itself to reveal the fullness and complexity of its total form. This is not a universe which could be finally mapped, even with a model of three or four dimensions; it is a universe which can ultimately be traced only as a process in the human mind.

The stages of that process may briefly be recapitulated. The original structure of Wordsworth's universe, we saw, was given by the Newtonian order of time and space which had dominated eighteenth-century thinking. In his youth, however, it had been learned about in conjunction with experiences of fear and tenderness in nature which established different emotional poles in his psyche. As the effects of these experiences waned, on the other hand, a strictly intellectual view had prevailed for a time and he had been left with an ineluctable dominating sense of the universe as a dead machine, submitting human creatures to the tyranny of law as they pursued their careers, heedlessly or otherwise, to the gulf of death.

From the nullities of this order, we have further argued, Wordsworth was enabled to release himself partly by Dorothy's immediacy of emotional response and partly by the aid of Coleridge's theory of consciousnesses, whereby the correspondences between phenomena in nature and man's emotions of sublimity and pathos were caught up into a further order in the universe, its central 'infinity' being no longer identified with an endlessness of Newtonian time or space, but seen rather as a self-renewing light-fountain, which corresponded in important respects to the inner nature of man's heart.

The fact that he could not know whether this 'primary' order was ultimately valid or not, however, transposed his view of humanity to a condition of intensified pathos. Even if he accepted the premises, it was still possible to interpret the experiences in question differently. The fear which he had come to see as a key to sublimity might turn out after all to be the outward and visible sign of an ultimate destructive psychic whirlpool; the suffering which revealed the nature of infinity might be not an accidental phenomenon in the universe of life but part of a permanent, blank wasting. Against that sort of nightmare such orders of the visible universe as the waxing and waning of the moon, the ebb and flow of the sea or the remoter motions of the planets were in their full process a happier portent; in them at least the universe of time was revealed not as a dead machine but as a process corresponding in a very straightforward sense to the workings of the heart.

If one remained solely under this restored dispensation, nevertheless, the sense of mercy might well be overtaken again by that of the machine. It was an additional bounty of the visible universe that its most characteristic workings were accompanied by intimations that splendour, not fear, tenderness, not suffering, constituted the ultimate order of nature. Listening to the sea, or contemplating the moon, one might hope to establish one's permanent point of reference in the mediating pattern of ebb and flow in each, while at the same time allowing the hoarse sublimity of the ocean's roar, or the tender fascination of moonlight to contribute intimations – at least – that the ebb and flow was a rhythm harking back to the gentler pulse of the spring and that the light of the moon was evidence of a mildness at the very heart of the sun, both offering true correspondence to the belief of some human beings that their own 'heart of hearts' was not a transient machine but a spring among springs.

This developed view of the universe offered a complex and comprehensive interpretation of Wordsworth's own experience; it also, however, possessed the concomitant disadvantage that it could not easily be rendered into poetry. Unless the reader had followed Wordsworth step by step through the full process, he would continually short-circuit such complex images of the ordinary universe by referring them back to simpler images from his own experience – reducing them, in the process, to banality. In this sense, what Hazlitt said of *Lyrical Ballads* ('Fools have laughed at, wise men scarcely understand, them'[14]) can sometimes be applied to his poetic achievement at large.

For the same reason, some of Wordsworth's most successful poems and passages are those in which he offers a small part or aspect of the total process in terms which the reader can appropriate directly to himself. In reading the following description of evening, for example, the reader who shares Wordsworth's knowledge of the classics and his scientific preoccupations will admire the way in which his post-Miltonic[15] use of the word 'punctual' contrives at once to fix the stars as points in space and suggest their ordered movement in time; and if he has followed Wordsworth's philosophy

further, the word 'admonition' will open a heart-contracting depth
near the end; yet even if he misses the wit of the one and the
profundity of the other the general sense of peace and order will still
be conveyed:

> the punctual stars,
> While all things else are gathering to their homes,
> Advance, and in the firmament of heaven
> Glitter – but undisturbing, undisturbed;
> As if their silent company were charged
> With peaceful admonitions for the heart
> Of all-beholding Man, earth's thoughtful lord. . .

Exc. viii 158–64

When, on the other hand, in a late poem, addressed to the sea,[16] he
writes

> Teach me with quick-eared spirit to rejoice
> In admonitions of thy softest voice!

the hint of the power of the sea to suggest to the human heart that its
expansions in joy and contractions in fear are yet contained by the
larger ebb and flow of its own systole and diastole is likely to escape
all but the most devoted reader. To read here is more like decoding a
shorthand, and the poetry, as poetry, suffers accordingly.

Occasionally in the later work one can actually see the process of
development in action, as Wordsworth modifies an early intensity
which now seems to him extravagant, and sounds the note of
reconciliation and admonition more openly. We have quoted, more
than once, the gnomic lines from *The Borderers*:

> Suffering is permanent, obscure and dark,
> And shares the nature of infinity.

When in 1837 Wordsworth decided to use these lines in an epigraph
for a new edition of *The White Doe of Rylstone*, he altered 'shares' to
'has' and added further lines which explicated his interpretation of
infinity in a more sober form:

> Yet through that darkness (infinite though it seem
> And irremoveable) gracious openings lie,
> By which the soul – with patient steps of thought
> Now toiling, wafted now on wings of prayer –

May pass in hope, and, though from mortal bonds
Yet undelivered, rise with sure ascent
Even to the fountain-head of peace divine.[17]

In such later additions Wordsworth's verse is almost wilfully sober: his concluding image of the fountain-head is projected through a verse which is straightforward to the point of monotony.

If this development is not welcome to the general reader, it is at least partly understandable in terms of Wordsworth's own experience. It bears a correspondence to a further factor in his creative experience – the knowledge that, in spite of his efforts to create a poetry which would contain the whole of his poetic universe, including the note of unpleasurable admonition, there had been times when the actualities of his life numbed the poetic faculty completely. Whereas the idea of death, in the Lucy poems, could sharpen the ambiguity between sublimity and nullity, producing an exciting counterpoint, the experience of real bereavement had sometimes, at the time, taken the wonder out of words altogether. Of the period after the deaths of Catharine and Thomas, he wrote,

> For us the stream of fiction ceased to flow,
> For us the voice of melody was mute.   PW III 282

The loss of these two children in 1812, the worst grief which Wordsworth had ever had to bear, was actually exacerbated, moreover, by his solitary surroundings. The permanences of nature, unrelieved, served only to perpetuate his prostration. Mrs Clarkson commented, perceptively,

> . . . I see in the effects of these losses upon them the evil of living so entirely out of the world. Especially in that country – I remember the effect which it had upon me – Those mountains give a character of permanency to any thing else. . . .[18]

In these months, it seems, Wordsworth's poetic universe failed him almost completely: sights which would normally have given consolation became part of a nightmare blankness.

One source of relief did, however, remain. Just as when the dream of the rock and the shell related in Book Five of *The Prelude* reached its point of nightmare the dreamer woke up into a world of actuality and found it less terrible, so there was a final possible appeal to the world of human affairs, which, going its own way according to man-made rules and well-wadded against metaphysical speculation, might act as a relief against unbearable losses in the world of human love.

These considerations throw light on the most banal act of Wordsworth's life. Early in 1812, he had approached Lord Lonsdale with a request for assistance in gaining financial means under terms which would enable him to continue as a writer. When the Distributorship of Stamps for Westmorland was offered him in December, a few weeks after the death of Thomas, it came as a timely relief. His own preparations to undertake the necessary duties (which also involved occasional tours of the district) helped to stir him from settled grief. His friends were pleased: Crabb Robinson said that he would 'lose those peculiarities of feeling which solitude and discontent engender . . .' and Mrs Clarkson wrote:

> . . . they need the sight of *equals* who are not intimate friends – in whose company they must put some restraint upon themselves and in return they w^d be won from their sadness by hearing of other things – the goings on of life in various ways. . . .[19]

At a human level, their diagnosis was correct: Wordsworth gradually became reconciled to the world again. But they did not realise what was also being sacrificed. Wordsworth was, to all intents and purposes, firmly retreating from the poetic universe which had proved such a stimulus to his poetry during the preceding years.

He did not, of course, cease to be a poet. In certain directions, indeed, he went on to acquire new strengths and new forms of rhetoric. In 'Laodamia' and other classically-based poems, for instance, he was to show how he could assimilate his view of humanity to the classical traditions of stoicism. Elsewhere, he can be seen reaching back to clutch at roots in the 'chaste diction' of late eighteenth-century verse.

What had changed was that he no longer *inhabited* the interpretative world which he had developed during and after his intimacy with Coleridge. During a decade, that universe had been for him rather like a world in a poetic romance, governed by distinctive laws, possessing its own language. The depth of his involvement had enabled Wordsworth to let his own poetry grow and acquire its own distinctive quality. His withdrawal from it was not total, of course. He could always re-enter it briefly (as in the Duddon sonnets) and use its imagery or language for particular purposes. What is missing is rather the sense that he belongs to it, that it is giving a distinctive turn to the rhythms of his poetry and even at times altering the texture of his diction. His firm point of central reference is now the world of actuality around him, and when his former imaginative universe appears it is as from outside. After the griefs of 1812 the course of time brought about a healing: once again the larger processes of nature came to the rescue. The lines quoted earlier continue,

> – But, as soft gales dissolve the dreary snow,
> And give the timid herbage leave to shoot,
> Heaven's breathing influence failed not to bestow
> A timely promise of unlooked-for fruit. . . .
>
> It soothed us – it beguiled us – then, to hear
> Once more of troubles wrought by magic spell;
> And griefs whose aery motion comes not near
> The pangs that tempt the Spirit to rebel. . . .   PW III 282

For all its healing power, however, romance had, we note, resumed its eighteenth-century status as a form of indulgence.

The withdrawal was by no means precipitate or sudden, either. If the estrangement from Coleridge and the deaths of his children finally drove him from his poetic universe, their effects had already been foreshadowed in the events of 1804–5, when the withdrawal of Coleridge to Malta had been followed by the death of John Wordsworth. It was during this period, we saw, that Wordsworth first began to fall back upon his permanent values of duty and affection. The events of 1812–13 were like a landslip which has long been foreshadowed by shifts and cracks. The full process of self-adjustment continued afterwards, moreover – involving, among other things, the very sections into which he arranged his poetic corpus; not until 1845, for example, was 'Goody Blake and Harry Gill' finally shifted from 'Poems of the Imagination' to 'Miscellaneous Poems'. Nor was the course of this long withdrawal without its interruptions. On rare occasions an image which had formerly moved within the context of his larger poetic universe might arise suddenly, and with unusual intensity – particularly to express a sense of loss.

This may be illustrated by a single example. Throughout Wordsworth's work there is a close connection between the image of the bird's nest and the work of the human heart. In itself this is not new. The traditional status of the nest as an emblem of pathos had already been recognised and intensified by poets such as Cowper in the eighteenth century; and the sudden leap of the heart on seeing a cluster of eggs gleaming in a wild and unexpected place is an experience common to all. But for Wordsworth there was a more intimate correspondence: the bird giving 'genial warmth' to the eggs in its nest could be an accurate image for the human heart sustaining the life-principle which it enclosed – heart and life together rebegetting the 'primal consciousness'. So the child Dorothy, approaching the sparrow's nest, 'still wishing, dreading to be near it', could be seen as expressing accurately the range of her early consciousness, her heart's affection opening out into a joy and fear that spoke from the life-force within herself. And Coleridge, in an even more developed use of the image, could promise to Sara Hutchinson that, living in the Wordsworth household, she should feel

> Even what the conjugal & mother Dove
> That borrows genial Warmth from those, she warms,
> Feels in her thrill'd wings, blessedly outspread –   CL II 798

and be so initiated into the full life-consciousness of the universe ('To thee would all Things live from Pole to Pole').

Wordsworth's counter-sense that the primary consciousness might also be a source of danger, particularly when it allowed human instincts to flourish unchecked by any sense of responsibility, extended to this image as well. Of a deserted mother he wrote, in *The Excursion*,

> She had built,
> Her fond maternal heart had built, a nest
> In blindness all too near the river's edge . . .   *Exc.* vi 1018–20

In his later poetry, also, his use of the image becomes more wary and conventional. But when he asks a skylark:

> Or, while the wings aspire, are heart and eye
> Both with thy nest upon the dewy ground?

concluding that it is a type of the wise who remain 'True to the kindred points of Heaven and Home!'[20] one can still trace a ghostly working of the idea; as also, much later, in a conversation with Lady

Richardson's mother,[21] who in 1841 heard him read his epitaph to Southey, which included the lines,

> Wide was his range, but ne'er in human breast
> Did private feeling find a holier nest

and objected that the last two words did not express 'a correct union of ideas'. Wordsworth took the criticism kindly, saying that the phrase had been much debated in his own mind and in his family circle; the phrase was duly changed. The fact that it had come so naturally to his mind, however, is a witness to the stubborn persistence of former trains of thought.

In an earlier poem of loss the reappearance of the image had been more striking. In January 1830 he wrote a poem[22] which stands out from the sequence of 'Miscellaneous Sonnets' by its directness of emotional utterance.

> Why art thou silent! Is thy love a plant
> Of such weak fibre that the treacherous air
> Of absence withers what was once so fair?
> Is there no debt to pay, no boon to grant?
> Yet have my thoughts for thee been vigilant –
> Bound to thy service with unceasing care,
> The mind's least generous wish a mendicant
> For nought but what thy happiness could spare.
> Speak – though this soft warm heart, once free to hold
> A thousand tender pleasures, thine and mine,
> Be left more desolate, more dreary cold
> Than a forsaken bird's-nest filled with snow
> 'Mid its own bush of leafless eglantine –
> Speak, that my torturing doubts their end may know!

Whether some deep stratum of former emotion was tapped in this poem (the memory of an agonising reunion during an adolescent love, possibly?) cannot be known; we can approach the poem only from the direction provided by his own official account. He and Dora had been walking across the vale of Grasmere when she had seen a bird's nest half filled with snow:

> Out of this comfortless appearance arose this Sonnet, which was, in fact, written without the least reference to any individual object, but merely to prove to myself that I could, if I thought fit, write in a strain that poets have been fond of.   PW III 435–6

For the present argument what is important is the fact that this chance sight could open up such a powerful vein of emotional utterance, and that in his later years such intensity is still associated (though now, inevitably, through sense of loss) with an image that traces a link between life and love in the work of the heart.

Poems such as this are a reminder that although, as we have seen, the deadening effects of loss were usually followed by some work of renewing life, there had been, at the deepest level, a further displacement of the emotional poles, making it impossible for the creative identity that had been developed during the years with Coleridge and Dorothy to re-emerge except in a negative mode. He would never again commit himself so fully to a cultivation of feelings, imagination and a sense of the 'one life'; his relationship not only to the human society around him but even to the natural environment itself was correspondingly changed.

The last change was in fact expressed very literally by a growing interest in landscape gardening: it is as if the energies which had struggled in his poetry to create an adequate presentation of the world now found a positive relief in designing alterations of the physical landscape which could affect the observer more simply and palpably. Just as his descriptions at Tintern had transformed the fashionable poetry of the picturesque into a mode more intimately related to the observer's emotions, moreover, his work on the landscape substituted for the 'improvements' on simple aesthetic principles undertaken by men such as Uvedale Price and Richard Payne Knight a work of transformation whereby the visible scene might be made to display a closer correspondence with inward human nature and its needs.

The development of his new attitude can be traced in the course of a friendship which has not so far been mentioned but which was particularly important to him during the crisis of loss in 1805. Two years earlier Coleridge had introduced the Wordsworths to Sir George and Lady Beaumont at Coleorton, in Essex, and during his absence in Malta the relationship had thrived. It has been convincingly argued that his respect for this country gentleman who was also a painter and distinguished amateur of the arts gave Wordsworth a growing sympathy for the landed interest as a force for the preservation of ancient values.[23] The Beaumonts were particularly kind to Wordsworth after the death of John, and such kindness, after many years of hostility from the Lowthers, may well

have brought home to him the possibility of hitherto unacknowledged virtues in a way of life which could, at its best, combine
respect for the land with an ordained courtesy. The old order, like
the mountains of his native countryside, might not always be
comforting, yet its abidingness offered a permanence, at least, to
which he could cling.

As in his poetry, however, he could not rely for long upon a
rock-like solidity without experiencing a revisitation from the
stream of romance. In this case, the relaxation can be traced in the
plan for the Winter Garden which (following the general scheme of
Addison's essay in the *Spectator*24) he planned for Lady Beaumont in
1806.25 The enterprise brought his creative instincts into action.
While giving room for the flowers, birds and insects of summer, its
main purpose involved the more complex requirement that it should
be attractive on days when all signs of visiting life were absent.

The garden was designed as a series of openings along a continuous path. For the first (since there was not a 'living stream bustling
through Rocks', as he would have preferred) Wordsworth proposed
a 'Stone-fountain of simple structure to throw out its stream or even
thread of water'. (He also expressed an 'old-fashioned' liking for *jets
d'eaux*, which, by catching the light, would give flashes of colour to
the scene.) The next, contrasting, compartment would be a glade
unelaborated and simple; the next an unvaried and secluded glade,
completely monotonous except for a central pool which would
contain two goldfish (the whole presenting, presumably, an extreme
contrast between life and stillness; colour and drabness). The fourth
compartment, a disused quarry, would also be made a pool, but one
open to the outer scene: it

> would reflect beautifully the rocks of the scar with their hanging
> plants, the evergreens upon the top, and, shooting deeper than all,
> the naked Spire of the Church.   WL (1806–11) 117

A final glade would contain a waterfall from the roots of a 'Witch
elm'; and the whole garden would be crossed by a laurelled, mossy
alley, 'soothing and not stirring the mind or tempting it out of itself'.
At the end of this alley would be a rising bank of green turf which
'would catch the light and present a cheerful image of sunshine; as it
would always appear to do, whether the sun shone or not'. Off this
long cross-alley, finally, there would be a 'natural Bower, or Parlour'. The garden would also be audibly enlivened, in spring by the

murmur of bees, and in winter by the movements of sheltering birds.

Each of these various artifices, it will be observed, offers a different relief from the world of death. The simple stone-fountain, the pool with its flashes of life; the next pool reflecting the upward thrust of rocks and spire; the sunlight-resembling turf – each quietly introduces a different aspect of the sun-like fountainous infinity of life itself. At each point, therefore, the winter observer would find that the most prominent feature of the scene directed his thoughts away from mortality in time.

It is equally typical of Wordsworth that, having suggested these features, he should have become conscious of the practical difficulties. Taking his cue from Addison, who said that if the makers of parterres and flower-gardens were the 'Epigrammatists and Sonneteers' of gardening, the 'Contrivers of Bowers and Grotto's, Treillages and Cascades' were the equivalent of romance writers, he continued his letter to Lady Beaumont:

> I am sensible that I have written a very pretty Romance in this Letter, and when I look at the ground in its present state and think of what it must continue to be, for some years, I am afraid you will call me an Enthusiast and a Visionary.   p. 119

The Winter Garden was duly laid out, nevertheless, and Wordsworth's mediating romance took physical form.

Wordsworth's interest in landscape was also a prominent feature of his own later life in Grasmere. Indeed it may not be far from the mark to say that he found in Sir George Beaumont himself a partial model for his own persona. Later visitors sometimes commented on his resemblance to a hale country squire, and although his share of the local property was small he became something of an arbiter of taste in the neighbourhood – a rôle which, we might say, mediated there between the doubtful sublimity of his private status as lonely, uncommunicating poet living away from the community and the banality of his involvement in local public affairs as Distributor of Stamps. When he and his family moved to Rydal Mount he not only laid out a terrace for his own composing but raised levels in order to improve the views, introduced a pool for fish, and, most dramatic of all, constructed a summer house which would surprise the visitor at a strategic point. Ellis Yarnall later reported the effect:

The moment we opened the door, the water-fall was before us, the summer house being so placed as to occupy the exact spot from which it was to be seen, the rocks and shrubbery around closing it in on every side. The effect was magical. The view from the rustic house, the rocky basin into which the water fell, and the deep shade in which the whole was enveloped made it a lovely scene.[26]

It was, among other things, a quiet revenge for the sense-dislocating pleasure-house filled with mirrors, which had disturbed him on a visit some years before to Dunkeld.[27] He would not, like the proprietor of that estate, employ machines and mirrors to distort the view and confuse his visitor; instead he would show him an actual scene of harmony – but in circumstances of contrast and surprise which invested it with sublimity. By this very simple device he could, at any time, achieve one of the effects which he had been aiming for all his life in his poetry.

His concern for the landscape was not confined to his own residences: he offered advice to his friends and neighbours on the lay-out of their grounds and helped readily with the planting of new trees and shrubs. He also kept a constant eye for any changes nearby. As an inhabitant of the vale later recalled.

'. . . he 'ud never pass folks draining, or ditching, or walling a cottage, but what he'd stop and say, "Eh dear, but it's a pity to move that stoan, and doant ya think ya might leave that tree?"'[28]

When asked if he could explain why this should have been so, the same man replied, memorably,

'He couldn't abear to see faäce o' things altered, ya kna.'

Despite its striking appositeness, however, this remark gives only half the truth. It applies to the side of Wordsworth which felt for the permanence of things, but not to the side which felt that the landscape could also be enhanced. His improving art extended even to chimneys. Another local resident, a mason, later said,

'. . . heéd a great fancy an' aw for chimleys square up hauf way, and round the t'other. And so we built 'em that how.'[29]

Canon Rawnsley, who recorded this, quotes relevantly from Wordsworth's own *Guide to the Lakes*:

Others are of a quadrangular shape . . . which low square is often surmounted by a tall cylinder, giving to the cottage chimney the most beautiful shape in which it is ever seen. Nor will it be too fanciful or refined to remark, that there is a pleasing harmony between a tall chimney of this circular form, and the living column of smoke, ascending from it through the still air.[30]

Wordsworth's aim in his advice and campaigning was not simply to conserve the *status quo*. He was equally anxious that those parts of nature which were open to human influence should be shaped to encourage a sense of peace and affection. It was important to him that the scenery of the vale should, by the harmonious arrangement of trees, shrubs and rocks, give a sense of quietness to the eye which might be reflected in the depths of the observer's being, and that even the chimneys, by the way in which they conveyed smoke from cottage fireplaces, should suggest the issue of a silent stream from the cell of every human heart. In a landscape dominated by large appearances of nature which could start a sense of wonder or give comfort by their permanence – but also, in other moods, terrify by violence or admonish by bleakness – the more immediate scenery would thus continue to remind the observer of less spectacular but more reliable mercies of the universe and direct his attention to the still centre at which all human beings could, according to Wordsworth, find a common point of peace and agreement.

9

The Long Perspectives

Wordsworth's devotion to landscape improvement was undertaken then not, like that of many of his contemporaries, as assistance to human complacency and self-assertion, but rather as a work of rescue and consolation. Against the doctrine that life in the midst of nature must be pleasant (a doctrine of the sentimentalists which would later thrive on a misreading of his own work) he, like Shakespeare, knew that such a life in its purest form must be that of 'unaccommodated man', exposed to the alien and uncaring processes of the universe at large; no response to the landscape which failed to acknowledge the fact could be adequate.

It was precisely this sense that had oppressed him on his walk across Salisbury Plain in 1793, and which he had tried to embody in his poem set in that place, a poem, it will be recalled, largely devoted to the dialogue between a traveller and a vagrant woman as they walked across the Plain all night. The woman's tale of her distress concluded at dawn with the words:

> And now across this waste my steps I bend
> Oh! tell me whither for no earthly friend
> Have I   no house in prospect but the tomb.[1]

The poet then left them with the words,

> Adieu ye friendless hope-forsaken pair
> Yet friendless ere ye take your several road
> Enter that lowly cot and ye shall share
> Comforts by prouder mansions unbestowed
> For you yon milkmaid bears her brimming load
> For you the board is piled with homely bread
> And think that life is like this desert broad

Where all the happiest find is but a shed
And a green spot mid wastes interminably spread.[2]

and moved into a concluding diatribe against contemporary wrongs
and injustices.

The vision set forth in that conclusion never left Wordsworth.
However much they might disguise the fact by retreating into large
cities and setting up warm self-protective cells, the ultimate condition of every human being, lost sight of at their peril, was to be 'a
traveller between life and death', carrying out a journey against the
background of a great cosmic machine which had little regard for
human wants. Against such a setting the Coleridgean notion of the
'one life' was of consolatory power: it helped, among other things,
to explain the bonds which could be seen to exist between all
members of the living creation and impulses of charity such as those
which led cottage-dwellers to relieve the wants of those who passed
by them on the road; in the end, however, his own vision stressed the
emblematic status of the road itself and of the lonely travellers who
passed along it. That status in turn emphasised the pathos, yet
strange impressiveness, of actual human beings when seen moving
in isolation against a great landscape.

Normal human life was not always in so desperate a case, of
course. Within a recognition of that basic condition, there was room
for frequent pleasure and delight in nature. Another of
Wordsworth's favourite images was of a country festivity taking
place against a background of large natural forms. In *The Excursion*
the narrator and the wanderer, walking along under the shadow of a
mountain, cast a casual glance across the valley and see

> a throng of people; – wherefore met?
> Blithe notes of music, suddenly let loose
> On the thrilled ear, and flags uprising, yield
> Prompt answer; they proclaim the annual Wake,
> Which the bright season favours.   *Exc.* ii 117–21

In *The Prelude*, the distancing is more dramatic still, beginning with
the opening of the eighth book:

> What sounds are those, Helvellyn, which are heard
> Up to thy summit? Through the depth of air
> Ascending, as if distance had the power
> To make the sounds more audible: what Crowd

Is yon, assembled in the gay green Field?
Crowd seems it, solitary Hill! to thee,
Though but a little Family of Men,
Twice twenty, with their Children and their Wives,
And here and there a Stranger interspers'd.
It is a summer festival, a Fair,
Such as, on this side now, and now on that,
Repeated through his tributary Vales,
Helvellyn, in the silence of his rest,
Sees annually, if storms be not abroad,
And mists have left him an unshrouded head.

By personifying Helvellyn (a device authorised by the inhabitants' own habit of ascribing different personalities to the mountains around them) Wordsworth humanises his scene: although distanced, the fair is not allowed to dwindle into insignificance. Instead, the mountain's presence gives proportion to the human activities; the scene is in marked contrast to the formless panorama of London which, looked at from detachment, had seemed to draw in and expel human beings from its various component parts as if in aid of some impersonal and mechanical process.[3]

The book which opens with the fair under Helvellyn is devoted to 'love of Nature leading to love of Man'; subsequent passages include memories of occasions when, under particular accidents of light and cloud, man had been seen not as puny but as splendid. Once, in childhood, on a day of mists and gleams of sunshine, he had walked along a 'narrow Valley and profound':

        . . . when, aloft above my head,
Emerging from the silvery vapours, lo!
A Shepherd and his Dog! in open day:
Girt round with mists they stood and look'd about
From that enclosure small, inhabitants
Of an aerial Island floating on,
As seem'd, with that Abode in which they were,
A little pendant area of grey rocks,
By the soft wind breath'd forward.   1805 viii 93–101

On a similar occasion in childhood he had first seen a shepherd teaching his dog to herd sheep

Through rocks and seams of turf with liquid gold
Irradiate, that deep farewell light by which

The setting sun proclaims the love he bears
To mountain regions.   1805 viii 116–9

In the more ecstatic moments of childhood and youth, at least, the seashore had intimated no threat and the distant rock-faces sometimes shone as if with their own inward light. If a child picked up a sea-shell then and held it to his ear he heard, not an 'Ode, in passion utter'd, which foretold/Destruction to the Children of the Earth',[4] but a delightful and mysterious harmony, expressing 'mysterious union with its native sea' and imparting

> Authentic tidings of invisible things;
> Of ebb and flow, and ever-during power;
> And central peace, subsisting at the heart
> Of endless agitation.   *Exc.* iv 1144

Yet even here a wisp of warning hovers. The word 'tidings' brilliantly reinforces its sense of good news with suggestion of the authoritative, tidal movement of the sea itself; previously, however, Wordsworth has described the shell as a 'monitor' – which, coming from him, can hardly be accidental. Is he perhaps denoting an initial moment of admonishment – suggesting, even, that before the child actually lifted the shell to his ear he had caught in the uncompromising cold fixity of its beautiful shape some intimation of his own mortality? Or that the audible note itself, before its rhythm was fully caught, had seemed alien?

Other experiences brought even more subtle undertones of warning, making nature's permanence a trouble to the mortal consciousness of the child. Even the glimpses of glory were by no means absolute. An episode in *The Prelude* indicates this with telling understatement: Wordsworth recalls how from his house on summer afternoons in childhood, a 'sparkling patch of diamond light' could be seen in a nearby wood, probably the reflection of a wet rock caught by the rays of the sun. He would visualise it sometimes as a burnished shield over the tomb of a knight buried in the wood, sometimes as a magic cave or palace –

> Nor would I, though not certain whence the cause
> Of the effulgence, thither have repair'd
> Without a precious bribe, and day by day
> And month by month I saw the spectacle,
> Nor ever once have visited the spot
> Unto this hour.   1805 viii 578–83

Although the view might be a source of wonder, he knew already (if only from eighteenth-century platitude) that that enchantment was 'lent' to it by distance and would be likely to disappear at close quarters. His canny avoidance of such disenchantment indicates a strong underlying sense of actuality; it also predicts the terms by which he would analyse his youthful optimism after the French Revolution:

> I had approach'd, like other Youth, the Shield
> Of human nature from the golden side
> And would have fought, even to the death, to attest
> The quality of the metal which I saw.   1805 x 662–5

Distance in time was in some ways a similar phenomenon. Under favourable conditions, some approach to the past was not impossible; but too 'actual' an attempt to regain it would merely confirm its inaccessibility to direct assault:

> . . . the hiding-places of my power
> Seem open; I approach, and then they close . . .   1805 xi 336–7

When memory of emotional experience did visit him in its own time, on the other hand, it brought with it a complete revival of the former sense. If its operation was not always to be won at will – it was a 'shy spirit'⁵ which visited only when it chose – its starting into the consciousness brought a pleasure which was correspondingly unassailable.

Christopher Salveson has discussed and demonstrated at length the importance of memory for Wordsworth,⁶ and there is no need for so full an account here. In the context of the present study, however, memory acquires a further significance: in its workings the existence of a force in the mind separate from that which observes, analyses and judges can most convincingly be traced. It was this phenomenon which was the most difficult to explain by the associationism of Hartley: if thought were merely vibration (as Hartley supposed) it was hard to understand how the little 'vibratiuncles' which were supposedly left in the system and revived in the act of remembering could so function without a continuous 'stream' to contain them. How, otherwise, could one account for the fact that memory acted so spontaneously – sometimes, even, like a gushing spring?

It was for this reason, perhaps, that when Wordsworth came to write his own poetic epic of the memory he found it rewarding to associate it closely with his friendship for Coleridge. (Throughout his lifetime, the poem bore on its title page the words 'Poem/Title not yet fixed upon/by/William Wordsworth/Addressed to/S. T. Coleridge'.7) Any doubt of the value of what he was writing, any sense of presumption at devoting so much poetic labour to the events of his own life, could be diminished both by the traditional acceptability of the 'address to a friend' as a form for intimate and informal discussion and (to his own mind at least) by recalling Coleridge's insistence on the significance of memory as a witness to the active power in all human knowledge.

It is in the second book that Wordsworth acknowledges his debt most openly. Having written, concerning the vividness of his earlier memories,

> . . . sometimes when I think of them I seem
> Two consciousnesses, conscious of myself
> And of some other being . . .   1799 ii 29–31

he goes on to use the fountain-image itself:

> Who knows the individual hour in which
> His habits were first sown, even as a seed
> Who that shall point as with a wand and say,
> This portion of the river of my mind
> Came from yon fountain?   1799 ii 245–9

and it is significant that this passage, with its suggestion of magic in 'wand', is immediately followed by reference to Coleridge himself as an intelligence who has come close to performing the miracle by his ability to distinguish between what is primary and what is secondary in the mind:

> Thou, my Friend! art one
> More deeply read in thy own thoughts; to thee
> Science appears but, what in truth she is,
> Not as our glory and our absolute boast,
> But as a succedaneum, and a prop
> To our infirmity. Thou art no slave
> Of that false secondary power, by which,
> In weakness, we create distinctions, then
> Deem that our puny boundaries are things

Which we perceive, and not which we have made.
To thee, unblinded by these outward shows,
The unity of all has been reveal'd . . .   1805 ii 215–26

Later in the poem the fountain/pool image recurs when he describes the involuntary action of his heart at the moment of dawn dedication:

Ah! need I say, dear Friend, that to the brim
My heart was full. . . .   1805 iv 340–1

When he describes the actual progress of the poem on the other hand, his imagery is more often that of a stream or river. Its opening, in retrospect, had been 'like a torrent sent/Out of the bowels of a bursting cloud/Down Scawfell';[8x] the later writing has been 'a less impetuous stream' which re-emerged 'last primrose-time'. In the opening lines of Book Nine the river-image is given full rein:

As oftentimes a River, it might seem,
Yielding in part to old remembrances,
Part sway'd by fear to tread an onward road
That leads direct to the devouring sea
Turns, and will measure back his course, far back,
Towards the very regions which he cross'd
In his first outset; so have we long time
Made motions retrograde, in like pursuit
Detain'd.

Wordsworth's preference for images which evoke an awareness of space and time, as compared with Coleridge's fondness for an imagery of ebullience, can be traced even in the famous phrase which Wordsworth uses for the benevolent work of memory: 'spots of time'. Both poets were fond of the term 'spot': Coleridge wrote of the 'repose' given by laudanum as 'A spot of inchantment, a green spot of fountains, & flowers & trees, in the very heart of a waste of Sands'.[9] A description in Bartram's *Travels* of an 'inchanting little Isle of Palms' in the midst of a lake as a 'blessed unviolated spot of earth!' and as an 'enchanting spot'[10] probably inspired both that passage and the note quoted earlier, envisioning a 'wilderness-plot, green and fountainous'.[11] But where Coleridge focuses upon the nature of the spot itself, Wordsworth's references usually seem to

contain reference to it as subsisting in a larger spatial context. The
opening of *Descriptive Sketches*:

> Were there, below, a spot of holy ground,
> By Pain and her sad family unfound . . .[12]

continued, it will be remembered, by suggesting that if such a place
might be found it would be in a large mountainous landscape; while
the consolation of human charity in the passage from 'Salisbury
Plain' was imaged as 'a green spot mid wastes interminably spread'.
     There are other uses for the imagery. Once, indeed, in the
Wanderer's speech in *The Excursion* about the 'active principle', it is
momentarily abolished: the 'Soul of all the worlds' that circulates
'from link to link' is described as a 'Spirit that knows no insulated
spot,/No chasm, no solitude'.[13] Elsewhere, the vision of a variegated
scene of human life expresses itself naturally in a number of interpenetrating variations, whether it is the lake pictured in 'Ruth',

> With all its fairy crowds
> Of islands that together lie
> As quietly as spots of sky
> Among the evening clouds.[14]

or the opening scene of *The Excursion*, exhibiting a landscape containing

> A surface dappled o'er with shadows flung
> From brooding clouds; shadows that lay in spots
> Determined and unmoved . . .   *Exc.* i 5–7

In *The Prelude*, where the early sense of refreshment amid waste is
stressed again, it is also transferred back into time. In Book Nine we
read of

>   each bright spot
>   That could be found in all recorded time,
>   Of truth preserv'd and error pass'd away.   1805 ix 373–5

The following book sees the sense encapsulated still further, in the
lines

>   And as the desart hath green spots, the sea
>   Small islands in the midst of stormy waves,
>   So that disastrous period did not want
>   Such sprinklings of all human excellence. . . .   1805 x 440–3

The phrase 'spots of time', which occurs two books later, finally telescopes it into an almost abstract formula which spatialises time, inviting us to see it spread out as a continuous plane, and to see the spots (if we visualise them at all) either as oases of greenery in an endless waste or as sunlit points picked out by stray sunbeams in a grey landscape on a cloudy day.

It is a matter of emphasis, not of distinction, however, for as soon as the formula has been stated the 'spot' is made fountainous, as it were, by reference to its powers of life-giving renewal:

> There are in our existence spots of time
> Which with distinct pre-eminence retain
> A vivifying Virtue, whence . . .
>   our minds
> Are nourish'd and invisibly repair'd,
> A virtue by which pleasure is enhanced
> That penetrates, enables us to mount
> When high, more high, and lifts us up when fallen.
>
> 1805 xi 258–60; 264–8

'Vivifying virtue' makes one think of a healing spring in romance; in a later poem[15] Wordsworth speaks of 'heart-moving words', 'words that can soothe, more than they agitate' –

> Whose spirit, like the angel that went down
> Into Bethesda's pool, with healing virtue
> Informs the fountain in the human breast
> Which by the visitation was disturbed.

It was the need to express this 'disturbing presence' as an essential element in his vision yet also to keep it at a distance which in fact made the large stream a particularly apposite symbol for Wordsworth: while it invoked a sense of the sea to which it was flowing and the spring from which it came (as with the waters of the Wye 'rolling from their Mountain springs/With a soft inland murmur') the river could more immediately be perceived as an extended phenomenon in space and time, stately and controlled in its progress, moving in time with a regularity like that of the stars themselves. And this image could be retained in the mind as a permanent consolation, for it reconciled itself immediately with the unconscious, hardly-perceived work of the bloodstream in the body.

A striking example of the more peaceful use occurs in the sonnet

'Composed upon Westminster Bridge', which opens with a picture
of London in the early morning and concludes with the reflection,

> Never did sun more beautifully steep
> In his first splendor valley, rock, or hill;
> Ne'er saw I, never felt, a calm so deep!
> The river glideth at his own sweet will:
> Dear God! the very houses seem asleep;
> And all that mighty heart is lying still!   1807 I 118

The idea of London as a 'mighty heart' has been enrolled too firmly
among the clichés of journalism to be easily extricated, and the
metaphors of houses 'asleep' and a river moving 'at his own sweet
will' offer themselves for dismissal as examples of pathetic fallacy.
Yet, examined in Wordsworthian terms, the language turns out to
have unexpected preciseness.

David Ferry has pointed out that the last lines suggest a city in
death;[16] that suggestion is not necessarily sinister or pessimistic if we
once see that the *total* image is of a city lying still and a stream moving
in peace. For the bodily state to which it would correspond is that of
arrested heartbeat accompanied by sense of an ongoing peaceful flow
– in other words, the experience of trance. If death, also, proved to
be like that, it would be a peaceful and even pleasant form of
immortality. The covert, consoling suggestion is reinforced by
other visionary intimations – notably the rising of the dayspring of
light, 'steeping' the whole scene (as the moonlight 'steeped in
silentness the steady weathercock' in 'The Ancient Mariner'). For a
moment the scene emblematises the idea of a stream that has always
run, unobtrusively, during life and might continue to flow even
when the visible signs of life are arrested.

It is impossible, obviously, for Wordsworth to know whether or
not the physical experience of trance will be thus finally consummated in the experience of death: it can be no more than an
intimation, and he ends it, as he did the first version of 'A slumber
did my spirit seal . . .', simply with an exclamation mark. As in that
poem, however, the very evocation of the trance-state relieves the
blankness of a mechanical universe, carrying human lives along in its
inexorable process, by setting the imagery of death in an alternative
context which recalls the 'active principle' in all life.

A similar relief is suggested elsewhere. In 'The Reverie of Poor
Susan', the illusion that 'a river flows on through the vale of

Cheapside' was a temporary comfort to her against the mechanical life of the city; in *The Prelude* he described his own pleasure when a sudden halt at the height of skating was succeeded not by a confused and whirling sense of the surrounding landscape but by the peaceful movement which his senses immediately began to impose:

> . . . still the solitary cliffs
> Wheeled by me, even as if the earth had rolled
> With visible motion her diurnal round. . .   1799 i 180–2

The involuntary action of the senses at such a moment simultaneously gives actuality to a process which in the Newtonian universe is always going on, and endows it with sublimity.

The sense of that underlying patient movement, surviving all vicissitudes of human life and civilisation, is in Wordsworth's eyes the most basic mercy of all. To this extent he can be seen at the end of a path which had begun in the seventeenth century with Hobbes's excitement at the idea that motion was a key to the nature of all phenomena. What was for Hobbes, living in a world which had been jolted from its Ptolemaic stability, a liberating idea, is rather for Wordsworth, buffeted by the contradictions of that same universe, a basic and kindly resource for the baffled consciousness to rest upon.

The idea was so important to him that it could sometimes lead him near absurdity. In the poem 'Gipsies', the sight of a crowd of gipsies who had not moved during the twelve hours since he last saw them provoked the stern reproof:

> The silent Heavens have goings on;
> The stars have tasks – but these have none.[17]

Coleridge, who shared the sense that the perceived motion of the heavenly bodies might relieve a tortured consciousness (as in 'The Ancient Mariner'), could not follow him as far as this: criticising the poem, he wrote of the various legitimate causes which might have forced a group of people to stay in the same place for twelve hours;[18x] but Wordsworth, it seems, had been too carried away by the overtones of his own image to admit unfairness. In later versions he altered the ending to suggest that society was to blame for the gipsies' torpor – but this hardly makes the point of the poem clearer unless one grasps why Wordsworth feels the benefits of movement so strongly in the first place.

The fact that Wordsworth's intentness upon larger concerns sometimes distracts him from considerations that would strike the ordinary observer as obvious is perhaps responsible for some of the common criticisms levelled against him. And while the justification for some criticisms falls away when the poetry is seen in its full process, grounds for disquiet may still be acknowledged. Is it indeed not true that Wordsworth's apparent preference for peaceful motion marks a serious limitation of his range as a poet? May there not be, for that matter, something basically lacking in a poetry written not from immediate inspiration but from the recreation and taming of earlier emotions? Blake's polemic against making Memory mother of the Muses comes disquietingly to mind,[19] and one is led on to ask whether there may not be an important limitation in Wordsworth connected with a rejection, or even fear, of immediate passion.

The question may most profitably be asked and answered, perhaps, in terms of passion between the sexes. In recent years the image of Wordsworth as arch-puritan and enemy of sexual pleasures has been successfully undermined. F. W. Bateson, for example, has drawn attention to his discussion of the celibacy of the clergy:

> If we would truly spiritualize men, we must take care that we do not begin by unhumanising them, which is the process in respect to all those who are now brought up with a view to the making of that unnatural vow.[20]

And F. R. Leavis draws attention to the letter to John Wilson in which he writes, of the various limiting bents and prepossessions that disqualify different readers, 'some cannot tolerate a poem with a ghost or any supernatural agency in it; others would shrink from an animated description of the pleasures of love, as from a thing carnal and libidinous . . .'[21] and the letter of 1816 'to a Friend of Robert Burns', in which he says, 'The poet, trusting to primary instincts, luxuriates among the felicities of love and wine . . . nor does he shrink from the company of the passion of love though immoderate'.[22] On the other hand, we cannot ignore the anecdote recorded in 1824 by Benjamin Robert Haydon:

> Once I was walking with Wordsworth in Pall Mall; & we ran in to Christie's, where there was a very good copy of the Transfiguration, which he abused through thick & thin. In the corner stood the group of Cupid & Psyche kissing. After looking some time, he turned round to me with an expression I shall never forget, and said, *'The Dev-ils!*'[23]

The difference may be partly explained by a growing puritanism over the years; Wordsworth, however, is rarely guilty of total self-contradiction in his attitudes, even over a long period. His attitude to passion, like many of his other attitudes, is better examined as a developing process with an inner consistency of its own.

His poetry of 1798–9 is particularly relevant here. Earlier in this study some of the Lucy poems were examined in terms of the questions raised by the idea of a young girl dying in the midst of a nature that had hitherto nurtured her. Other poems of the group, however, have roots in a slightly different context: Wordsworth's meditations, during his winter in Germany, upon the passionate experiences of his own youth. Early versions of 'She dwelt among the untrodden ways' and 'Strange fits of passion' were sent to Coleridge in a letter[24] which also contained three passages describing moments of passionate experiences in boyhood (skating, the stolen boat, nutting), two of which eventually found a place in *The Prelude*.[25] The two Lucy poems are more elegiac in quality, but a similar note of passion may be traced in them also, a note which reveals itself primarily in vividness of image and metaphor. The girl was compared to a flower by a river or (like Burns's sweetheart) to a rose in June; one of her lover's fits of passion took the form of a hypnotic experience under the moon. The state that is being recalled, in fact, is itself, in retrospect, rather like that of a luminous body in a black sky: it suggests the power of love to endow its possessor with an emotion that is itself quiet, vivid and isolated.

The other passages in the letter, later to be used in *The Prelude*, differ only in the fact that the contrast with passionate activity is focused not in a death but in the order of nature beyond man's intervention. In the skating episode, the energised movement on the ice is matched by a sense of the quietness of the landscape beyond; in the episode of the stolen boat, the passionate strokes of the rowing boy are overtaken by the silent stride of the mountains; and in the nutting episode the contrast is so striking that Wordsworth cannot be sure that he is not 'confounding his present being with his past' when he recalls that

> Even then, when from the bower I turned away,
> Exulting, rich beyond the wealth of kings –
> I felt a sense of pain when I beheld
> The silent trees and the intruding sky.... WL (1787–1805) 242

The note of veiled puritanism throughout this episode is reinforced by echoes of Milton's *Comus*. In her speech of reproof, the
Lady paints the picture of 'swinish gluttony' which

> Ne'er looks to Heaven amidst his gorgeous feast,
> But with besotted base ingratitude
> Crams, and blasphemes his Feeder.   ll. 777–9

In 'Nutting' Wordsworth has taken the issues a stage further by
making a woodland glade like that where Milton's Lady was tempted the actual object of his rape. The youth (as David Ferry points
out[26]) approaches as a knowing voluptary, delaying his pleasure, and
then falling to with violence and 'merciless ravage'. Meanwhile,

>   the shady nook
> Of hazles, and the green and mossy bower,
> Deformed and sullied, patiently gave up
> Their quiet spirit.

This boy 'blasphemes the feeder' in an even more literal sense than
Comus, for he eats his fill and destroys the glade's harmony without
once coming anywhere near appreciating its 'spirit', its existence in
another dimension of peace and organic growth. One need not recall
Comus to find overtones of sexuality in the episode, moreover: the
suggestion of a lusty and violent youth ravishing a quiet and patient
girl who never responds but simply feels herself 'deformed and
sullied' by the event is clearly there in Wordsworth's own language.

In one of her earliest references to her brother Dorothy spoke of 'a
sort of violence of Affection' in him;[27] in his more mature poetry,
however, this tension between violence and affection more often
falls into sequential form: the rendering of a moment of passion is
followed by a check, a sense of loss or admonition, which transposes
the poem into a different key. The openings of the Immortality Ode
and of 'Resolution and Independence' are good examples. Capti-
vated by the rhythmic power which Wordsworth exhibits on such
occasions, the reader may well be disappointed that it is so quickly
thwarted; yet for Wordsworth himself the check is essential. It
results not so much from a wish to deny the power of his emotion as
from a concern to find images which will reconcile what he has
experienced in the moment of passion with his equally powerful
sense of nature's ultra-human order. Images such as that of the star
across which he skates or the flower to which he compares a loved

girl fulfil this aim for him by exhibiting the isolated vividness which characterises his moments of passion but also setting it in a totally benevolent form, exempt from danger of madness or violence.

Although Wordsworth puts his final trust in these reconciling images, however, it remains true that they could not have been seen as such in the first place had it not been for his earlier experiences in nature. Some wildness, some exercise of passion was necessary if the human being was to grow, through interplay of opposites, into a wiser consciousness. This is recognised as late as the Duddon sonnets. Among these there is a curious poem, presented as a legend about a girl looking into a pool and seeing a primrose reflected from a steep rock above as a 'starry treasure from the blue profound'.[28] (The bright spectre of a Coleridgean idea walks in his description of the primrose: 'that Rose, which from the prime/Derives its name, reflected as the chime/Of echo doth reverberate some sweet sound'.) The relationship between star and flower in the Lucy poems, commented on earlier, is revived in this emblem, and the poem is followed by another, 'Sheep-washing', which describes the shoutings and clamour of shepherds as they wash their sheep in the river, concluding

> . . . nor need *we* blame the licensed joys,
> Though false to Nature's quiet equipoise:
> Frank are the sports, the stains are fugitive.   xxiii, 12–14

The moral implication is fairly obvious: exercise of pure animal spirits in a natural setting is not necessarily reprehensible. In an earlier manuscript the next poem begins by celebrating the energy of the butterfly with a similar indulgence.

> The lightsome vigour sprung from heavenly seed
> That loves the intensest heat the Sun bestows
> Yon butterfly may boast and scorn repose
> Of which we men who tread the earth have need. . . .[29]

In the butterfly, the exercise of natural energy is almost etherealised. Young men are more earth-bound, more at risk, yet in their case too the indulgence of animal spirits, even in a crude form, is seen as beneficial, so long as it is contained within certain bounds of expression.

Milton's own puritanism had not been altogether different. He had represented Adam and Eve before the Fall as enjoying the sensuous delights of marriage, and had seen the difference after the Fall not in the introduction of the sexual act, or of its accompanying pleasure, but in the *kind* of pleasure that was now enjoyed. The effect of the fruit was to inflame 'carnal desire':

> hee on *Eve*
> Began to cast lascivious Eyes, she him
> As wantonly repaid; in Lust they burn.   PL ix 1013-5

Blake felt Milton had been mistaken in making such a distinction, and said so;[30] in our own post-puritan society it has become incomprehensible to many readers.[31x] In the seventeenth century, on the other hand, it offered a considerable modification of sterner traditions. Wordsworth believed, with Milton, that there was a point at which sexual passion ceased to be humanising and turned into destructive lust – which may explain why he was so vehement about the Cupid and Psyche statuary. On the other hand, he was willing to relax his attitude still further than Milton had done, to a point where it could include the bawdy of Chaucer and Burns. Such a position could be justified on the ground that both Milton and Burns (though at opposite extremes) had stood for a sexuality of the heart. Wordsworth was attracted by such a concept: for him, too, a passion which was mediated through the heart was automatically humanised: it was *heartless* passion, self-originating and self-sustaining, that was truly devilish.

The preoccupation is particularly evident in his attitudes to previous literature. If it authorised a delight in the work of Chaucer and Burns it found its chief point of reference in the writings of Shakespeare and Milton, poets who, for all their differences, had each seen deeply and sympathetically into the human heart. It gave him a particular delight in the George Herbert of poems such as 'Love bade me welcome . . .' or the Sidney of the sonnet that ends '"Fool!" said my Muse, to me, "look in thy heart, and write."' The original setting of the phrase 'humorous stage', similarly, which he quoted in the Immortality Ode to describe the imitative power of the child, is a poem by Samuel Daniel:

> I doe not here upon this hum'rous Stage,
> Bring my transformed Verse, apparelled
> With others passions, or with others rage;
> With loves, with wounds, with factions furnished:

But here present thee, onely modelled
In this poore frame, the forme of mine owne heart. . . .[32]

Against such an honourable tradition the continuing creation of a
'poetry of the heart' might seem to present few problems. The true
difficulties, however, sprang not from his attempts to portray in
simple fashion the workings of the 'one human heart' but from his
more comprehensive attempts to relate the operations of the heart to
those of mind and body. His discussions with Coleridge had encouraged the production of a view of human nature which would show
its instinctive workings to be both justified and harmonised when
allowed to flourish within an ordained commitment of the heart
itself.

Many twentieth-century moralists would, no doubt, disagree,
arguing that to place so much stress upon the heart, whether
literally or metaphorically, while ignoring the claims of other passions (particularly of course the sexual) to exist in their own right, is
to introduce a hurtful imbalance into the organisation of behaviour.
And the justice of such a view receives some support from the
apparent effects of this attitude upon the members of Wordsworth's
own circle. Although Coleridge was ready to give a more important
place to the workings of the sexual instincts, it seems likely that the
close connection set up by both poets between the life of the passions
and the workings of the heart was checked by an unwarrantable fear
of certain manifestations of instinct – which in turn set a corresponding strain on other areas of their emotional life. The dangerously
intense workings of emotion which characterised both William and
Dorothy Wordsworth from their earliest years have already been
commented upon.

One cannot say this, however, without observing how far the
pendulum has swung in the opposite direction during the present
century. Contemporary literature has become so preoccupied with
more violent aspects of the instinctive life of man that references to
the workings of the heart are now normally treated exclusively as
metaphor. Wordsworth's bias is towards actualising them as far as
possible. Just as a twentieth-century poet may find himself drawn to
interpret the less rational aspects of his contemporary society by
studying the behaviour of his own phallus – its pistol poise, its snaky
lapse, its cocky jubilance, its semi-alien ebullience – so Wordsworth
tried to throw light on the nature of human relationship in his time

by paying attention to the workings of his own heart as he observed them. The results of that study are apparent in the almost incredible number and variety of references to it in his poetry. We have already drawn attention to images which liken its state to that of a fountain, lake or sea, and to verbs, such as 'draws', 'fastens' and 'is attached', which suggest the imagery of magnetisation. Elsewhere, at one point or another, the heart works, plays, leaps, bounds and whispers.[33] It sickens, trembles, dies – and recovers, is stung, pressed upon, wasting or plagued.[34] It shrinks with sadness or dilates with joy; it kindles, pants, is fiery, shines and runs wild.[35] Sensations sweet are 'felt in the blood and felt along the heart'; the fever of the world hangs 'upon its beatings'; when Peter Bell hears the ass bray, joy 'knocks at' it.[36] In what is perhaps the most characteristic refinement of his image Wordsworth speaks here and there of an emotion – or person – being, simply, 'at' someone's heart.[37] And all this in addition to the more conventional ranges of imagery associated with freezing, melting, lightness, heaviness, dancing, fluttering, heaving and breaking, where Wordsworth's obsession breathes new life into old clichés. Even when full allowance has been made for literary reminiscence and metaphorical usage one is left with an extraordinarily high literal content. Wordsworth clearly believed, from intent observation of his own heart, that it was – in physical actuality as well as in traditional metaphor – the true centre of emotional life.

If this were so, however, a certain degree of indulgence – and even delight – in human weakness was sometimes authorised. That the Farmer of Lothbury Vale did all that he did 'in the *ease* of his heart' was a strong point in his favour. One of Wordsworth's less characteristic poems, 'The Two Thieves', is about a very old man and a three year old child who live in a village and spend their time stealing small things such as wood and turf. While careful to point out that everything is repaid by the old man's daughter, Wordsworth displays an inordinate delight in their behaviour – licensed evidently by his sense of its ultimate innocence. For the child is not old enough to be responsible, and the old man acts purely from the restricted potencies of age:

> He once had a heart which was moved by the wires
> Of manifold pleasures and many desires . . .   PW IV 246

As a result, the single passion of cupidity has now taken over and is exhibited (rather like a vice in some medieval woodcut) with un-canny clarity. What he reveals has a value of its own, therefore:

Long yet may'st thou live! for a teacher we see
That lifts up the veil of our nature in thee.

To see him now is to see in harmless form one of the passions which are normally, in a good man, harmonised by the heart, and so to learn more of the heart's importance as an ultimate centre of con-cord. Besides being a subdued spring, pulsing in the steady flow of the bloodstream, mediating between the aridity of the analysing mind and the chaos of unchecked passion, moreover, the heart plays an invaluable part in ennobling human experience: Wordsworth not only recognises a 'grandeur' in its beatings but declares that it 'magnifies this life'.[38] These observations, coupled with his belief that humanity may be evolving towards the developed heart-culture of a 'milder day' to come, stand behind his characteristic note of 'manly cheer'. When oppressed by the desert of the world he can draw strength from oases of behaviour which remind him of the heart's apparently limitless resources.

Later in the century, such cheerfulness would have been less easy. By then the compelling idea of 'survival of the fittest' had under-mined the Romantic idea that humanity might be automatically evolving to a state of universal love. Instead, the inexorability of the natural order, now seen as working through laws of heredity as well, had resumed sway as an oppressive presence. Thomas Hardy, in fact, was to produce a darker version of the Wordsworthian uni-verse, constructing a whole art around the belief that human affec-tion did not correspond to any perceptible order in the world at large, and must therefore be either a cruel sport devised by the gods or a value to which God himself had not attained – at least so far as his outward dealings with men were concerned.[39] In this more sombre vision the importance ascribed to the human heart produces a concentrated and hardly relieved pathos. For Hardy, as for Wordsworth, the sight of a human being against a vast landscape is impressive, but for him there is no comparable hint of the sublime. When Elizabeth-Jane watches Henchard moving away at the end of *The Mayor of Casterbridge* her sense of space is complemented by the narrator's sense of time's necessities and time's weatherings:

She watched his form diminish across the moor, the yellow rush-basket at his back moving up and down with each tread, and the creases behind his knees coming and going alternately till she could no longer see them. Though she did not know it Henchard formed at this moment much the same picture as he had presented when entering Casterbridge for the first time nearly a quarter of a century before; except, to be sure, that the serious addition to his years had considerably lessened the spring of his stride, that his state of hopelessness had weakened him, and imparted to his shoulders, as weighted by the basket, a perceptible bend.[40]

As Henchard moves on his way, moreover, further forces take over, so that his course becomes a bitter comment on the very world that Wordsworth had created; his is not a general 'filial bond' but a specific and paternal one, subject to a literal, and tragic, force of 'gravitation':

> He intended to go on from this place – visited as an act of penance – into another part of the country altogether. But he could not help thinking of Elizabeth, and the quarter of the horizon in which she lived. Out of this it happened that the centrifugal tendency imparted by weariness of the world was counteracted by the centripetal influence of his love for his stepdaughter. As a consequence, instead of following a straight course yet further away from Casterbridge, Henchard gradually, almost unconsciously, deflected from that right line of his first intention; till, by degrees, his wandering, like that of the Canadian woodsman, became part of a circle of which Casterbridge formed the centre. In ascending any particular hill he ascertained the bearings as nearly as he could by means of the sun, moon, or stars, and settled in his mind the exact direction in which Casterbridge and Elizabeth-Jane lay.[41]

In *The Mayor of Casterbridge*, Hardy rescues this part of his narrative from protracted pathos only by his presentation of Henchard himself; sardonic, proud, unbending, a figure who is finally blasted but never voluntarily bows, his final will and testament[42] a defiant assertion of his own rights as an individual.

Wordsworth's version of such a figure had been less uncompromisingly stark. The Old Cumberland Beggar, he said, was representative of a class of persons who had been observed 'with great benefit to my own heart, when I was a child', and consisted of 'poor, and, mostly, old and infirm persons, who confined themselves to a stated round in their neighbourhood, and had certain fixed days, on which, at different houses, they regularly received alms, sometimes in money, but mostly in provisions'.[43] In his poem the emphasis is placed only initially on the figure himself, before being transferred to the pattern of country life which his round maps out spatially. At every point, it is suggested, a mutual interchange of good takes place: passers-by who help him also benefit themselves; the housewife who regularly puts her contribution of flour into his scrip returns with 'exhilarated heart'. By the end of the poem the old man's ministrations have come to resemble those of the stars: just as their movements redeem the universe from stasis, so his keep human links alive. For all the limitations of Newton's laws, it was his achievement to have established a sense of moving cosmic relationship; it is the old man's to demonstrate, in a smaller orbit, relationship humanised.

Even if he gave them less prominence, however, Wordsworth, as much as Hardy, knew the rigours of the universe in which he lived; otherwise the logical implications of such compassion and forgiveness might well have led him to a limited anarchism, an antinomianism of the heart. As it is, his furthest excursion in this direction is to be found in his poem *The Waggoner* (which may explain why he kept the poem so long in manuscript).[44] Benjamin, the hero of the story, who was noted for his skill in bringing great loads over Dunmail Raise in a single large waggon, also had a love of strong liquor. His downfall came on a stormy night when he took pity on a sailor's wife and baby and transported them, followed by her husband and an equipage which included a large model of Nelson's *Vanguard* and an ass, to the next hostelry, where he fell a victim to his old weakness. When his master, worried by the delay, came out to meet him next morning, he was greeted by a strange caravan: to the tail of the waggon were now attached not only his own mastiff but the sailor's ass (which had kicked the mastiff on the way) and the model of the *Vanguard*, 'following after in full sail'. Enraged, he dismissed Benjamin from his service. But since no one could handle the team of horses as he had done, this convenient form of transport soon ceased to operate altogether, being replaced by a train of lighter carts.

The poem is written partly out of affection for a local character. (The themes of affection and locality were reinforced in an early manuscript by a long passage concerning the Rock of Names, where various members of Wordsworth's community had cut their initials as a remembrancer of 'genial feeling'.[45]) But it also springs from his fascination with a man who was 'larger than life'. Here, once again, a poem conceived in affection seems to have been fertilised by Coleridge's imagination. The meeting with Benjamin's real-life counterpart took place when the two poets were out walking together. They discussed with him the disappearance of the great waggon, whereupon he commented: 'They could not do without me; and as to the man who was put in my place, no good could come out of him; he was a man of no *ideas*.'[46] Coleridge's delight at this word is readily comprehensible: it was not merely unexpected and incongruous, but bore closely on his interest in the possible relationship between strong animal spirits and strong genial spirits. Genius, he could argue, was not confined to the artist; the waggoner's instinctive ability to handle horses was of the same order as that which inspired more abstract and intellectual achievements. That Coleridge reasoned on these lines is further suggested by Wordsworth's next comment: 'The fact of my discarded hero's getting the horse out of a great difficulty with a word, as related in the poem, was told me by an eye-witness.'[47] Coleridge's insistence on the power of the word when employed by a 'man of genius' can seldom have received such literal illustration.

If I am right in seeing these arguments of Coleridge's at work in the poem, their impact may further be traced in the fact that Benjamin is not only himself an imaginative figure, but seems to act as focus for all the workings of that power about him. The names of inns, 'The Dove and Olive-bough', 'The Swan' and 'The Cherry-Tree' (which suggest the efficacy of vivid images in attracting the potential drinker) are matched in the poem by other examples of the working of the popular imagination in this locality: the naming of the mountains, for example ('The Astrologer', 'The Ancient Woman'); the attractions of the village 'Merry-Night'[48]; and the admiring response to the model of Nelson's *Vanguard* in the inn. The strong sense of history and space conveyed by mention of the legendary burial of King Dunmail at the top of Dunmail-Raise and the frequent reference to states of the sky and stars all help to give Benjamin semi-epic status: even his waggon suggests the wain-figure that human imagination has imprinted on a simple pattern of the stars. As usually happens with Wordsworth these ideas, while fully available to an imaginative reader, are suggested rather than defined; they give further colouring, nevertheless, to his own final words of regret for the loss of the waggon. Having told of the

'scruples' which have prevented him from taking the poem further,
he justified his poem as an operation of the spirit of fancy:

> Nor is it I who play the part,
> But a shy spirit in the heart,
> That comes and goes – will sometimes leap
> From hiding-places ten years deep;
> Or haunts me with familiar face,
> Returning, like a ghost unlaid,
> Until the debt I owe be paid.   iv 209–15

The spirit's insistence, clearly, is associated with something more
than a desire to pass on an amusing anecdote; it is the vivid ideas
inherent in the story that continue with a sprightly daemonism to
haunt his imagination. This man and his waggon were carrying on
the work of the Old Cumberland Beggar in a more majestic form,
helping, like him, to redeem the landscape from temporal stasis:

> In him, while he was wont to trace
> Our roads, through many a long year's space,
> A living almanack had we;
> We had a speaking diary,
> That in this uneventful place,
> Gave to the days a mark and name
> By which we knew them when they came.   iv 218–24

They were also a memorable physical image in their own right:

> . . . I, and all about me here,
> Through all the changes of the year,
> Had seen him through the mountains go,
> In pomp of mist or pomp of snow,
> Majestically huge and slow:
> Or, with a milder grace adorning
> The landscape of a summer's morning;
> While Grasmere smoothed her liquid plain
> The moving image to detain;
> And mighty Fairfield, with a chime
> Of echoes, to his march kept time. . . .   iv 225–35

The authentic Wordsworthian note emerges there in the picture of
the waggon passing by Grasmere, reflected in a lake which by its

stillness arrests the moving image in the observer's mind, while echoes from Fairfield remove all suggestion of dead fixity, substituting by their resonance a sense of grandeur and infinity.

For the inhabitants of the vale, the waggon was a great organising 'idea', imposing a welcome and familiar pattern on the succession of days; it was also a moving image, giving resonance and significance to their existence in a limited framework of time and space; most important of all for Wordsworth, however, was the fact that in it the workings of a great human heart were at once emblematised and realised. The waggon's great capacity was matched by Benjamin's greatness of heart and genius: so that now Wordsworth's greatest regret comes when

> . . . sitting by my fire, I see
> Eight sorry carts, no less a train!
> Unworthy successors of thee,
> Come straggling through the wind and rain:
> And oft, as they pass slowly on,
> Beneath my windows, one by one,
> See, perched upon the naked height
> The summit of a cumbrous freight,
> A single traveller – and there
> Another; then perhaps a pair –
> The lame, the sickly, and the old;
> Men, women, heartless with the cold;
> And babes in wet and starveling plight;
> Which once, be weather as it might,
> Had still a nest within a nest,
> Thy shelter – and their mother's breast!   iv 248–63

Had Blake written this he would probably have ended with a hymn of defiance to Benjamin's master as a blind servant of Urizen. Wordsworth had too great a respect for the established order to go so far as that. Instead he simply voices regret – and leaves his reader to respond to a great image for the activity of the human heart itself, proceeding powerfully on its way, succouring and sheltering the distressed, giving human existence its savour, and redeeming the human consciousness from over-oppressive consciousness of its own mortality.

The Waggoner was a great favourite with Charles Lamb, who expressed a wish that Wordsworth would write more often in the same vein and was surprised that he did not publish it sooner.[49] In doing so he showed himself to have a finger on the pulse of his own time. *The Waggoner* foreshadows the forms of later fictions; what Wordsworth had attempted in his portrayal of Benjamin would be further realised in some of the characters of Charles Dickens. To go further in this direction would have required an imagination less consumed by other preoccupations, however. Wordsworth had neither Dickens's flair for establishing a *rapport* with his audience nor his ear for all the shades of voice and character around him in a large community. He was not even, one might argue, particularly interested in representing human beings unless they were in some clear way related to the areas or forces of nature that surrounded them. Benjamin earned his major place in the gallery, therefore, not by reason of his warm human charity, still less by his amiable weaknesses. What made him truly memorable in Wordsworth's eyes was that as an ordinary human being he had mastered one of the great human arts – that of living and moving against the distances of a great and wild landscape with simple grandeur.

10

The Stately
and the Quixotic

Given the complexity of Wordsworth's development, it is not
surprising that by 1815 his contemporaries hardly knew what to
make of him. The poetry which he had written in the 1790s had in
itself been unusual, standing away from the Godwinianism to which
it was a response; when modified as a result of all that had happened
to him in subsequent years the body of his work became, at a direct
approach, still more bewildering.

To those who shared the prevailing liberal sentiments of the
Regency decade Wordsworth's attitudes were particularly unpalata-
ble. His earlier sympathies with France and his immediate feeling for
all human beings without regard to class or property should have
made him a prophet of reform; yet his mature convictions were
enlisted behind a far more conservative view, sympathetic to the
landed interest. Some noted with disquiet his friendships with men
such as Sir George Beaumont: Hazlitt, for instance, describing his
later poems as 'a departure from, a dereliction of, his first principles',
commented knowingly,

> They seem to have been composed not in a cottage at Grasmere,
> but among the half-inspired groves and stately recollections of
> Cole-Orton.[1]

Wordsworth's increasing puritanism found no better favour
among writers of the new generation. Shelley's satire in *Peter Bell the
Third*, including the description of his hero as 'a kind of moral
eunuch' and comparison of his timidity and coldness with the 'frank,
warm, and true' love of Robert Burns,[2] was clearly aimed at Peter
Bell's creator.

Even those who responded with more enthusiasm failed to appreciate the full course of Wordsworth's development. Keats found *The Excursion* one of 'three things to rejoice at' in his age,[3] but the effects in his work suggest that the passages composed earliest, such as the description of the Pedlar's boyhood and the vision of Apollo in Book Four, were those which particularly caught his imagination.[4] When, meeting Wordsworth in 1817–18, he found the lover of humanity cold and egotistical and the celebrant of Greek mythology unreceptive to *Endymion*,[5x] he was understandably disenchanted.

The disappointment more commonly felt by those who had admired Wordsworth's poetry aligned itself with that implicit in Lamb's judgment of *The Waggoner*. How did it come about that one who apparently valued human nature so highly was so unwilling to permit himself a broad indulgent look at human diversity? Why were the poet's eyes fixed upon so narrow a range of human experience?

Those who understood Wordsworth best found in the very intensity of Wordsworth's commitment to the heart, an explanation of the warmth of enthusiasm with which he greeted evidences of its w~rk. Some of De Quincey's accounts have already been quoted. Even Byron identified one Coleridgean source of Wordsworth's fervour with surprising accuracy when he described the latter in 1818 as

this new Jacob Behmen, this ★★★★★★ whose pride might have kept him true, even had his principles turned as perverted as his *soi-disant* poetry.[6]

Hazlitt, who had known Wordsworth in the heady days of 1798, was able to approach more closely and sympathetically to the particularity of his stance. His essay in *The Spirit of the Age* was partly characterised by faint praise and hesitant admiration, yet he caught the opposing forces of Wordsworth's psyche very exactly when he wrote of his air as 'somewhat stately and quixotic'.[7] And both extremes, it will be observed, were equally characteristic of Wordsworth's refusal to fall in with the fashionable. Where most poets contrive to exist in a kind of loose fellowship with their contemporaries, picking up here an idiom, there an acceptable tone, Wordsworth drew upon few such resources. Instead, he alternated along the course mapped by Hazlitt's phrase, sometimes making quixotic sorties into the world of the heart's affections, sometimes retiring into older modes of discourse, authenticated by eighteenth-century practitioners of pure diction or, still further back, by seventeenth-century poets such as Herbert, Daniel and (above all) Milton.

Not all his friends disapproved of his refusal to compromise with current literary fashions. Coleridge, indeed, came to feel that he had not withdrawn enough. Discussing the matter towards the end of his life he said,

> I think Wordsworth possessed more of the genius of a great philosophic poet than any man I ever knew, or, as I believe, has existed in England since Milton; but it seems to me that he ought never to have abandoned the contemplative position which is peculiarly – perhaps I might say exclusively – fitted for him. His proper title is *Spectator ab extra*.[8]

Despite the acuteness of this criticism, however, it has to be recognised that the position to which Coleridge was trying to restore him (one which he himself had originally helped to foster) had not been altogether beneficial to him. By encouraging his friend to 'assume the station of a man in mental repose, one whose principles were made up, and so prepared to deliver upon authority a system of philosophy',[9] he had encouraged him in the withdrawal which made it hard for him to communicate readily with his fellows. The programme which he said it was agreed that Wordsworth should pursue (that of 'informing the senses from the mind, and not compounding a mind out of the senses') invested the poet with an inner authority which actively encouraged a turning away from popular modes. The implied picture of him as a figure on an eminence, surveying mankind from outside, is not altogether reassuring.

As Wordsworth grew older, the tendency among many of his admirers to treat him as an elevated seer grew. He himself did little to discourage the movement – partly, no doubt, because he felt it consonant with his own conception of himself as a teacher, and also, perhaps, because such veneration suited his own impulse to solitude. He was not even, we learn, fond of casual fireside conversations with acquaintance and neighbours; in a candid poem entitled 'Personal Talk'[10] he writes:

> These all wear out of me, like Forms, with chalk
> Painted on rich men's floors, for one feast-night.

What he prefers is silence:

> To sit without emotion, hope, or aim,
> By my half-kitchen my half-parlour fire,
> And listen to the flapping of the flame,
> Or kettle, whispering its faint undersong.

The scene corresponds to his sense of himself at its most peaceful: the irregular flapping of the flame in the quiet breath of air, the kettle's undersong both harmonise with the music produced from his own subconscious. There is acknowledgement here of a fact honestly accepted: that the music of his own being, when attuned to natural sounds, is so satisfying as to make ordinary human discourse seem a worthless distraction.

There is also, however, as David Ferry has pointed out,[11] a dangerously high element of self-absorption. Coleridge had noticed this tendency as early as 1799, when he complained that his friend appeared to him to have 'hurtfully segregated & isolated his Being'; later, he wrote with bitterness and affection of Wordsworth's domestic life,

> I saw him . . . living wholly among *Devotees* – having every the minutest Thing, almost his very Eating and Drinking, done for him by his Sister, or Wife – & I trembled, lest a Film should rise, and thicken on his moral Eye.[12]

Wordsworth's egotistical behaviour during his London visit of 1817–18, which alienated many contemporaries, has often been described;[13] there are also accounts of his tightfistedness with money, including his servant's story that when completely absorbed in poetic composition he could be brought to meals only by someone breaking a plate outside his room,[14] and Coleridge's account of their visit to hear the organ at Haarlem in 1828. A party was formed, but Wordsworth declined to contribute to the fee. After some time Coleridge, becoming aware of a draught from the doorway, turned to catch sight of a familiar profile, which slipped behind one of the pillars, and removed itself just before the end.[15]

There are mitigating features, however, even to Wordsworth's cautiousness with money. Along with other sobrieties, it had been prompted in part by an early recognition that if he was to be a 'dedicated spirit' he could not afford to give unnecessary hostages to fortune. Although the attitude persisted, moreover, it was accompanied by an important discrimination in favour of the needy: years later a guest complained of the difficulty of obtaining cream in his household by comparison with the lavishness with which milk was distributed to the local poor.[16] And in the end, any uneasiness at his judicious meanness must be overtaken by awareness of his awesome sense of responsibilities – to the circle of his dependants, to his vocation as a poet and to humanity at large. Responsibility is not always a good friend to poetry: it can choke the creative act and make the poet's own words rebarbative to him; yet without it the poet forfeits some of his own humanity. When responsibility is to a private vision as well as to other people, it is a still more complicated factor, forcing the reader to watch the shell of caution for signs of the hidden generosity it may be guarding.

For Coleridge, certainly, any human defects in Wordsworth were dwarfed by a sense of his central power – 'the vision and the faculty divine' as he put it, quoting Wordsworth himself. What he did not, perhaps, perceive was that his friend was unwilling to think of that vision simply as open power and radiance: his aim was rather to find a mediant point where its power could be reconciled with the weakness – and even the darkness – of human existence. It was not for nothing that he had made the moon a central private symbol.

He could hardly expect such a vision to be readily appreciated by the world at large; indeed it could hardly have been generated in the first place, except by an individual who had found a strong security of private being. No one, he said in 1812 – not even Coleridge – had completely understood him who was not happy enough to enter into his feelings. 'I am myself of the happiest of men, and no man who lives a life of constant bustle, and whose felicity depends on the opinions of others, can possibly comprehend the best of my poems.'[17] This, we perceive, was not as complacent as it might at first sound. Wordsworth thought it his duty, as a happy man, to live in solitude and face the fact of human suffering. It was an advantage of the Pedlar's quiet cheerfulness (an advantage which, he said, Coleridge did not share[18x]) that

> he could *afford* to suffer,
> With those whom he saw suffer.   *Exc.* i 370–1

He could even trace in suffering a mode of genius. Coleridge saw the act of creation as a positive and dialectical process, the idea rising in its own organic form to the music of vital energy, which endowed it with a dimension of infinity.[19x] Wordsworth, in *The White Doe*, had explored a different mode, whereby a pure and luminous image of love was sustained by a kind of negative energy. It is primarily the reader's response to Emily Norton's suffering which causes the image of the doe to 'share the nature of infinity'.

This version of genius carried the advantage that it did not, like that of Coleridge or Blake, lay itself open to charges of artistic arrogance. It also linked itself naturally to his puritanism and love of peace. *The White Doe* was, therefore, in terms of his concerns taken as a whole, a brilliant *tour de force* of reconciliation: to the committed Wordsworthian, or the reader willing to enter sympathetically into Wordsworth's vision, it would remain peculiarly satisfying.

The success of such a negative mode must however to some degree rest upon the reader's predisposition to accept certain corresponding positives – in this case a belief in affectionate love as the central value in the universe. That belief – though very attractive to some in the century that followed – would never, however carefully redefined and developed, gain general acceptance. And in the harsher atmosphere of the twentieth century it would actually come to be regarded by many as an insidious doctrine, encouraging human beings to turn their back on the realities of an industrial civilisation in order to listen to a private music of their own.

The weight of such charges must be acknowledged. Few would now be willing to propose cultivation of the heart's affections as an answer to society's ills: to do so would be to ignore all that has come to be recognised of the limitations of a psychology that centres on those instincts without allowing for the health of others. It would also be to ignore the danger of a philosophy centred in the search for peace, for that might end logically in the conclusion that true perfection was to be found only in self-isolation and death, when the human heart, weary from attempting to fit the external universe to the grandeur of its own desires, could find in final stillness a union with the 'central peace, subsisting at the heart of endless agitation'.[20]

In Wordsworth's own thought and personality there were, of course, strong elements that resisted such a conclusion: too much subterranean energy was at work to allow him to lapse to such acceptance. In his art as much as in his life, he needed to be in movement as much as he needed his times of stillness. And it is this which reveals the inadequacy of Coleridge's attempt to place him simply as 'Spectator from without'. We hardly understand Wordsworth at all, in fact, unless we see that his apparently quiet and statuesque character bears the lineaments of a journeying man, one who has moved through nature and the local resorts of human society in the guise of a questioner and listener. His great moments are not those of a man in stillness, in whom illumination rises effortlessly, but (to adopt the memorable characterisation with which Geoffrey Hartman opens his study of Wordsworth) those of a 'halted traveller' – whose finest enlightenments may come when he has been overtaken by mist.

One of the most typical patterns in his poetry, accordingly, is that of regular movement unexpectedly arrested. Out for a quiet country walk he is stopped by the sight of an unusual human figure; the repetitive hooting of owls in response to his own mimicry ceases, leaving silence; while dealing with the ordinary business of life he is brought news of a sudden death. In the moment of arrest, expectation is thwarted, to be replaced by extreme agitation or overwhelming illumination. The experience is one of crucial significance; yet no less significant is the quiet work of the heart, which still continues underneath, to be perceived in the end as the most universal and dependable resource of all.

It is, from one point of view, a scandalous way of coming at things, since it is by definition available only to those few human beings who are prepared to believe that they may be more themselves when they are alone than when they are working or playing with the tribe. Yet it cannot be dismissed as a solipsistic mode, since it carries with it a complementary sense of relationship. Still less is it simply static in quality: a formality conceived in the moment of arrested energy is preserved from that accusation, for it remains charged with some of the power that preceded its shaping.

The image of the halted traveller has its negative side as well, of course. A thwarted and inhibited native vigour was, we have seen, characteristic of both the Wordsworths. It is suggested even by one of the most curious features of their old age. In her dotage Dorothy became increasingly addicted to large fires, even in the heat of the summer. Mrs Wordsworth complained of the expense, and said that she could not sit near her in such heat, but she was implacable. And after Dora's death in 1847, Wordsworth himself succumbed to the same passion, becoming 'to the full as great a lover of a large fire as his Sister'.[21]

Mary Wordsworth's agitation probably owed something to the fact that brother and sister were forsaking the frugal pattern of living which they had undertaken in their youth, and to which she, as manager of the household expenses, had in turn devoted herself.[22] There was no doubt something alarming about their sudden departure from so deep-rooted a habit, and it is tempting to see in this late obsession of the Wordsworths a forced and involuntary recognition of the inner core of spontaneous energy which they had damped down or avoided throughout life.

In Wordsworth's case, certainly, further evidence of such repressed emotion is not lacking. His need to walk up and down while composing, so as to impose some order on the tumults of his inner emotion, is eloquent of a phenomenon which was commented on by various of his friends, including Isabella Fenwick:

> What strange workings there are in his great mind, and how fearfully strong are all his feelings and affections! If his intellect had been less powerful, they must have destroyed him long ago.[23]

Miss Fenwick's observation not only supports the sense of conflicting forces at work in Wordsworth, but throws light on the significance of his devotion to the intellect. If the twofold thrust which we traced from his early encounter with Coleridge, the one directing him towards exploring all manifestations of the universal human heart, the other encouraging him to believe in the originality of his own standpoint, had brought him, at one extreme, to a high valuation of the powers of the human mind, this was not simply a matter of asserting, after all, the superiority of abstract reason. The mind was seen rather as an instrument of justice and mercy, needed, among other things, to restrain the over-reaching demands of the passions and instincts. Nor was this a light matter. From the nature of its inner argument, one might have expected *The Prelude* to end in a proclamation of the power of universal love; instead it concludes, in 1805 as in 1850, with an affirmation of the mind's transcendence over nature. The poet's task is to instruct his fellow mortals

> how the mind of man becomes
> A thousand times more beautiful than the earth
> On which he dwells, above this Frame of things
> (Which, mid all revolutions in the hopes
> And fears of men, doth still remain unchang'd)
> In beauty exalted, as it is itself
> Of substance and of fabric more divine.

These lines, on the other hand, must be read in the context of the last book as a whole, where the vision of the moon from Snowdon comes to be seen as 'the perfect image of a mighty Mind,/Of one that feeds upon infinity'.[24] Like the moon, the mind is no sooner viewed as transcendent than it is seen to exist in dependency, no sooner exalted than it is humbled. Its function, in fact, is not to conquer but to mediate, to transmit the idea of a principle of beauty which interpenetrates all things, and which, once apprehended, will extend itself into the field of human relationships as well.

Confronted by Wordsworth's massive self-absorption in his later years, one may be tempted to follow F. W. Bateson in seeing it as the prime cause of his growing political conservatism after 1799. As we have come to see, however, the full process is much more complicated. The conservatism itself was by no means absolute: he was still expressing republican opinions late in his life. And his self-absorption appears in a less damaging light once it is seen to have been devoted towards establishing the transcendence of the human mind in a way that would make men and women responsive to the demands and interdependencies of the human heart. *The Prelude* was to be seen always as a forerunner to the great poem which would have had as its centre *The Excursion.* If equality between men were to be achieved, it could come, he thought, only through extension of the links between one heart and another: like Swinburne later, and Forster later still, he rested his hopes on 'Love, the beloved Republic'.[25] Yet these links could be established only through the co-operation of the mind.

The austerity of the resulting attitude might inhibit him from easy commerce with the country people around him, but they were not excluded from his consciousness. In pursuit of his argument that they were, Bateson quotes Eliza Fletcher's report of Wordsworth's funeral:

> Every Grasmere face you know of the upper grade was at the funeral, but I was sorry not to see any of the peasantry, he was so peculiarly the poor man's friend.[26]

He continues,

> Once upon a time, in the 1790s, he had been the poor man's friend, but for the last fifty years of his life he had been too much preoccupied with himself to spare much time for the poor – or indeed the not-so-poor.[27]

This is surely unjust. Wordsworth had turned his back on political radicalism but not on human need. Despite his noted stringency with money, he always gave to beggars who called for alms and when, in old age, his cook complained of their ingratitude, he told her to 'go on giving, and some day the right beggar will come'.[28] It is true, nevertheless, that the charity was invariably given to individuals, just as his support of reforms was always offered for specific objects. His political cynicism, which was directed rather at theories of general human improvement through political action, sprang not from lack of human sympathy but from distrust of all courses of action which were not mediated through the human hearts of the participants.

It is in a political context, in fact, that his most extended critique of human action and passion occurs. Towards the end of the Cintra pamphlet there is a long passage which shows the extent of his reflections on the subject. Any passion, operating in pure form and unmodified by sensibility, creates misery. That is the assumption on which his argument is based. But his other point is less pessimistic. He also believes that the force *behind* the passion is, in itself, by no means ignoble – rather the reverse, for its existence is an answer to those who believe that 'the hearts of the many *are* constitutionally weak; that they *do* languish; and are slow to answer to the requisitions of things'. So he gives a long catalogue of public violence and then turns to the passions of the individual, continuing,

> . . . the long calenture of fancy to which the Lover is subject; the blast, like the blast of the desart, which sweeps perennially through a frightful solitude of its own making in the mind of the Gamester; the slowly quickening but ever quickening descent of appetite down which the Miser is propelled; the agony and cleaving oppression of grief; the ghost-like hauntings of shame; the incubus of revenge; the life-distemper of ambition; – these inward existences, and the visible and familiar occurrences of daily life in every town and village; the patient curiosity and contagious acclamations of the multitude in the streets of the city and within the walls of the theatre; a procession, or a rural dance; a hunting, or a horse-race; a flood, or a fire; rejoicing and ringing of bells for an unexpected gift of good fortune, or the coming of a foolish heir to his estate; – these demonstrate incontestibly that the passions of man (I mean, the soul of sensibility in the heart of man) – in all

quarrels, in all contests, in all quests, in all delights, in all employ-
ments which are either sought by men or thrust upon them – do
immeasurably transcend their objects.   PrW I 338–9

The little parenthesis near the end is crucial. The passions, at their
point of origin in the heart, are transposed – but only there – into the
'soul of sensibility'. It is that reservation that holds Wordsworth
back from the fuller celebration of energy and desire to be found in a
writer like Blake. When Blake, in his early Prophetic Books, wrote
in favour of political liberty it was on the assumption that such
liberty, once achieved, would realise itself as a consummation of
energy's inherent ability to find new forms for itself and express
human identity more vividly. Wordsworth's belief in political liberty is based upon a divergent conviction. He clings to ordained
structures, believing that even they provide no more than a fragile
defence for human sensibility against the discordant energies that are
always threatening it. The difference from Blake is apparent even in
the handling of a simple image like that of the spider's web. For
Blake it is a straightforward emblem of the way in which the human
brain, if isolated, weaves abstractions until they become an imprisoning mesh. For Wordsworth (readier to see the optimistic aspect of
nature) the web is a more kindly symbol, showing the genial ability
of human sentiment to produce itself into a form which, though
weak, is reinforced by its own elaboration:

>   The outermost and all-embracing circle of benevolence has
> inward concentric circles which, like those of the spider's web, are
> bound together by links, and rest upon each other; making one
> frame, and capable of one tremor; circles narrower and narrower,
> closer and closer, as they lie more near to the centre of self from
> which they proceeded, and which sustains the whole. The order of
> life does not require that the sublime and disinterested feelings
> should have to trust long to their own unassisted power. Nor
> would the attempt consist either with their dignity or their
> humility. They condescend, and they adopt: they know the time
> of their repose; and the qualities which are worthy of being
> admitted into their service – of being their inmates, their compan-
> ions, or their substitutes. I shall strive to shew that these principles
> and movements of wisdom – so far from towering above the
> support of prudence, or rejecting the rules of experience, for the
> better conduct of those multifarious actions which are alike neces-

sary to the attainment of ends good or bad – do instinctively prompt the sole prudence which cannot fail. The higher mode of being does not exclude, but necessarily includes, the lower; the intellectual does not exclude, but necessarily includes, the sentient; the sentient, the animal; and the animal, the vital – to its lowest degrees. Wisdom is the hidden root which thrusts forth the stalk of prudence; and these uniting feed and uphold 'the bright consummate flower' – National Happiness – the end, the conspicuous crown, and ornament of the whole. PrW I 340–1

Because of its beautifully intricate unity in diversity, the web of benevolence is stronger than it might seem. But because of its vulnerability to violent attack, it may still need the whole force of the state to defend it against enemies who would not allow it to elaborate itself in the first place. Wordsworth in his pamphlet criticises the government for its weakness; yet he is also, at every point, referring back to a further principle which he believed to be valid internationally as well as nationally: that a state or civilisation is to be judged by the degree to which it allows its members to live in liberty, and encourages them to express themselves in benevolence.

In his own time, he was forced to recognise, the progress of social and political life was giving little grounds for hope that his ideal of a civilisation which could reconcile purity of domestic life with large and generous social ideals (through a common culture of the heart) would in fact be realised. The true potentialities of the heart, he feared, were too slow to realise themselves: accordingly the critique of passion quoted just now ends with a sentence full of tragic foreboding:

> The true sorrow of humanity consists in this; – not that the mind of man fails; but that the course and demands of action and of life so rarely correspond with the dignity and intensity of human desires: and hence that, which is slow to languish, is too easily turned aside and abused. PrW I 339

In time, it seems, passion realises its own pathos. Yet when he turned back from the waste of human potential in his civilisation to look at the resourcefulness that could be displayed by a single human being or family, he was struck by the power of the human heart to preserve its integrity in spite of all the squalid courses of action to which it was beckoned or the sufferings to which it was subjected. It was for this reason that he placed so much stress upon the quality of 'fortitude' –

and that the sight of a single human being, devoid of friends or relations, barely able to provide its own sustenance, yet moving on through a large landscape with resoluteness of heart, would always be for him so impressive a spectacle – and one offering more hope for the future of humanity than the most detailed and comprehensive plans for social improvement by the application of general theories, however subtle or elaborate.

The same conviction gave him a firm point of reference in judging the urban civilisation of his time. We remarked earlier that in the Racedown period he showed signs of becoming a Juvenalian poet, castigating the shortcomings of his age; Coleridge had expected this to be a feature of *The Recluse*:

> . . . then he was to describe the pastoral and other states of society, assuming something of the Juvenalian spirit as he approached the high civilisation of cities and towns, and opening a melancholy picture of the present state of degeneracy and vice. . . .[29]

As we saw, however, Wordsworth seems from an early stage to have felt that the cultivation of such modes might prove self-defeating, by discouraging the growth of better feelings. His later exercises in the mode were reserved particularly for his patriotic verses, therefore – as in his 1802 sonnet on the speed with which French devotion transferred itself to Buonaparte:

> Is it a Reed that's shaken by the wind,
> Or what is it that ye go forth to see?
> Lords, Lawyers, Statesmen, Squires of low degree,
> Men known, and men unknown, Sick, Lame, and Blind,
> Post forward al, like Creatures of one kind,
> With first-fruit offerings crowd to bend the knee
> In France, before the new-born Majesty.
>
> 1807 I 128 (PW III 109)

More often he came to practise a blend of ridicule and affection which looked forward to Victorian ironists such as Newman and George Eliot and which appears particularly in connection with scenes connected with his own youth, when his eye was more sharply focused on hypocrisies and affectations. His description of academic life in Cambridge, for example, ranges from the humorous picture of the older dons,

                    Men unscour'd, grotesque
        In character; trick'd out like aged trees
        Which, through the lapse of their infirmity,
        Give ready place to any random seed
        That chuses to be rear'd upon their trunks . . .   1805 iii 574–8

to a more biting commentary on academic politics in general:

        Feuds, Factions, Flatteries, Enmity, and Guile,
        Murmuring Submission, and bald Government;
        The Idol weak as the Idolater;
        And Decency and Custom starving Truth;
        And blind Authority, beating with his Staff
        The Child that might have led him. . . .   1805 iii 636–41

A similar satire, with humour and sharpness more closely blended, is
aimed at the typical fashionable preachers in London at the time:

        There have I seen a comely Bachelor,
        Fresh from a toilette of two hours, ascend
        The Pulpit, with seraphic glance look up,
        And, in a tone elaborately low
        Beginning, lead his voice through many a maze,
        A minuet course, and winding up his mouth,
        From time to time into an orifice
        Most delicate, a lurking eyelet, small
        And only not invisible, again
        Open it out, diffusing thence a smile
        Of rapt irradiation exquisite.   1805 vii 547–57

One cannot help wishing that Wordsworth had indulged this particular gift more often. For reasons already indicated he drew back
from a course that might have given us further scathing portraits of
men who, like the fashionable preacher, were responsive neither to
the forces of nature nor to the resources of their own minds and
imagination and those sensibilities were, in consequence, doubly
unreal, so that he could never allow himself the kind of sharp
comparison between men and the organisms of the natural world
that gives bite to a poem such as Lawrence's 'Lizard':

        A lizard ran out on a rock and looked up, listening
        no doubt to the music of the spheres.

> And what a dandy fellow! the right toss of a chin for you
> and swirl of a tail!
>
> If men were as much men as lizards are lizards
> they'd be worth looking at.[30]

Wordsworth's instinct draws him always to the mediating course, to the points of continuity between the natural world and the human. The comparison between Wordsworth and Lawrence is worth taking up again here, in fact, for it is, as before, mutually illuminating. At an earlier stage we saw how sharply the courses of the two men diverged. Wordsworth set his sights by affection and imagination; Lawrence, by contrast, renounced the cultivation of affection which he had known in adolescence with Jessie Chambers, and followed to a logical conclusion of his own the idea of the 'one life'. Instead of assuming that that life must be mediated through the affections and the heart, he located it in the workings of the instincts, assuming that in a good culture the instincts could do no wrong and that true living depended first, therefore, on attending to them in their own right. Where Wordsworth stressed relationship, Lawrence stressed individuality, believing that the first task of every human being must be to find, and keep faith with, his or her own individual nature.

    In view of the common cultural matrices from which both men developed, on the other hand, it is not surprising that there should sometimes have been striking coincidences of theme. We need only turn to one of Lawrence's late poems of visionary despair, 'Nothing to Save':

> There is nothing to save, now all is lost,
> but a tiny core of stillness in the heart
> like the eye of a violet.[31]

Close as this is to Wordsworth, nevertheless, it has reached its point of concurrence by a quite different route, bearing the marks of its journey even in the informality of its expression. And on the way, Lawrence sometimes criticised Wordsworth sharply. Although, with his unerring eye for strong imaginative achievement, he had from an early age seized upon the Immortality Ode as a favourite,[32] he could not bear with Wordsworth's belief in natural innocence, or his readiness to fuse himself with the objects of nature about him. 'The simple innocent child of nature does not exist,' he maintained:

If there be an occasional violet by a mossy stone in the human sense, a Wordsworthian Lucy, it is because her vitality is rather low, and her simple nature is very near a simpleton's.[33]

In similar iconoclastic mood he attacked the implications of Wordsworth's remark on Peter Bell's inability to see a primrose as anything more than a primrose:

Wordsworth gathered it into his own bosom and made it part of his own nature. 'I, William, am also a yellow primrose blossoming on a bank.' This, we must assert, is an impertinence on William's part. He ousts the primrose from its own individuality. He doesn't allow it to call its soul its own.[34]

Amusing as this is, Lawrence misses the subtlety of Wordsworth's attitude, which is one not of self-appropriation but of a vital relationship like his own – differing only in being mediated by the heart. Elsewhere, however, he could be more perceptive. When he wrote of those in whom 'the greatest utterance of Love has given expression to Love as it is in relation to the Law', Wordsworth's name was there, numbered with those of Rembrandt, Shakespeare, Shelley, Goethe and Tolstoy.[35]

Lawrence, sardonic and vitalist, could find his way forward only by means of an elected isolation, against which relationships with his wife and friends must take their chance. Wordsworth also courted solitude, but balanced this with regular retreat into the company of those to whom he was attached by bonds of affection, encouraging his faith in the coming of 'the milder day' and his belief that the human heart was ultimately on its side. Despite the unrealistic elements in that belief, it guarded him against the kind of extravagance to which Lawrence could sometimes give rein, as when he wished for the destruction of all those members of the human race who had 'gone utterly sunless'.[36] Lawrence was no doubt being rhetorical, but Wordsworth would not have allowed himself the indiscretion in the first place.

There was, in fact, a radical disagreement between the two men concerning the nature of the heart itself. Writing of 'Space', in his poem of that name,[37] Lawrence wrote,

... somewhere it has a wild heart
that sends pulses even through me;
and I call it the sun;

and I feel aristocratic, noble, when I feel a pulse go through me from the wild heart of space, that I call the sun of suns.

For Lawrence the heart of the universe was not love but life. His vision of the universe, correspondingly, was not of an ultimate harmonic order, but of a vital chaos, sometimes lit up by visions, sometimes not. Human civilisation, he believed, failed because it tried to ignore that chaos by setting up an enclosing fabric around itself to shut it out altogether. The task of the artist, therefore, was to slit the fabric so that the true nature of things was revealed again: only so could life be revealed again by the light of the visionary gleam. Yet when he looked for an illustration to his thesis it was, tellingly, to Wordsworth's primrose that he at once turned:

> The joy men had when Wordsworth, for example, made a slit and saw a primrose! Till then, men had only seen a primrose dimly, in the shadow of the umbrella. They saw it through Wordsworth in the full gleam of chaos. Since then, gradually, we have come to see primavera nothing but primrose. Which means, we have patched over the slit.[38]

Wordsworth still might not have recognised his own vision of the primrose in this. For him the marvel of its existence lay rather in its ability to flourish with a life of its own in the midst of contending natural forces that might be expected to banish or stifle all spontaneity. Yet in another way Lawrence's intuition was right. Wordsworth's sense of contending energies and his efforts to find points of possible correspondence between nature and individual human beings, made it impossible for him ever to finally settle down or to regard even Rydal Mount as more than shelter – a temporary resting-place for the halted traveller. However far he might proceed towards a settled composure, any renewed evidence of the riddle in all things would urge him back into fresh questionings, new reorderings. He could not finally turn his back on the wildness of nature.

It is the same sense of journeying and questioning that gives his poetry as a whole its surviving challenge. For twentieth-century readers he has become primarily a great poet of human consciousness, registering in *The Prelude* and elsewhere the conflicts and illuminations of a human being who is trying to come to terms with the significance of his existence in time. The Wordsworth of the Grasmere poems is less readily approachable: his stately diction can look impossibly old-fashioned, while his cultivation of the heart's affections is, to some post-Freudian readers, simply embarrassing.

Yet once we penetrate the text to discover the process by which the product was reached, we discover that Wordsworth's attitudes acquire an immunity against critical attitudes which rest solely upon a view of the heart as sentimental metaphor. Wordsworth, we come to feel, has, by his own experience, won the right to talk about certain areas of emotional experience – to suggest that the etymology of 'courage' might not be altogether empty, that the patient ongoing movements of life deserve to be contemplated and wondered at in their own right, that there might be occasions of human encounter when it would be true to say that 'heart speaks to heart'. And in acknowledging that, one is also forced to recognise that for all its shortcomings, no equivalent language has been evolved in the twentieth century to deal seriously and directly with such things. Instead, they are subsumed into the categories of social theorising or regarded as somewhat illusory, not to be thought of except in terms of other physiological factors.

To say this is not to argue for uncritical acceptance of what Wordsworth is saying, obviously: it is rather to assert that there can be no such thing as a simple critique of Wordsworth. An intricate and subtle approach is required even when dealing with his most obvious shortcomings. And in general it could be said that those shortcomings are most apparent when Wordsworth departs from what he knows in experience, and passively accepts attitudes and beliefs handed down from his predecessors, or when, carried along by contemporary optimistic attitudes, he allows himself to generalise unduly from the correspondences between nature and the workings of his own heart which he has sometimes experienced, particularly in trance-like states.

Even in his own time statements of his which relied upon the latter kind of insight sometimes disturbed his contemporaries. Blake, for example, was sharply critical. Reading Wordsworth's lines about how he hoped to show

> How exquisitely the individual Mind
> (And the progressive powers perhaps no less
> Of the whole species) to the external World
> Is fitted: – and how exquisitely, too –

Theme this but little heard of among men –
The external World is fitted to the Mind. . .

he wrote, 'You shall not bring me down to believe such fitting &
fitted. I know better & please your Lordship'.[39x] Wordsworth went
on:

Such grateful haunts foregoing, if I oft
Must turn elsewhere – to travel near the tribes
And fellowships of Men, and see ill sights
Of madding passions mutually inflamed;
Must hear *Humanity in fields and groves*
Pipe solitary anguish; or must hang
Brooding above the fierce confederate storm
Of sorrow, barricadoed evermore
Within the walls of cities – may these sounds
Have their authentic comment; that even these
Hearing, I be not downcast or forlorn!

Blake commented bitterly, 'Does not this Fit, & is it not Fitting most
Exquisitely too, but to what? – not to Mind, but to the Vile Body
only & to its Laws of Good & Evil & its Enmities against Mind.'[40] He
was roused, evidently, not simply by the harmonising intent of the
verse, but by the suggestion that the sufferings described were
inevitable and not (as he himself would have argued) the effects of
failures in the human spirit which could be rectified.

Of all those who puzzled over Wordsworth, in fact, Blake was the
most baffled. 'I see in Wordsworth the Natural Man rising up against
the Spiritual Man Continually,' he wrote,[41] and went so far as to
wonder whether some of his prose had not been written by someone
else. What he did not perceive, perhaps, was the acutely penetrative
power of Wordsworth's sensibility – that he could not write of
humanity piping 'solitary anguish' without feeling that anguish
himself; that his composing was undertaken not to surround himself
with a comfortable blanketing harmony but to save himself, very
literally, from being left 'downcast or forlorn' by his entry into the
sufferings of others.

Blake's puzzlement was no doubt intensified by his recognition
that Wordsworth, whom he regarded as the foremost poet of the
age, was, with his declared belief in 'the Vision and the Faculty
divine', closest to himself. He could also perhaps discern in him a

shared conception of life as 'mental travel', the process of which he described in *Milton*:

> . . . every thing has its
> Own Vortex, and when once a traveller thro' Eternity
> Has pass'd that Vortex, he perceives it roll backward behind
> His path, into a globe itself infolding like a sun,
> Or like a moon, or like a universe of starry majesty,
> While he keeps onwards in his wondrous journey on the earth,
> Or like a human form, a friend with whom he liv'd
>   benevolent.[42x]

Wordsworth knew those vortices and englobings well: they were inherent for him in every true human encounter. But sometimes, as in his feeling for Dorothy, the vortex could not be left behind. The heart remained moved and unsatisfied. It was precisely because the emotional area between pulse and englobulation could be rendered so agonizing by his own engagement and responsibility that he needed to catch the whole up into a larger sense of ebb and flow, accompanied by a devotion to peace and stillness which Blake would regard as disablingly quietist.

For all that, there were continuing moments of halted encounter when he would find himself in an ultimate place as poet and as man – a place that was truly inviolable. The immediate vision and joy of childhood he had long regarded as marvellous but wasting assets; the power of the mind, though more dependable, must gradually fail; even memory itself might fade. But in the unfailing impulse of his heart at any corresponding expression from another he could recognise a resource that persisted: in that he remained, unalterably, the Wordsworth of 'Salisbury Plain'. His nephew describes how on a wet night, returning from dinner with the widow of Richard Watson, Bishop of Llandaff, they met a woman in the road:

> She sobbed as she passed us. Mr Wordsworth was much affected with her condition: she was swollen with dropsy, and slowly hobbling along with a stick, having been driven from one lodging to another. It was a dark and stormy night. Mr Wordsworth brought her back to the Low-Wood Inn, where, by the landlord's leave, she was housed in one of his barns.[43]

In those later years Hazlitt, who wrote in the essay mentioned earlier, 'His Muse . . . is a levelling one', blamed him for departing from his first principles. For others, he was, – far more completely and straightforwardly than for Browning himself[44x] – 'the Lost Leader'. The evidence of an incident such as this, however, as of many in his life and poetry, is that even if his muse was not what Hazlitt and others would have liked her to be, she had an identity of her own, in which she remained a leveller – and that in that identity she was not finally betrayed.

Notes

(The suffix *x* to a note indicator in the text signifies that the note contains further information, as opposed to simple references and cross-references.)

Preface

1. Since one or two reviewers complained that I had not given sufficient attention to Norman Fruman's study of Coleridge's plagiarisms, I must reiterate what I said in my preface: that this question is not particularly relevant to the topics and period under discussion there – though it would clearly call for further comment in a study of the later thought. For a preliminary discussion of Mr Fruman's book – including some account of his inaccuracies and omissions, the reader may be referred to my review of it in the *Review of English Studies* 1973, N.S. xxiv, 346–53). Thomas McFarland's 'Coleridge's Plagiarisms Once More' (*Yale Review*, Winter 1974, 252–84), should also be consulted.

Chapter 1

1*x*. Quoted by F. W. Bateson, *Wordsworth – A Re-Interpretation* (1956), p. 65, citing E. Whately, 'Personal Recollections of the Lake Poets', *The Leisure Hour*, 1 Oct. 1870, p. 653. Bateson also mentions a less convincing version in William Knight's *Life of Wordsworth* (1889, Vol. I, p. 38) which Knight had heard from a nephew of Southey's.

2*x*. CN III 4243. Coleridge also referred, more succinctly, to 'the attorneysonship of the Trismegist'.

3. See e.g. Exod. xxv, 2; Psalm xiv, 1; Ezra vii, 10.

4. See e.g. (respectively) Psalm xliv, 12; Prov. vi, 18; Mark xi, 23; Matt. xi, 19.

5. See e.g. (respectively) Job xxiii, 16; Mark xvi, 14; 1 Sam. xxv, 36; Psalm xiv, 13; 2 Chron. xvii, 6; Psalm xxxiv, 18.

6*x*. He also pointed out that such an attitude carried with it certain advantages. 'It is always a bad method of reading the hearts of others to affect to hide your own.' *Confessions* (Bk ii), ed. A. S. Glover (1938), Vol. I, p. 92.

7. George Ticknor's *The Sorrows of Young Werther* (by J. W. von Goethe), ed. F. G. Ryder (N.Y., 1966), p. 60.

8. For an extended discussion see A. H. Cash, *Sterne's Comedy of Moral Sentiments:*

the Ethical Dimension of the Journey (Pittsburgh, Pa., 1966).

9. L. Sterne, *A Sentimental Journey through France and Italy*, ed. G. D. Stout, Jr. (Berkeley and L.A., 1967), pp. 68–9.

10. 'The Passport, Versailles'. Ibid., 219.

11. Letter to Mathews, 3 Aug. 1791 (WL (1785–1805) 56–7).

12. Note appended to MS of 1842 (PW III 441–2).

13. 1805 vi 13–14.

14. See (respectively) his 'Epitaph on my own friend . . . Wm Muir . . .', l.5; 'The Lament', l.13; 'Lines sent to Sir John Whiteford', l.4; 'Lord Gregory —', l.17; 'The Author's Earnest Cry and Prayer', l.8.

15. 'For the Author's Father', ll.5, 6.

16. 'Epistle to Davie', ll.116–18; 'On the death of Sir J. Hunter Blair', l.17.

17. Cowper, 'To Miss —', ll.66–8, 85–92.

18. *The Task*, iii, 241; iv, 24.

19. 'Progress of Error', l.43.

20. 'Charity', ll.376, 610.

21. 'Tirocinium', l.722.

22. *The Task*, v, 779–84; 785–90; 796–846.

23. J. P. Muirhead, 'A Day with Wordsworth' (1841); *Blackwood's Magazine*, 1927, CCXXI, 736.

24. St. vii (PW II 236).

25. J. P. Muirhead, *loc. cit.*, p. 735.

26. *The Task*, iii, 303–5.

27. *Coleridge's Poetic Intelligence*, 1977, p. 33 and n; p. 45.

28. Descartes, *Discourse on Method* (1637), Part v.

29. 'Tintern Abbey', l.28 (PW II 260).

30. 'Jones! when from Calais . . .', ll.6–7, 1807 I 129 (PW III 110).

31. *Milton* 24:72; 29:21–2 (BW 510, 516–17).

32. 'Home at Grasmere', *The Recluse* I, i, 1–18 (PW V 313). Cf. 1799 ii 156–78.

33. Moorman I 125.

34. Preface to *Lyrical Ballads* (1802) (PrW I 139).

Chapter 2

1. PW II 387–8.

2. 'Autobiographical Memoranda' (PrW III 372).

3. De Quincey, 'Recollections of the Lakes and the Lake Poets', Ch. iii (DQW II 144).

4x. They were the passages sent to Coleridge in December 1798 (WL (1787–1805) 238–42).

5. 1805 iii 80–1 (1850 iii 81–2).

6. 1805 iii 294–328 (1850 iii 296–324).

7. Erasmus Darwin, *The Botanic Garden* (1789–91), ii, 29.

8. Mark Akenside, *The Pleasures of Imagination* ii, 103–20 (1744, pp. 51–2).

9. Ibid., ii 158–65 (pp. 54–5).

10x. Cf. 1805 vi 681–end. Mary Moorman's account (Moorman I 128–49) indicates that their pleasure in what they saw did not stop the companions from going on as fast as they could to reach the Alps.

11. WL (1787–1805) 282. For Annette's letters to William and Dorothy in March 1793 see Moorman I 180–1.
12*x*. The rules for marriages between Catholics and Protestants seem to have been less rigorous then than later, however.
13. 1805 x 904–40 (1850 xi 331–70).
14. BW 148–9.
15. See Enid Welsford's *Salisbury Plain: A Study in the Development of Wordsworth's Mind and Art* (Oxford, 1966).
16. Preface to 'Guilt and Sorrow' (PW II 95).
17. For the various versions of this see *The Salisbury Plain Poems*, ed. Stephen Gill (The Cornell Wordsworth I), 1975.
18. 1805 x 577–85 (1850 xi 11–17).
19. PW IV 357–8, corrected from MS at Dove Cottage.
20. Dove Cottage MS 19, p. 12.
21. D. H. Lawrence, *Complete Poems*, ed. V. de Sola Pinto and W. Roberts, (1964), I, p. 36.
22. D. H. Lawrence, *Sons and Lovers*, Ch. iv (1913), pp. 60–1.
23*x*. See D. H. Lawrence, *The Trespasser*, esp. Ch. xiii, and contrast Helen Corke, *Neutral Ground* (1933), pp. 221–3. Cf also *The Prelude* (1805 x 291–307; 1850 x 315–30), and PW I 307 on the sunset cannon at the Isle of Wight in 1793.
24. Letter to Lady Cynthia Asquith, *c.* 31 Jan. 1915. *Letters*, ed. H. T. Moore (1962), I, pp. 309–10.
25*x*. The parallels continue in the decisions of both writers to live in seclusion in the west of England during the upheaval of war, followed in both cases by the suspicions of the local inhabitants and by Government investigations. Wordsworth and Coleridge, planning their poem 'The Brook', were thought of as French spies and their question whether the local river was 'navigable to the sea' was immediately seized on as evidence of subversive intent (CBL I, 126–9 and A. J. Eagleston, 'Wordsworth, Coleridge and the Spy' (1908), reprinted in *Coleridge: Studies by several hands . . .* , ed. E. Blunden and E. L. Griggs (1934), pp. 71–88). In the same way Frieda Lawrence's Hebridean songs were mistaken for German by the local inhabitants and the wreck of a vessel off the coast was put down to their activities (see H. T. Moore, *The Intelligent Heart* (Harmondsworth, Middx., 1960), pp. 295–6). By the time that we think of Wordsworth in the Lakes and Lawrence in Mexico the contrasts have become almost overwhelming. Only the instinct to move away from the great centres of modern civilisation and the impulse to build a secluded community unite the two men – and even there Lawrence's community relies on a strenuous balancing polarity between individuals, whereas Wordsworth builds on the more conventional foundations of the family and domestic affection.
26. See *Chronology*, 145–6 and nn.
27. W. Gilpin, *Observations on the River Wye, Etc.* (1792), p. 46.
28. Mark Akenside, *The Pleasures of Imagination*, iii, 599–608, (1744, p. 124).
29. See my essay 'Blake, Coleridge and Wordsworth: Some cross-currents and parallels, 1789–1805', in *William Blake: Essays in honour of Sir Geoffrey Keynes*, ed. Paley and Phillips (1973), pp. 233–4; 239–43.
30*x*. 1850 i 129. (Cf. Milton's desire to engage with 'Some Graver subject': 'At a Vacation Exercise', l. 30.)

258 *Notes to Pages 34–56*

31. PW I 302–6.
32. PW V 379–99. For a more accurate text and full discussion see Jonathan Wordsworth, *The Music of Humanity* (1969).
33. PW I 128–225. Robert Osborn has recently edited the texts of this for Volume III of the Cornell Wordsworth. For the early text used here see the Textual Note at the beginning of the volume.
34. Act III, v, 66–70.
35x. In the 1847 version, however, Marmaduke/Mortimer is made to reply, 'Truth – and I feel it'.
36. Roger Sharrock, '*The Borderers*: Wordsworth on the moral frontier', *Durham University Journal* (1964), LVI, 170–83.
37. Donald E Hayden, 'Toward an Understanding of Wordsworth's *The Borderers*', *MLN* (1951), LXVI, 1–6, citing ll. 1529–30 (PW I 188).

Chapter 3

1. See *Chronology*, 167 and 167–8nn.
2. Cf *Salisbury Plain Poems*, 38.
3. Cf ibid., 154. For further discussion, see my essay, 'Coleridge, the Wordsworths and the state of trance', *The Wordsworth Circle* (1977), VIII, 12–38.
4. Particularly in *Coleridge's Poetic Intelligence* (1977), Ch. ii–iv, etc.
5. Boehme, *Aurora*. . . , tr. J. Sparrow (1656), xi, 32.
6. William Law, *A Demonstration of the Gross and Fundamental Errors (&c)* (1769), p. 209 (*Works*, IV).
7. Rousseau, *Eloisa* (translated from the French) (1795), I, p. 72.
8. See Lane Cooper, 'The power of the eye in Coleridge' (1910, reprinted in his *Late Harvest* (Ithaca, N.Y., 1952), p. 75).
9. For further accounts, see Robert Darnton, *Mesmerism and the End of the Enlightenment in France* (Cambridge, Mass., 1968) and my *Coleridge's Poetic Intelligence*, Ch. iv.
10. See the Preface to my edition of Coleridge's *Poems* (1974), pp. vi–viii.
11. H. W. Piper, *The Active Universe* (1962), pp. 61–74.
12. See above p. 33.
13. Ibid., 77–8, quoting *Exc.* iii 808–12.
14. III, iii, 32; II, ii, 47; cf. my *Coleridge the Visionary*, 1959, pp. 213–14, 217–22.
15. Enid Welsford, *Salisbury Plain* (1966), pp. 57–65.
16. John Jones, *The Egotistical Sublime* (1954), pp. 76–8.
17. See Moorman I 17–18, citing 'Address from the Spirit of Cockermouth Castle' (PW IV 23).
18. De Quincey, 'Lake Reminiscences from 1807 to 1830', *Tait's Edinburgh Magazine*, 1839, VI (N.S.), 94. See my *Wordsworth in Time* (1979) ch. ix.
19. LB II 80–1 (PW II 217).
20. PW IV 240 and note, p. 447.
21. R. Mayo, 'The Contemporaneity of the *Lyrical Ballads*', *PMLA*, 1954, LXIX, 486–522. Reprinted in *Wordsworth*, 'Lyrical Ballads', Casebook ed. A. R. Jones and W. Tydeman (1972), pp. 79–126. Cf. John E. Jordan, *Why the 'Lyrical Ballads'?* (Berkeley and Los Angeles, 1976), Ch. v.

22*x*. Margaret Drabble, *The Garrick Year* (1964), p. 222. For a Victorian counterpart, cf. Mrs Transome in George Eliot's *Felix Holt* who when young 'had been thought wonderfully clever and accomplished, and had been rather ambitious of intellectual superiority . . . had laughed at the Lyrical Ballads and admired Mr Southey's Thalaba'. (Ch. i, Cabinet ed., I, 40).
23. Fenwick note (PW II 478).
24. See my *Coleridge's Poetic Intelligence* (1977), pp. 160–1.
25. Ibid., pp. 161–75.
26. LB I (1798) 25, ll. 53–8 (CPW I 184).
27. LB (1798) 59–62 (PW I 92).
28. LB (1798) 63–9 (CPW I 264–7).
29. LB (1798) 69 *(bis)* – 84. Cf. 'Salisbury Plain', stanzas xxvi–xliv (*Salisbury Plain Poems*, 28–34).
30*x*. The scene she paints seems at the end to carry an echo of that on the cliffs near Dover in *King Lear* (VI, ii, 11–22).
31. LB (1798) 85–93 (PW IV 173).
32. E. Darwin, *Zoönomia* (1794–6), II, 359. See my *Coleridge's Poetic Intelligence*, pp. 50–7, 74–7.
33. LB (1798) 95–7 (PW IV 59).
34. LB (1798) 98–104 (PW IV 60).
35. Godwin, *Political Justice* (2nd ed., 1796), I, p. 130.
36. LB (1798) 105–9 (PW I 241).
37. LB (1798) 110–4 (PW I 236).
38. Fenwick note (PW I 362).
39. LB (1798) 115–6 (PW IV 58).
40. LB (1798) 117–32, 133–8 (PW II 240, 43). See my *Wordsworth in Time* (1979) ch. vi.
41. LB (1798) 141–6 (PW II 107) ('Her Eyes are Wild').
42. LB (1798) 191–6 (PW II 40).
43. See J. L. Lowes, *The Road to Xanadu* (1927), pp. 493, 553; S. Hearne, *Journey . . . to the Northern Ocean* (1795), pp. 223–4; 346.
44. Ibid., pp. 202–3.
45. 1800 Preface (PW II 388n).
46. For other instances of this usage, see my *Wordsworth in Time* (1979), Ch. viii.
47. LB (1798) 189–90.
48. PW IV 247. The restricted title was used from 1800 onwards.
49. CBL II 6.
50. LB (1798) 201–10 (PW II 259–63).
51. Colin Clarke, *Romantic Paradox* (1963), pp. 44–53.
52. J. G. Zimmermann, *On Solitude* (translated 1797), pp. 197, 177, 102.
53. See my *Coleridge's Poetic Intelligence* (1977), pp. 125–6.

Chapter 4

1. Fenwick note, PW II 517.
2*x*. See the famous statement on the primary imagination as 'a repetition in the finite mind of the eternal act of creation in the infinite I AM' (CBL I 202) (struck out in one copy, ibid., 202n) and its antecedent in a letter of January 1804 where

he describes imagination as 'a dim Analogue of Creation, not all that we can *believe* but all that we can *conceive* of creation' (CL II 1034). For 'Kubla Khan' see my *Coleridge the Visionary* (1959), pp. 256–66.

3. Cudworth, *Intellectual System of the Universe* (1743), I, p. 465. Quoted by J. D. Gutteridge in his unpublished Oxford D.Phil. Thesis, 'The Sources. Development and Influence of Coleridge's Conversation Poems, 1793–1798.'

4x. 1799 i 433. This becomes in 1805 (i 631) 'the impressive discipline of fear'.

5x. This phrase is from a letter of Coleridge's to his brother, 10 March 1798 (CL I 397). For a partial source see Milton, who claims it among the virtues of the songs in the Bible that they are able 'to allay the perturbations of the mind, and set the affections in right tune' (*Reason of Church Government*, ii, Preface), *Works*, ed. F. A. Patterson (N.Y. 1931), III, p. 238.

6x. This was believed in a more absolute sense at the time: cf. Coleridge's letter to his son Derwent, 7 Feb. 1807: '. . . Before you were born, for eight months together every drop of Blood in your Body, first beat in HER Pulses and throbbed in HER Heart.' (CL III 2).

7. F. R. Leavis, *Revaluation* (1936), pp. 160–1.

8x. For an account of the critical reception, see John E. Jordan, *Why the 'Lyrical Ballads'?* (Berkeley and Los Angeles, 1976), Ch. iii. Jordan's account suggests that critical reactions for and against were fairly evenly balanced, but that the standards by which the judgments were reached were disappointingly ordinary, and even trite.

9x. See, e.g., *Hints towards the Formation of a more Comprehensive Theory of Life* (1848), pp. 74–86, and my discussion in *Coleridge's Poetic Intelligence* (1977), pp. 53–5 and 231–59. I hope to return to the questions involved (including the relationship between Coleridge's ideas on the subject and those current in contemporary Germany) in a subsequent study.

10x. LB II 103–16 (PW II 227–35). The text of this and subsequent such entries is from the 1800 version, the line references from PW.

11. See, e.g., Dorothy's complaint on the subject, WL (1785–1805) 229–30.

12. LB II 52 ('Song') (PW II 30).

13. F. W. Bateson, *Wordsworth: A Re-Interpretation* (1959), p. 33. Cf. Cleanth Brooks, 'Irony as a Principle of Structure' (1949) and Geoffrey Hartman's discussion of both in *Beyond Formalism* (New Haven, 1970), pp. 43–4 et seq.

14. 'He lived amidst the untrodden ways . . .'. Quoted by Bateson (*op. cit.*, 2) from *Notes and Queries*, 19 June 1869, III (NS) p. 580 (cf. 24 July 1869, IV (NS) pp. 85–6).

15. See Bateson (*op. cit.*, 34) citing H. E. Rollins, *The Keats Circle* (Cambridge, Mass., 1948), II, p. 276.

16. LB II 136–8 (PW II 214).

17. 'The Little Girl Found' (BW 113–5).

18. LB II 19–41 (PW II 1–11).

19x. Wordsworth's note (PW II 2n) acknowledges his indebtedness to a description of the Calenture by William Gilbert, author of *The Hurricane*. For the relationship between Gilbert's poem and Coleridge's theories see *Coleridge's Poetic Intelligence*, pp. 96–9.

20x. Wordsworth's later poem 'The Somnambulist' (?1828) (PW IV 49–54), a romance in which a lady is seen sleep-walking by the bank of a river, its torrent

sounding throughout, seems to be a late throwback to this early interest.
21x. For a full account of the lines, which may have been projected originally as a separate poem 'The Pedlar' and which were later subsumed into the opening of *The Excursion*, see Jonathan Wordsworth, *The Music of Humanity* (1969), pp. 157–241. My text is taken from the one reproduced in that study, pp. 172–83.
22. LB II 163–4 (PW II 244).
23. LB II 69–75 (PW II 238).
24. 1807 I 77–9 (PW II 222).
25. PW II 225–6.
26. 1807 II 145–58 (PW IV 279–85).
27. 'The Immortality Ode', *The Liberal Imagination* (1951), pp. 129–59.
28x. Ibid., 146. It should be noted that the *Prelude* lines (1850 ii 245–8) appear only in the late version, when Wordsworth was emphasising the frailty of the baby.
29x. 'What got into *Coleridge on Imagination* was a sort of free reconstruction. I wasn't so much concerned to say what Coleridge had thought as to suggest what might be done with what he had said.' 'Beginnings and Transitions: I. A. Richards Interviewed by Reuben Brower' in *I. A. Richards: Essays in his Honor*, ed. Brower, Vendler and Hollander (N.Y., 1973), p. 33.

Chapter 5

1. LB II 151–62 (PW IV 234–40).
2x. Coleridge, Letter to Lady Beaumont, 3 April 1815 (CL IV 564); F. R. Leavis, *Revaluation* (1936), pp. 179–81; Jonathan Wordsworth, *The Music of Humanity* (1969). Quotations from the poem are taken from the latter study, pp. 33–49.
3. 1805 ii 125–35 (1850 ii 118–28).
4x. The Packman whom he had known and talked to at Hawkshead. Sara Hutchinson was influenced similarly by a pedlar called Mr Patrick, and described his 'tenderness of heart, his strong and pure imagination and his solid attainments in literature (chiefly religious)' to Wordsworth (PW V 373–4). He also found a passage in praise of such men in Heron's *Journey in Scotland* and quoted it in a note (PW V 412).
5. PW II 331–82.
6x. Originally Wordsworth intended to include a passage in which Peter Bell snatched up a penny which had been thrown to a cripple by a passing horseman; he removed it however, and transferred the incident to a separate poem, 'Andrew Jones', where the incident is related by a narrator who shows abhorrence for the deed, hoping that the youth will be removed from the village by the press-gang (see PW II 463 and nn). Wordsworth may have felt that the deed would be too heinous for such a man as Peter Bell, suggesting a sense of humanity too broken to be revivified even by events such as he was to describe.
7x. It may also be noted, however, that the two poets seem to have visualised the albatross differently. In his note concerning the poem, Wordsworth recalls Shelvocke's description of albatrosses with wing-span of twelve or thirteen feet (PW I 361). Recent evidence turns out to support J. L. Lowes's suspicion (*The Road to Xanadu* (1927), pp. 226–7) that Coleridge himself had in mind the small 'sooty albatross' – which could more easily be hung about the neck and drop from there into the sea. My conjecture would presuppose that

Wordsworth was combatting his own image rather than Coleridge's, therefore.

8. E. Darwin, *Zoönomia* (1794–6), I, p. 151–2.
9. CN I 330; Darwin, *op. cit.*, I, p. 423–6.
10. *Table Talk*, 31 May 1830 (CPW I 193, l.164).
11. Between lines 515 and 516 in 1819 version: see PW II 354 (app. crit.).
12. 'My First Acquaintance with Poets' (HW XVII 118).
13x. This idea may have played its part in Blake's motifs of the 'moon-ark' and of the feathered glory around the head of visionary man (cf. my *Blake's Visionary Universe*, 1969, figs. 47–50 and 36; and the commentary, pp. 34, 372, 374). It should be added, however, that if these ideas were circulating in late eighteenth-century London they perhaps arose there as well: I have not so far found any suggestion of the connection in travel-books emanating from North America.
14. De Quincey, 'On Wordsworth's Poetry' (DQW V 260–1).
15. 1805 iv 400–504. See also the drafts, *Prel.*, pp. 536–9.
16. 'Nuns fret not . . .' (PW III I); 'Composed in one of the Catholic Cantons' (PW III 173). A. S. Byatt first drew my attention to the prevalence of cell-imagery in Wordsworth's poetry.
17. 'Lines written as a school exercise . . .' (PW I 260); 'The Convict' (PW I 312).
18. 1850 x 406; *Peter Bell*, ll.513–5 (PW II 354).
19. 'Vernal Ode', ll.97–100 (PW II 311); PW IV 152.
20. 'The Kitten and the Falling Leaves', ll.96–8, 1807 I 50 (PW II 172).
21. See *Descriptive Sketches*, 1793 vn, l.627 (1849, 523) (PW I 78–9) and n. quoting Cowper, *The Task*, vi, 11–12.
22. 'The Church of San Salvador' (PW III 180).
23. 'The Cuckoo at Laverna', ll.71–3; 82–102 (PW III 218–25).
24. 1807 II 11–13 (PW III 77).
25x. Later published in his *Tours to the British Mountains* (1824), p. 12. De Selincourt, who cites the accounts of Wordsworth and Dorothy, quotes a slightly different form, copied into one of Wordsworth's commonplace books by Wilkinson himself. PW III 444–5.
26. 'The Sun has long been set . . .', 1807 II 41 (PW IV 9).
27. 'Jones! when from Calais . . .', 1807 I 129 (PW III 110).
28x. Since I use this phrase several times in the pages that follow I should perhaps emphasise that it is not an actual quotation.

Chapter 6

1. E. P. Thompson has suggested this in an unpublished lecture.
2. 1807 I 68–9 (PW II 30–1). Cf. Wordsworth's comments on his return to England in 1800: WL (1787–1805) 259.
3. De Quincey, 'Recollections of the Lakes and the Lake Poets', DQW II 136.
4. Ibid., 146.
5. E.g. *Journal*, 17 March 1802 (DWJ 103).
6. Letter to Jane Marshall, 10–12 Sept. 1800 (WL (1787–1805) 298).
7. 'The Knight's Tale' (*Canterbury Tales* I(A) l.2779: *Works* ed. F. N. Robinson, 1957, p. 44). My text is from Robert Anderson's *British Poets* (Edinburgh 1793,

p. 24) the edition of Chaucer read by Wordsworth (and Dorothy – see her journal) during the winter of 1801–2.

8. 'The Sparrow's Nest', 1807 II 54 (PW I 227).

9. CL I 449.

10. 10 Nov. 1801 (DWJ 57).

11x. Cf. his praise for the sonnet: '. . . the melody/Of this small lute gave ease to Petrarch's wound' ('Scorn not the Sonnet', PW III 20) and his line 'Thus Elidure, by words, relieved his struggling heart' ('Artegal and Elidure', PW II 18).

12x. See e.g. the address to his own tears in 'The Vale of Esthwaite': 'Flow on, in vain thou hast not flow'd,/But eas'd me of a heavy load;/For much it gives my heart relief/To pay the mighty debt of grief' (PW I 280); and 'Guilt and Sorrow', ll. 534–5: 'and while her heart/Struggled with tears nor could its sorrow ease' (PW I 121). It would be interesting to trace the literary ancestry of the idea; by 1824 it was so established in Wordsworth's mind that a single phrase, 'one heart-relieving tear', could encapsulate it ('Cenotaph', PW IV 255).

13. See above, pp. 63–4.

14. LB II 1–13 (PW II 249–54).

15. G. Bürger, 'The Chase', and 'William and Helen', tr. W. Scott (1796), p. 14.

16. Psalm xlii, 1–2.

17. See his 1797 note to line 44 of 'Religious Musings' (CPW I 110).

18x. E. Darwin, *Zoönomia* (1794–6), I 492–509. As Enid Welsford points out (*Salisbury Plain* (1966), p. 34), other thinkers of the time, such as Diderot, Robinet, and Priestley, had spoken of evolution as a purposeful development of the spirit of nature. The question is further discussed by H. W. Piper (*The Active Universe* (1962) – see especially his Appendix A on Coleridge's opinions) and, very fully in relation to Erasmus Darwin, by D. King-Hele, *Erasmus Darwin* (1963), pp. 63–96.

19. See above, pp. 82–91.

20. PW I 315–6; Jonathan Wordsworth, *The Music of Humanity* (1969) pp. 5–6.

21. De Quincey, 'Recollections of the . . . Lake Poets' (DQW II 203).

22. Ibid., 64.

23x. PW II 505. The lines are dated by De Selincourt in the summer of 1798. This invites comparison between the 'houseless being in a human shape' of these lines and the 'vagrant dwellers in the houseless woods' of *Tintern Abbey*. In both cases there seems to be some connection with the 'wild eyes' and gipsy-like behaviour of Dorothy, as if Wordsworth were trying to establish the significance of 'wildness', and its relationship to the peace of nature, through what he observed of her.

24x. *As You Like It*, II, vii. The words are used by Orlando, when he has burst in with drawn sword upon the peace of Duke Senior and his courtiers at their woodland meal, in order to stress that he is not an uncivilised man but has been driven to his action by his own and Adam's hunger.

25. PW IV 423, quoting from MS M (1803–4).

26. F. W. Bateson, *Wordsworth: a Re-Interpretation* (1954), pp. v, 143, 156–7.

27x. The denial in the second edition (1956, p. 143) seems to be categorical, but in a letter to the TLS some years later (9 April 1976, p. 430) Mr Bateson returned to the point, maintaining that the deletions in Dorothy's MS journal probably hid evidence of sexual activity and should be subjected to examination by infra-red techniques. After some further skirmishes, Jonathan Wordsworth restored a sense of proportion to the discussion by producing (21 May, p. 614) a spoof entry which he claimed to have discovered under deletions in Dorothy's journal, recording the birth of a baby; shortly afterwards (28 May, pp. 646–7) Robert Woof recorded that he had deciphered nearly all the deleted passages, and that they contained nothing which was relevant to the issue. Mr Bateson's comment during the same correspondence that his book had been written when he took Wordsworth's poetry 'rather more seriously than I find I can today' (p. 430) is perhaps revealing.

28. ''Tis said that some have died for love . . .', LB II 76–9 (PW II 33–4).
29. Song of Solomon, ii, 10–12.
30. LB (1798) 95 (PW IV 59).
31. Song of Solomon, ii, 8–9.
32. 17 March 1802 (DWJ 102–3); Psalm cxxvii, 2.
33. Song of Solomon, iv, 12.
34. PW V 347. This is one of several fragments extracted by Professor Knight from Dorothy's journals.
35. Pope, 'Eloisa to Abelard', ll.88–90.
36. D. H. Lawrence, *Sons and Lovers* (1913), Ch. vii, pp. 160–1.
37x. 26 Dec. 1801 (DWJ 74). Cf. Wordsworth's comment on Chaucer to Miss Fenwick in a letter of c.1840 (WL (L.Y.) II 1001–2).
38. Bateson, *op. cit.*, p. 153.
39. CN III 3304.
40. 'There is an Eminence . . .', LB II 186 (PW II 115).
41. 1807 I 77 (PW II 224).
42. See above, p. 104.
43. Entry for 10 June 1800, recording an incident on 27 May (DWJ 26–7).
44. Cf. Blake's 'He who binds to himself a joy/Doth the winged life destroy.', BW 179, 184.
45. 1807 II 39–40 (PW I 226).
46. 1807 II 53–4 (PW I 227).
47. 21 March 1802 (DWJ 105).
48x. 17 March 1802 (DWJ 103); Dorothy 'tried to write verses' on the following evening, but was too tired (Ibid., 104): this makes me think the lines quoted are her own.
49. 1807 I 19 (PW II 54–5).
50. 1807 II 109–14 (PW II 56–9).
51. 16, 17 March 1802 (DWJ 102, 103) and see above, pp. 154–5.
52x. Ibid., 84. A poem written two months later, on 18 April, 'The Redbreast chasing the Butterfly' (1807 I 16–18), suggests that the passage in that book describing Adam's first sight of destruction between animals after the Fall had also impressed them. (See the note added in 1815, PW IV 149 (app. cr.).
53. 1807 I 14–15 (PW II 213–4).
54x. The recently discovered letters between William and Mary Wordsworth from 1812 to 1820 bring out further the depth of his passion. Separated from her he writes, 'every hour of absence is a grievous loss. . . . The fever of thought and longing and affection and desire is strengthening in me. . . . Last night I

suffered and this morning I tremble with sensations that almost overpower me.' (*Sunday Times*, 8 Jan. 1978, p. 3).

Chapter 7

1. See Moorman I 551; G. Whalley, *Coleridge and Sara Hutchinson and the Asra Poems* (1955), pp. 11; 119–22.
2. Letter to Sara Hutchinson 4 April 1802, 133–43 (CL II 793).
3x. It is unlikely that any engagement, or even 'understanding' existed between Sara and John. The arguments against such a hypothesis have been presented by Alethea Hayter (*A Voyage in Vain* (1973), pp. 57–8). On the other hand Coleridge was well placed to perceive a covert attraction between them, even if it had not yet been openly acknowledged. His belief in the possibility – and even desirability – of such a marriage is indisputable (see, e.g. CN II 2517, 2861).
4. Letter from Dorothy Wordsworth to Catherine Clarkson, 6 Nov. 1806 (WL (1806–11) 86).
5. Letter to Richard Wordsworth, 19 March 1805 (WL (1785–1805) 571). Cf. p. 540.
6. 1807 II 141–4 (PW IV 258–60).
7. 'Elegiac Stanzas', l.15; see next note.
8. Letter from Dorothy Wordsworth to Mrs John Marshall, 15–17 March 1805 (WL (1806–11) 559).
9x. 1807 II 117–8 (PW II 34). After Coleridge's death in 1834 Wordsworth changed 'this consecrated fount' to 'that consecrated fount'.
10. WL (1806–11) 87 (see note 4).
11. Letter to Wordsworth, 21 May 1808 (CL III 110).
12. Letter from Dorothy Wordsworth to Catherine Clarkson, 12 April 1810 (WL (1806–11) 399) (foreshadowed by a less severe comment to Lady Beaumont on 25 Feb., ibid., 390–1).
13. Coleridge, letter to Wordsworth, 4 May 1812 (CL III 397). Cf. p. 382.
14x. G. Herbert, 'Virtue': *Works*, ed. F. E. Hutchinson (Oxford, 1941), p. 87. The implications of Wordsworth's metaphor in the 'Recluse' passage are explored at length in M. H. Abrams's *Natural Supernaturalism* (1971).
15. T. Whitaker, *History and Antiquities of the Deanery of Craven*, 2nd ed. (1812), pp. 449–50. Quoted, in part and *variatim*, in Wordsworth's note to the poem (PW III 535).
16. PW III 281–340.
17. Letter to Wrangham, 18 Jan. 1816 (WL (1812–20) 276).
18. 8 Nov. 1805 (DWJ (De Sel) I 415), quoted Moorman II 111.
19x. The 'lily in June' may perhaps be compared with the 'rose in June' of Burns's 'O my Luve's like a red, red rose' and of Wordsworth's own 'Strange fits of passion . . .'; it provides a complement to the more positive passion of those poems.
20. Henry Vaughan, *Works*, ed. L. C. Martin (1914), II, 425.
21. Moorman II 112 and n, citing CPW I 217 (ll.48–52) and DWJ 7 March 1798.
22. See above, p. 166.
23. PW III 542.
24. 13 March 1802 (DWJ 103).

25. Cf. my *Blake's Humanism* (1968), pp. 76–82.
26. Jessie Chambers ('E.T.'), *D. H. Lawrence: a Personal Record* (1935), p. 223.
27. Letter from the Duke of Argyle to Rev. T. S. Howson, September 1848; quoted PW II 517. Dorothy's own verses on the subject, written some years earlier, should also be noticed, however: Moorman II 491–2.
28. *Recollections of the . . . Lake Poets* (DQW II 134).
29. Ibid., 136.
30. LB II 199–225 (PW II 80–94).
31. 11 Oct. 1800 (DWJ 44).

Chapter 8

 1x. Supposedly in the orchard at Racedown. See letter to Coleridge, 16 April 1802 (WL (1787–1805) 348 and n).
 2x. 1807 II 57–9 (PW II 207–8). The line 'about, and all about', which (like a contemporary journal entry of Dorothy's (29 Dec. 1801, DWJ 75)) has a Coleridgean ring, was later changed to 'At once far off, and near' – which while emphasising the main point, forfeits some of the 'magical' connotations.
 3. *Prel.* pp. 571–78.
 4. PL x 318.
 5. LB II 195–6 (PW II 118).
 6. See below, p. 215.
 7x. Both this and the incident of the ram reflected in the lake are described in drafts for *The Prelude*. In the latter instance, Wordsworth takes up a stone to break the image of the ram, and then desists. See note to 1805 viii 497 (*Prel.* 581).
 8. *Exc.* iv 422–3.
 9. 'Point Rash-Judgment', LB II 190–4 (PW II 115–7).
10x. In the later version, this passage is shortened to end, 'That skimmed the surface of the dead calm lake,/Suddenly halting now – a lifeless stand!' – which sharpens the anticipation of the later point at the expense of the opening sense of life.
11. See above, p. 150.
12x. 1805 vii 620–22. The old man of 'Resolution and Independence', who seemed 'like a man from some far region sent,/To give me human strength, by apt admonishment', was playing a still more active part in carrying through the experience.
13. 1805 vi 617–57. Cf. my *Wordsworth in Time* (1978), Ch. vii.
14. Hazlitt, 'Mr Wordsworth', para. 2 in *The Spirit of the Age* (HW XI 87).
15. Cf. PL vii 23: 'Round this opacous earth, this punctual spot'.
16. 'On a high part of the Coast of Cumberland' (PW IV 2–3).
17. Preface to *The White Doe of Rylstone*, 1815 (PW III 283).
18. Letter to Crabb Robinson, 29 March 1813 (HCR *Corr* I 76) (quoted Moorman II 248).
19. HCR I 125 (24 March 1813); HCR *Corr* I 77. Quoted Moorman II 249.
20. 'To a Skylark', PW II 266.
21. From a record by Lady Richardson (PrW (Gr) III 438).
22. PW III 51. The unusual intensity of this sonnet was first called to my attention by Professor W. B. Gallie.

23. B. Ifor Evans, 'The European Problem' in *Wordsworth: Centenary Studies*, ed. G. T. Dunklin (Princeton, N.J., 1951), pp. 119–22.
24. Addison, *The Spectator*, No. 477, ed. D. F. Bond (Oxford, 1965), IV, 199.
25. Letter to Lady Beaumont, *c.* December 1806 (WL (1806–11) 112–20).
26. Ellis Yarnall, *Wordsworth and the Coleridges* (New York and London, 1899), p. 45. Quoted *variatim* by Russell Noyes, who gives a full account of the changes at Rydal: *Wordsworth and the Art of Landscape* (Bloomington, Indiana, 1968), pp. 126–35.
27. See Dorothy's journal for 8 September 1803 (DWJ (De Sel) I 358–9) and Wordsworth's 'Effusion in the Pleasure-ground on the banks of the Bran, near Dunkeld' (PW III 102–5); and cf. my *Wordsworth in Time* (1979), Ch. vi.
28. Transactions W. Soc. VI 178.
29. Ibid., 170.
30. Wordsworth, *Complete Guide to the Lakes* (1835) (PrW II 202) (Quoted variatim, Transactions W. Soc. II 171).

Chapter 9

1. 'Salisbury Plain', st. 44 (Cf *Salisbury Plain Poems* 34). See also Enid Welsford, *Salisbury Plain, a Study in the Development of Wordsworth's Mind and Art* (Oxford, 1966), pp. 14–15.
2. Ibid., st. 47.
3. 1805 vii 692.
4. 1805 v 97–8.
5. 'The Waggoner', iv, 210 (PW II 204).
6. C. Salveson, *The Landscape of Memory* (1965).
7. Reproduced, *Prel.*, facing p. 1.
8. 1850 vii 6–7; 8–12. The 1805 version suggests that there had been more power in the intermediate writing.
9. Letter to George Coleridge, *c.*10 March 1798 (CL I 394).
10. W. Bartram, *Travels through North and South Carolina* (1792), p. 155.
11. J. L. Lowes, *The Road to Xanadu* (1927), pp. 364–5, quoting Gutch Notebook (=CN I 220).
12. 1793 version (PW I 42).
13. *Exc.* ix 13–14.
14. ll.69–73, PW II 229.
15. 'Lines suggested by a Portrait by F. Stone', ll.125–9 (PW IV 124).
16. D. Ferry, *The Limits of Mortality* (Middletown, Conn., 1959), pp. 12–15.
17. These lines appeared from 1807 to 1815 (PW II 227n).
18x. CBL II (Ch. xxii) 110–1. Cf. Hazlitt's criticism and Keats's comment in a Letter of 30 Oct. 1817: *Letters of John Keats, 1814–21*, ed. H. E. Rollins (Cambridge, Mass., 1958), I, 173–4.
19. See e.g., his annotations to Reynolds (BW 452 etc.), and his criticism of Wordsworth himself: 'Imagination has nothing to do with Memory' (BW 783).
20. Letter to W. F. Hook, 5 Feb. 1840 (*Life and Letters of W. F. Hook* (1881), p. 304; quoted Bateson, *op. cit.*, 155n).
21. Letter to John Wilson, 7 June 1802 (WL (1787–1805) 354). Quoted (but misdated 1800) by F. R. Leavis, *Revaluation* (1936), p. 169.

22. PrW III 124.
23. B. R. Haydon, *Diary*, ed. W. B. Pope (1960), II p. 470.
24. Letter of Dec. 1798 (WL (1787–1805) 235–43).
25. The third appeared as 'Nutting' (LB II 132–5; PW II 211–12).
26. David Ferry, *op. cit.*, pp. 23–4.
27. Letter to Jane Pollard, 16 Feb. 1793 (WL (1787–1805) 87).
28. PW III 255–6.
29. PW III 256a, app. crit.
30. See HCR I 330 and my *Blake's Humanism* (1968), p. 31.
31x. William Empson, e.g., says, 'Milton . . . follows St Augustine in believing that the Fall produced a bad kind of sex, though he insists that it is not the only kind. Evidently there is some broad human truth here, but it is hard to say what.' (*Milton's God* (1961), p. 188.)
32. Samuel Daniel, Preface to 'Musophilus', ll.1–6. (*Complete Works*, ed. A. B. Grosart (1885), I 223).
33. PW II 56 (14), II 232 (161), I 226; 1850 vi 517; PW III 255 (xxi, 1).
34. *Exc.* vii 131; 1850 v 22; PW I 240–1 (61), II 199 (77), I, 178–80 (1262, 1306); *Exc.* i 875; PW III 382 (xlii, 2).
35. PW III 129 (viii, 13), I 74 (560), III 143 (xxxviii, 12), III 354 (517), II 214 (ix, 2); *Exc.* ii 885; PW IV 68 (3).
36. PW II 260–1 (28, 54), II 351 (468).
37. Cf. 'The Brothers' (above, p. 100) and *Exc.* i. 264.
38. 1805 i 441 (PW IV 96 (12)).
39. See e.g., the last chapter of *Tess of the D'Urbervilles* and the poem, 'God's Education' (*Collected Poems* (1976), p. 278).
40. *The Mayor of Casterbridge*, Ch. xliii (Library ed. (1950), pp. 360–1).
41. Ibid., Ch. xliv (p. 368).
42. Ibid., Ch. xlv (p. 384).
43. Fenwick note; and note to original poem (PW IV 445).
44. PW II 176–205 and note, pp. 497–8.
45. PW II 499–500.
46. Note of 1836 (PW II 97).
47. Ibid.
48. Canto i, 52 and ii, 21–2; i, 170–9; ii, 23–30; ii, 113–63.
49. *The Letters of Charles and Mary Lamb*, ed. E. V. Lucas (1935), II, p. 249 (cited Moorman II 369).

Chapter 10

1. Hazlitt, 'Mr Wordsworth', para 5. In *The Spirit of the Age* (HW XI 90).
2. Shelley, *Peter Bell the Third*, IV, xi–xiii (*Poetical Works*, ed. T. Hutchinson (1934), p. 354).
3. Letter to Haydon, 10 Jan. 1818 (cf. his similar statement in letter to George and Thomas Keats, three days later). *Letters of John Keats, 1814–21*, ed. H. E. Rollins (Cambridge, Mass., 1958), I, pp. 203, 205.
4. For good accounts of the relationship between the two poets, see Sidney Colvin, *John Keats, His Life and Poetry* (&c.) (1917), esp. pp. 125–6, 220 and 233–4; and John Middleton Murry, 'Keats and Wordsworth', *Studies in Keats,*

2nd ed. (1939), pp. 123–45 (repeated in *Selected Criticism 1916–1957* (1960), pp. 127–45).

5x. 'I am sorry that Wordsworth has left a bad impression wherever he visited in town – by his egotism, Vanity and bigotry – yet he is a great Poet if not a Philosopher.' Letter to George and Thomas Keats, 21 Feb. 1818 (*Letters*, op. cit., I, p. 237). After Keats read his 'Hymn to Pan' Wordsworth commented, 'A very pretty piece of Paganism': *The Keats Circle*, ed. H. E. Rollins (Cambridge, Mass., 1958), II, pp. 143–5.

6. Byron, letter to Thomas Moore, 1 June 1818. *Byron: a Self-Portrait*, ed. P. Quennell (1950), II, 431.

7. Loc. cit. (HW XI 91). In 1798 (XVII 118) he was 'gaunt and Don Quixote-like'.

8. Coleridge, *Table Talk*, 21 July 1832 (1835, II, 71–2).

9. Ibid., 70.

10. Untitled, 1807 II 119–22; later called 'Personal Talk' (PW IV 73–5).

11. D. Ferry, *The Limits of Mortality* (Middletown, Conn., 1959), pp. 53–6.

12. Letters to Poole, 6 May 1799 and 14 Oct. 1803 (CL I 491, II 1013).

13. See e.g. W. J. Bate, *John Keats* (1963), pp. 272–3.

14. Transactions W. Soc. II, 189.

15. J. C. Young, *Memoir of C. M. Young* (1871), I, pp. 182–3.

16. Harriet Martineau, *Autobiography* (1877), II, pp. 235–6 (Cited Moorman II 581).

17. HCR I 73.

18x. '[Coleridge] could not afford to suffer with those whom he saw suffer.' Remark by Wordsworth quoted in Barron Field's 'Memoirs' (MS BM); PW V 412–3.

19x. Cf. the last stanza of 'Kubla Khan'. A more absolute example may be found in his description of Shakespeare's genius: *Shakespearean Criticism*, ed. T. M. Raysor (1936), I, p. 126. Here the process is described as 'silent' but carries suggestions of an inner music in the sun. (Cf. my *Coleridge the Visionary* (1959), pp. 89–90, 163–4).

20. *Exc.* iv 1146.

21. *Letters of Mary Wordsworth*, ed. M. E. Burton (Oxford, 1958), pp. 165, 298.

22. See, e.g., Transactions W. Soc. II, 179.

23. Letter to Henry Taylor, 4 Jan. 1839. Quoted, Edith Batho, *The Later Wordsworth* (Cambridge, 1933), p. 37n.

24. 1805 xiii 69–70.

25. Swinburne, 'Hertha' (*Collected Poetical Works* (1924), I, p. 739); Forster, *Two Cheers for Democracy* (1951), p. 79. (See also W. Stone, *The Cave and the Mountain* (Stamford, Calif., 1966), pp. 61–2, for further references.)

26. Eliza Fletcher, *Autobiography* (Edinburgh, 1875), p. 283.

27. F. W. Bateson, *Wordsworth – A Re-Interpretation* (1956), p. 174.

28. Edith Batho, *The Later Wordsworth* (Cambridge, 1933), p. 45 (cited Moorman I 471).

29. Coleridge, *Table Talk*, 21 July 1832 (1835, II 71).

30. D. H. Lawrence 'Lizard', *Complete Poems*, ed. V. de Sola Pinto and Warren Roberts (1964), I, p. 524.

31. Ibid., II, p. 658.

32. 'Hymns in a Man's Life', *Phoenix II*, ed. Warren Roberts and Harry T. Moore (1968), p. 597.

33. 'On Human Destiny', ibid., p. 624.
34. Ibid., p. 447.
35. *Phoenix*, ed. E. D. McDonald (1936), p. 513.
36. 'Democracy', *Complete Poems*, op. cit., I, p. 526.
37. Ibid., p. 525.
38. Preface to *Chariot of the Sun* by Harry Crosby: *Phoenix* (1956), p. 256.
39x. Blake, Annotations to *The Excursion* (BW 784). It should be noted that this passage was quite possibly not drafted until 1806; if so, Blake's critical antennae may be picking up a note of willed affirmation, following the doubts raised by John Wordsworth's death (see above, pp. 167–8). For the successive versions of the Prospectus and a discussion of the dating problem see M. H. Abrams, *Natural Supernaturalism* (1971), pp. 465–79.
40. BW 784. The underlining in the Wordsworth passage is Blake's.
41. Annotations to Wordsworth's *Poems*, Ibid., 782.
42x. *Milton* 15: 21–27 (BW 497). For a detailed discussion of this passage in relation to contemporary scientific theories see Donald Ault, *Visionary Physics: Blake's Response to Newton* (Chicago, 1974), pp. 154–6.
43. C. Wordsworth, *Memoirs of William Wordsworth* (1851), II, 474 (cited Moorman II 581).
44x. Replying to a query by A. B. Grosart, Browning said that he had used the 'great and venerable personality of Wordsworth as a sort of painter's model, one from which this or the other particular feature may be selected and turned to account' but denied that any full scale reference had been intended in his poem: he did not believe, for example, that material considerations ('handfuls of silver and bits of ribbon') had ever influenced Wordsworth's politics. Letter of 24 Feb. 1875, *Letters*, ed. T. L. Hood (1933), pp. 166–7. I am grateful to John Woolford for this reference.

Index

(Page-references in bold type indicate central discussions; (sel.) indicates selected references on a pervasive topic.)

271

Index   277